THE ECONOMIC ILLUSION

Also by Robert Kuttner:
REVOLT OF THE HAVES

Robert Kuttner

THE ECONOMIC ILLUSION

False Choices Between Prosperity
and Social Justice

Houghton Mifflin Company   Boston   1984

Library of Congress Cataloging in Publication Data

Kuttner, Robert.
The economic illusion.

Includes index.
1. Economics. 2. Comparative economics. 3. Social
justice. 4. Efficiency, Industrial. 5. Welfare state.
I. Title.
HB72.K84 1984   330   84-10856
ISBN 0-395-35347-5

Printed in the United States of America

S 10 9 8 7 6 5 4 3 2 1

Book design by Ann Schroeder

for Sharland

Study economics to avoid being deceived by economists.
— Joan Robinson

CONTENTS

THE ECONOMIC ILLUSION

The political problem of mankind is to combine three things: Economic Efficiency, Social Justice, and Individual Liberty.

— John Maynard Keynes, 1925

INTRODUCTION

THE ECONOMIC ILLUSION is the belief that social justice is bad for economic growth. That illusion is held today by nearly all political conservatives and by most professional economists. In their view, gains to the common welfare that result from the workings of the marketplace are good, while welfare effects of social tinkering are inefficient, unnatural, and in any case unsustainable. This book will argue, to the contrary, that prosperity and social justice can be reconciled; and that they can be mutually reinforcing.

The claim that equality harms efficiency underpins the stunning resurgence of laissez-faire ideology throughout the West. It is the essence of much conservative folk wisdom about how the economy works. "Don't punish the rich: They make jobs," warns an op-ed writer in *The New York Times*. "In order to succeed," declares George Gilder, "the poor most of all need the spur of their own poverty." And when Ronald Reagan says, "You know how to spend your own money better than the government," he appeals to everyone's common sense. The gross maldistribution of "our" economic resources seems beside the point.

All of these claims have rejoinders. Are the rich the *only* source of jobs? The best source? What good does the spur of poverty do when jobs are not to be had? We may know how to spend our money better than the government does, but where do we turn when we are sick, or old, or unemployed — and out of money? And why is "our" money so unevenly distributed? Unfortunately, the claims make better one-liners than the rejoinders. Today the voting public is no longer quite so innocent about the promise of affirmative government. The public wonders what killed prosperity. If equality is truly bad for growth, then equality must wait.

In economic and "games theory" parlance, a zero-sum game is one in which the sum of everybody's winnings and losses adds up to zero, as in a poker game; for each winner, there must be a loser. A positive-sum game is one in which the game itself helps the pie to expand, and everybody, at least in theory, can gain simultaneously. A positive-sum game offers a more attractive and cooperative prospect because there need be no losers, only relatively greater and lesser winners. Many orthodox economists believe they want to promote economic growth; yet their models are based on the assumption that the economy is a zero-sum game, in which distribution must come at the expense of other goals, and life is a series of "tradeoffs." Even many American liberals and their economic advisors have fallen into the trap of assuming that in order to restore growth, it is first necessary to sacrifice equity: they suggest that we emphasize economic recovery now, and worry about redistribution after the fact.

Whenever an idea takes hold that is contrary to the apparent self-interest of most people, it invites very close examination. Predicating economic efficiency upon gross social inequality is such an idea. In this book, I shall argue that the supposed incompatibility of equality and efficiency is a myth, and a politically useful one at that. It is convenient indeed for the wealthy and the powerful that economic recovery should depend on their further enrichment. Self-interest is successfully masquerading as a technical imperative. Ideology has appropriated the costume of value-free positive economics.

This is not to deny the deep flaws in the contemporary welfare state. The pathology of welfare capitalism is a recurring theme of this book. Often the compromise between the logic of the market and the logic of social entitlement manages to blunt both welfare and efficiency. But just as often social justice produces positive-sum economic gains — outcomes that enhance both goals. There are good political reasons why some social policies succeed and others fail.

Admittedly, economic growth has slowed throughout the West, in nations with big welfare states and with small ones. However, a careful comparison of social policies in different Western nations casts substantial doubt on the claim that redistributive excess killed prosperity.

*   *   *

The relationship of equality to efficiency is of course one of the Big Issues of political economy. It leads to other big issues: Why socialism and political democracy have never been successfully combined. Why capitalism has such a stormy, ambiguous relationship to freedom. Whether the greater practical threat to personal liberty for most ordinary people is too much state or too much market. Whether personal effort thrives on security or insecurity. Whether the impasse of welfare capitalism is best resolved by sacrificing some capitalism, or some welfare. This is the contested terrain of several disciplines — economics, sociology, political science, moral philosophy, social psychology — and several ideologies as well.

In challenging the idea that equality harms efficiency, I propose to weigh the theoretical claims against the practical policy experience of different industrial nations. My own approach is primarily that of a journalist working in the tradition of comparative political economy. In examining how countries go about providing social security, collecting taxes, promoting full employment, enhancing economic development, stimulating productive investment, and influencing the distribution of income, it is difficult to resist two evident conclusions:

First, the relationship of equality to efficiency is at worst indeterminate: a wide range of equality/efficiency bargains exists. Some improve equality at the expense of efficiency; some improve efficiency at the expense of equality; others creatively maximize both; still others make a hash of things and worsen both. One can find efficient transfer programs that broaden the self-reliance of the nonrich. One can find labor-market strategies that expand national output as they reduce inequality. One can identify pension schemes that increase wealth, even as they broaden its distribution. One can find tax loopholes that further enrich the rich by steering their money into absurdly unproductive uses. Equality and efficiency coexist in all manner of relationships. A concrete discussion of these different social bargains is the main subject matter of this book.

Second, all of these issues are deeply political. The policy sphere is almost never autonomous. The range of equality/efficiency bargains that present themselves and the design of social institutions to carry them out reflect balances of political power. Few if any of the choices are merely technical, though they are often so disguised.

Economic distribution is far too important to leave to economists. Most of mainstream economics and much of the newer discipline of public policy, wittingly or unwittingly, serve as handmaidens of deep political conservatism. For the usual efficiency paradigm is premised on the distributive status quo. And fifty years after Keynes, the conventional view of tradeoffs is curiously static.

Economic orthodoxy is doubly impenetrable. It uses a technical, esoteric idiom spoken only by other economists; and it often operates by tautology. If we assume, axiomatically, that markets are mostly self-correcting and that all resources are or soon will be optimally deployed, then it follows logically that people get just what they deserve and that all redistributive efforts are as futile as they are arrogant.

Based on its faith in markets, much of the economics profession shares the premise of political conservatism that egalitarianism must harm economic growth. The market, admittedly, generates winners and losers. But tampering with market outcomes is said to depress economic performance in multiple ways. Redistribution, in theory, undermines incentive, thrift, savings, investment, creativity, the efficient use of labor, and the optimal allocation of capital. We may desire a more equal society on political grounds, but we shall pay a heavy economic price. It is only a short leap to the further conclusion that redistribution harms not only economic performance, but personal liberty as well.

The convenience of tautology is that it defies awkward practical detail. Much of contemporary neoclassical economics represents the easy victory of assumption over evidence. Mainstream economics tends to obscure the deeply political nature of most economic questions. Who gets what is seldom merely a technical issue. The realm of political choice is largely beyond the competence of positive economics. When economists advise that equality must harm efficiency, they have taken leave of social science and are wielding recondite models in the service of ideological claims.

*　　*　　*

For three decades after World War II, there was broad political and intellectual consensus that equality *improved* efficiency. Full employment meant full production; eliminating poverty meant more purchasing power to keep factories humming. Social justice reduced social conflict. Redistribution, within limits, enjoyed substantial legitimacy, not just as decent social policy, but as sensible economics.

Economic events often transform political assumptions. In the celebrated "end of ideology" of the 1950s and 1960s, ideological détente was concluded on surprisingly egalitarian terms. During the three postwar decades, political liberty, economic opportunity, and social security came to be seen as mutually reinforcing. Democracy ceased to mean only the negative liberties of the Enlightenment. Instead, a series of positive rights were to be guaranteed by a benign state: the right to a job, to education, to health — to a minimal standard of living notwithstanding one's personal fate in the marketplace. In the Western democracies, these new economic rights did not require a sacrifice of older political liberties, though they did expand the domain of the state. In effect, economic entitlements became an extension of basic civil rights. The English social philosopher T. H. Marshall described this new conception of freedom aptly, as "social citizenship."

Today, economics again pervades politics; but the logic has been thrown into reverse. After a decade of economic stagnation, social citizenship is fatally discredited as a practical economic failure. In a culture that prizes growth, inequality has regained ideological currency not as a morally attractive ideal but as necessary economics. High taxes are said to have killed personal thrift. A costly public sector is held responsible for depressing private investment. The redistributive state is blamed for stunting individual initiative. The pragmatic critique of the welfare state, in turn, has breathed new life into some hoary propositions about the sanctity of private property, the relationship between democratic liberty and laissez-faire, the absolute rights of the individual against the organized community, and the other musty themes of classical economics.

Thus, the resurgence of political conservatism as a social philosophy rests more on a utilitarian premise than on a spiritual one. Conservative ideas are not ascendant because of a sudden mass revulsion against "statism" — for personal liberties are no more circumscribed by the state than they were four decades ago; on the contrary, there is a strong case that civil and political liberties have been enlarged since 1950. The difference is that the economy is no longer booming, and the welfare state is held to blame. Stripped to its essentials, much of the appeal of Margaret Thatcher, Ronald Reagan, and company rests on the simple idea that the economy performs better when government doesn't attempt to alter market outcomes.

The utilitarian basis of contemporary conservatism is a slender pillar, one worth reflecting upon. When the top 0.8 percent of families owns 40 percent of the property wealth and the bottom 25 percent owns no wealth, it becomes extremely difficult to defend that outcome as inherently desirable or inherently just. Even if I.Q., personal effort, and individual contributions to the Gross National Product are distributed unequally, the gross extremes of actual economic life are disproportionate to any conceivable concept of personal economic "worth."

Long ago, economic and social inequality was rooted in aristocratic or feudal values; it was simply a function of a social order in which classes were deemed fundamentally unequal, and inequality itself was the basis of personal security. But two hundred years after the French and American revolutions, few conservatives anywhere in the West would justify gross social inequality primarily on ethical grounds. In a democratic age, the case for inequality stands or falls mainly on the pseudo-technical claim that equality retards efficiency. And in a society where the professed civic values are democratic the practical burden of proof must be on the inegalitarians.

*   *   *

This book is mainly a concrete examination of the politics of equality and efficiency in different industrial nations, in the several policy areas of economic life. I count myself an egalitarian, but this is not intended as a philosophical brief for greater equality. Other books have performed that task eloquently, most recently Michael Walzer's *Spheres of Justice* and William Ryan's *Equality,* both of which demonstrate why many realms of human life must necessarily exist outside the market's ruthless allocational criteria of commodity and exchange.

I happen to agree with Walzer and Ryan that more equality is philosophically defensible and ethically desirable; but I will leave that sphere of the argument to them. Exactly how much equality can be justified *morally* is a normative question — one more for social philosophers than for economists. It is an issue for the political arena rather than the technical one. But a good deal more equality than what we now have can surely be attained without sacrificing the common goal of economic growth. The precise blend of equality and efficiency is seldom a mechanistic "tradeoff" but a matter of political choice, institutional form, and the distribution of power.

Egalitarian societies have an interest in devising social bargains that reconcile equality with economic performance. Unequal societies tend to resist such positive-sum bargains, for their leaders have a material and ideological stake in perpetuating inequalities. In such societies, equity-enhancing social bargains are shunned — not because they would harm growth but because they would transform relationships of privilege and power.

As it turns out, there is one set of economic bargains in the industrial countries with strong labor and social democratic roots and quite a different set in countries where labor movements are weak or divided and business ideologies are dominant. It will surprise many conservatives and neoclassical economists to learn that positive-sum gains tend to be statistically superior in societies where labor and business operate more as equals and where egalitarian values are better entrenched. In practice, redistributive measures take more of a toll on economic efficiency when they are carried out grudgingly, in the inhospitable climate of business supremacy and social conflict. In America, where the ideological and institutional reach of business is immense even in more liberal hours than this, redistributive efforts tend to be hobbled; in turn, they hobble economic efficiency. In Northern Europe, where social democratic parties often govern, where trade unions exercise more influence and more responsibility, and where egalitarian professional economists (*not* an oxymoron!) have opportunities to do practical policy work, redistribution and efficiency are blended more happily.

This is not to say that we have only to emulate the technical approaches of the Swedes or the Austrians (or, for that matter, the Japanese). A decade ago, it was too easy for American egalitarians to counsel facile imitation of Western Europe, where the welfare state was indeed broader and the rate of economic growth nonetheless higher. Two things are wrong with that advice. First, the entire West, including those countries that managed positive-sum bargains before 1973, is experiencing the strains of global slowdown. Settled social compromises are coming unglued. Even the most successful nations are refining their strategies in the face of changed circumstances. Second, economic institutions need to grow in their own political soil. A socialized health program that evolved within a political culture where organized medicine is weaker, or a program of wage restraint that reflects a tradition of labor solidarity, or a pension system that mirrors egalitarian values, cannot easily be imported as a technical fix.

The economic illusion is the vision of static tradeoffs; the idea that we must sacrifice well-being in the present for investment in the future; social justice for economic rationality; work satisfaction for labor discipline; decent wages for international competitiveness. The value of comparative political economy is to demonstrate that policy approaches which improve equality can also improve efficiency. I offer these illustrations not as a policy cookbook but as an illustration of democratic possibility and as a corrective to the mechanistic "tradeoff" mentality. If, as I believe, the distribution of wealth and income is essentially a political choice, there is little reason to tolerate the gross economic injustices that exist today; and laissez-faire must find another ethical basis to justify its brutal medicine.

Chapter 1, EQUALITY AND EFFICIENCY, places the equality/efficiency debate in historical context. It discusses the brief Keynesian interlude and the current fiscal wreckage of welfare capitalism. It points to differences in the social contracts of various Western nations.

Chapter 2, CAPITAL, considers the claim that redistribution of wealth and income must depress savings and investment. It finds, to the contrary, that a variety of policies exists for promoting savings, some of which broaden the distribution of wealth while others narrow it. It also discusses the efficiency consequences of politically allocated investment.

Chapter 3, TRADE, reconsiders the holiest ground of laissez-faire economics, free trade. It finds that free trade, within limits, promotes efficiency and growth; but that anarchic trade and excessively mobile private capital recreates the worst dilemmas of nineteenth century capitalism: falling wages and competitive deflation — with severe consequences for both equality and efficiency.

Chapter 4, LABOR, suggests that full employment is the best means of reconciling economic justice with economic growth. It compares wage policy, trade unionism, and labor market approaches in various nations and finds several exemplary equity/efficiency bargains. It concludes that certain forms of trade unionism improve equity/efficiency outcomes.

Chapter 5, TAXES, considers equity/efficiency issues in tax policy. Several countries succeed in reconciling high and progressive tax systems with high rates of savings and growth. Others manage to botch both their tax system and their economic performance. In Britain and America, many politically popular tax preferences have heavy costs to both equality and efficiency.

Chapter 6, WELFARE, compares different approaches to guaranteeing income, in such policy areas as social security, child allowances, health care, et cetera. Universalism in social services is essential to program success, but expensive. The welfare state does not necessarily wreck the productive economy, though as public spending increases, so do fiscal contradictions. Socializing income without socializing productive capital has its limits.

The Epilogue, POLITICS, considers the political underpinnings of different equality/efficiency bargains. Social democratic Europe is having difficulty in maintaining its social contract in the face of economic slowdown. Individualist America is not conducive to finely tuned social contracts. But there are some positive-sum bargains that do not go against the American grain. The difficult questions are political, not technical.

To approach the question of economic equality is to enter a region haunted . . .

— R. H. Tawney

1

EQUALITY AND EFFICIENCY

POLITICAL DEMOCRACY and market capitalism exist in an uneasy marriage. The democratic state proclaims equality. The market generates inequality. The ideological champions of the market *celebrate* inequality. In the civic realm, the first democratic freedom is citizenship — membership in a political community, which implies security and an equal voice in governance. In the market realm, the first freedom is freedom of exchange — the liberty to achieve personal economic success or failure. Absolute freedom of exchange thus creates extremes of social inequality. By market standards, inequality is not a regrettable necessity, but a virtue. In theory, the dynamism of the market and its unequal outcomes are logically inseparable. And the dynamism supposedly makes up for the social imbalance.

The conflict between polity and market is most acute with respect to the distribution of wealth and income. In a democracy, the rights of citizenship are supposed to be equally distributed and broadly diffused. They necessarily exist in a realm beyond the reach of personal economic differences. But the gross inequality generated by the market, at some point, compromises the ideal of political equality; for citizens cannot enjoy an equal political voice when they live at vastly different standards of material security. At some point unequal wealth purchases unequal influence.

By laissez-faire standards, liberty is simply the absence of coercion. But unequal economic relationships themselves open the way to new forms of coercion by the haves, at the expense of the have-nots: coercions to take lower wages or lose a job, to vacate an apartment, to suffer the loss of community because higher profit opportunities happen to exist elsewhere. "In liberal [laissez-faire] thought, exchange is conflict-free," writes Charles E. Lindblom in his classic *Politics and Markets.*

> Everyone does what he wishes. [But, adds Lindblom] a person whose style of life and family livelihood have for years been built around a particular job, occupation, or location finds a command backed by a threat to fire him indistinguishable in many consequences for his liberty from a command backed by the police and the courts.

The authority of the market can be as coercive as that of the state.

It is a truth that neither classic liberals nor classic socialists like to admit that civil society and personal liberty can be threatened by either excesses of the state — or of the market. Fashioning a democratic political economy that maximizes both the civil and social liberties of the polity and the sense of economic possibility of the market, is no easy matter.

EQUITY VERSUS ECONOMICS

In conventional economic theory, the tension between state and market is simply the tension between equality and efficiency writ large. For classical economists, the political arena is the realm of equality; the market is the realm of efficiency. Any shrinkage of the market realm tends to distort the allocation of economic resources by subjecting them to political criteria. In a liberal democratic state, some "safety net" concessions to economic equality may be necessary; but the greater the concessions, the greater the real economic cost. Therefore, in this theory, whosoever gratuitously expands the political sphere at the expense of the market sphere is behaving perversely; the result will be lower living standards for all, and particularly for the downtrodden whom the misguided egalitarian seeks to uplift. Even opponents of redistributive policies like Milton Friedman insist that the inequalities of laissez-faire are really more egalitarian, for they will lead to more growth and hence to broader economic prosperity in the long run. Thus do the defenders of inequality seek legitimacy for their approach by invoking the egalitarian ideal. The sociologist Philip Green terms this logical twist "the homage that vice self-confidently pays to virtue."

In this respect, professional economists are very useful ideological allies of political conservatives. Both believe that redistribution departs from the libertarian principle of reward for effort. Economists find that departure inefficient; conservatives find it unjust as well. Economists worry that the state will allocate resources less efficiently than the market does; conservatives worry more about the personal usurpation. If private property is the ultimate bulwark of liberty, any taking of property is the taking of a liberty. Thus does capitalism go with freedom — and with economic growth, human possibility, and hence with more freedom.

These arguments are spoken with particular force and self-confidence in the 1980s, but they are hardly new. Some of the recent case for inequality is a reaction against the postwar welfare state, but much of the argument reiterates an older set of claims about the sources of wealth and the dynamics of personal motivation. This is how the English economic historian R. H. Tawney characterized the laissez-faire case against redistribution, writing in the fateful year 1929:

> Measures — so the argument runs — which have as their object the diminution of inequality, have as their effect the depletion of capital and the discouragement of enterprise. Their ultimate victims are not only those upon whom taxation is levied, but those for whose benefit it is imposed. The latter lose as workers what they gain as citizens, and pay for illusory improvements in their social conditions in the hard cash of lower wages and increased unemployment. Thus the wealth of the few is the indispensable safeguard for the modest comfort of the many, who, if they understood their own interests, would not harass the rich with surtaxes and death duties, but would cherish and protect them.

How durable are the utilitarian arguments for inequality? In the 1920s, Tawney's opposition were the social Darwinist disciples of Herbert Spencer. But except for the formal Edwardian prose, Tawney's discussion sounds utterly contemporary. It is as if Tawney were engaging not Spencer, but George Gilder. As Tawney himself lived to witness, the greatest era of sustained economic growth was the postwar era of social democratic economics. But to pursue the argument, let us complete Tawney's list of why "measures which have as their object the diminution of inequality" are supposedly bad for economic performance.

Incentive and Desert

The first premise is that in a free market people get more or less what they deserve. If the state tampers with the principle of desert, the most efficient producers may well stop working so hard, while those who happen to be inefficient will be overcompensated for their meager contribution, and they may stop producing at all. This is why the poor presumably "need the spur of their own poverty," while the rich are presumed to deserve their riches. John Kenneth Galbraith, writing in the sly spirit of Anatole France, described the even-handed majesty of Reaganomics: "The poor need the incentive of lower benefits, while the rich require the incentive of lower taxes."

Neoclassical economists render this same argument in terms of the theory of marginal productivity. Prices are deemed to be efficient signals of what the last unit of labor or capital is "worth" in the marketplace. If you believe this is how markets actually work, then the market price for labor as well as the market-determined return to capital are by implication "fair," as well as optimally efficient; and so is the resulting distribution of life's material goods. When no one's position can be improved without worsening someone else's, the situation is said to be efficient — or "Pareto-optimal," a concept of Vilfredo Pareto, the Italian-Swiss political economist. Within this framework of assumptions, subsidies, transfers, taxes, and trade unions distort market price signals; thus they have costs to economic efficiency.

What is intriguing is that the ultraconservatism of a Gilder or a

Herbert Spencer is only a slight exaggeration of the cherished assumptions of mainstream economics. Arthur Okun, a moderately liberal and moderately Keynesian economist, made the definitive case in his 1975 book, *Equality and Efficiency: The Big Tradeoff:*

> The contrasts among American families in living standards and in material wealth reflect a system of rewards and penalties that is intended to encourage effort and channel it into socially productive activity. To the extent that the system succeeds, it generates an efficient economy. But that pursuit of efficiency necessarily creates inequalities. And hence society faces a tradeoff between equality and efficiency.

Inequality, for Okun, is both a measure of success and a precondition for success. He adds,

> Tradeoffs are the central study of the economist. "You can't have your cake and eat it too" is a good candidate for the central theorem of economic analysis. . . . We can't have our cake of market efficiency and share it equally.

Much of his uneasy essay can be read as a contest between Okun's egalitarian instincts as a citizen and his inegalitarian training as a professional economist.

But of course you *can* have your cake and eat it, too — if you decide to bake a second cake. And you may well find that baking two cakes does not take twice the work of baking one. Nor does it necessarily hold that society will get more pastry if Smith gets all the cake while Jones gets just the crumbs. Economists confuse tradeoffs with social choices. Life always entails choices, but it does not always require static tradeoffs. Formal economic analysis has a very hard time dealing with dynamic gains.

The economists' case for inequality rests on several tacit assumptions that are presumed true by definition. To begin with, the argument assumes that the actual distribution of economic prizes closely reflects the real value of individual contributions to economic output. Moreover, even when wealth does not reflect worth, as in the case of unearned windfall or unearned misfortune, the argument further presumes that substantial interference with market outcomes would nonetheless wreck the system of incentives and expectations. Thus, whether or not outcomes are truly "earned," altering them must depress work effort by rich and poor alike, distorting the optimal allocation of capital investment as well.

Both premises fail to withstand careful scrutiny. First, even if we agree that markets are "efficient" at responding to price signals, at best they are efficient only at serving an a priori distribution of purchasing power, which reflects all sorts of historical accidents. One of those accidents is the pre-existing distribution of wealth, which is far more unequal than the distribution of income and often bears little relationship to actual economic contributions, however defined. "Property is not theft," Tawney writes, "but a good deal of theft becomes property. The owner of royalties who, when asked why he should be paid £50,000 a year from minerals he has neither developed nor worked but only owned, replies, 'But it's property!' " The legitimacy of private property in our system has multiple virtues, but it should not be confused with desert.

If we were to radically redistribute personal means and begin the economic game again, the textbook market would immediately resume responding to price signals, with its usual marvelous "efficiency." Indeed, if we truly believe in the value of incentives, it makes no sense to deny them to the children of the rich. To the extent that advocates of laissez-faire concede the necessity of any taxes at all, they should logically begin with very high inheritance taxes on great private fortunes. From an efficiency point of view, an inheritance tax is superior to any tax on real economic activity, since it taxes away wealth that was reaped with neither effort nor risk, let alone the virtuous self-sacrifice of "patient accumulation."

Even if we believe that market-determined distributive outcomes bear some rough relationship to social contributions, it is extremely difficult to find a utilitarian — let alone an ethical — basis to justify the *extremes* that exist. What theory of personal worth or social contribution could possibly justify material rewards for Smith that are many hundred times those bestowed on Jones? When something like half of the great fortunes are inherited, it is very hard to contend that this unequal market "voting power" literally reflects real contributions.

T. H. Marshall once observed with his usual understatement, "The more you look on wealth as conclusive proof of merit, the more you incline to regard poverty as evidence of failure — but the penalty for failure may seem to be greater than the offense warrants."

Luck

In practice, a good deal of the outcomes produced by the market reflect nothing more than luck — good or bad. An investor happens to hold the right stock at the right time; an autoworker finds himself in the wrong trade in the wrong decade. The unexpected passing of a rich aunt produces a windfall for one family, while the untimely death of a husband produces hardship for another. Prudent citizens who save and invest sometimes lose their shirts; diligent and loyal workers often lose their jobs. People reap fortuitous windfalls or suffer devastating reverses that have nothing to do with their social contribution or their personal effort.

Perform the following thought experiment about three households, each in late midlife, all stalwarts of the American middle class:

In one lives the widow of a successful small machine-tool manufacturer. During his prime her husband contributed jobs and products to the nation's commerce, and the couple lived well. Late in his career, he introduced a bold new product line, only to see it undermined by shifts in demand and a swing to imported products. His health failed not long afterwards; insurance paid only part of the costs of nursing-home care, which consumed their savings. The widow was left with only $50,000 in life insurance. She moved to a smaller apartment, but it was condominiumized. Today, she lives on a total income of about $700 a month, in fear that she will be evicted from her present two-room apartment if rents are raised much.

The second includes a retired steelworker and his wife. He got out of the navy, worked in the local mill 32 years, put three children through college. She worked as a bank clerk. But the plant closed, and at age 56 he went on relief; as the regional economy declined, the bank consolidated branches. Finally, they had to sell their house, in a depressed market. Today, the couple lives modestly but decently thanks largely to social security and his union-negotiated pension. But for Medicare, they would soon incur insurmountable health bills.

In the third is the widow of a salesman. They always "lived up to their income" and never saved very much. In 1966, his best year, they splurged on a very lavish house, which cost an astronomical $90,000. After he died in 1981, she sold it for $375,000, and put the proceeds into Treasury bonds, then yielding 15 percent. Luckily, she sold the house and bought the bonds at the peak of both markets. Last year, her aged father died, leaving her $450,000. Today, she lives quite nicely.

These are hardly unusual hypotheticals; on the contrary, they are typical of the unpredictable courses that actual lives take. But to what extent are these outcomes "just," ethically or economically? To what extent do the current economic circumstances of the two widows reflect their actual contribution or that of their spouses to the nation's economic well-being? Does the plight of the manufacturer's widow or of the ex-steelworker's family simply reflect their own improvidence? Does the well-being of the salesman's widow, who happened to have her capital in a house rather than in the stock market and who inherited money from her father, represent anything more than luck? More pertinently, to what extent do efforts to shelter ordinary people from unearned reverses (or unearned windfalls) necessarily interfere with the incentive principle and the efficient performance of the market? It is also revealing to appreciate that, even in America with its minimalist welfare state, the rather limited economic security of the nonrich depends heavily on post-1933 institutions that trample criteria of laissez-faire efficiency: social security, Medicare, and trade unions. Would the economy really be more "efficient" by any definition — would it really grow faster — if we scrapped these institutions?

In theory, capitalism offers an opportunity to cash in on innovation. That prospect is deemed a fair reward for risks incurred. Innovation is the social justification for inequality. Even if the rewards sometimes seem excessive, supposedly they are not a large price for society to pay for the dynamism that is engendered. But in practice, just as many personal reverses do not reflect personal improvidence, most concentrations of wealth do not reflect the patient accumulation, the self-denial, and the daring risk-taking of the textbook economy. Some wealth is simply inherited. More subtly, many rapid accumulations of new wealth typically represent lucky breaks, which are only partially "earned."

In his early book, *Generating Inequality,* Lester Thurow persuasively explained the windfall origin of most new fortunes. In theory, markets are in equilibrium; but in the real world, they are in constant flux and disequilibrium. Some investments earn much higher returns than others. As markets seek to equilibrate, a company that is earning an above-average rate of return is a candidate for a big stock run-up, which can be cashed in for a capital windfall. Thurow concludes:

> Large, instant fortunes are created when financial markets capitalize new above-average rates of return. . . . Patient savings and reinvestment have little or nothing to do with rapid fortunes. To become very rich one must generate or select a situation where an above-average rate of return is about to be capitalized.

As Thurow notes, once lucky fortunes are accumulated, they need to earn only normal rates of return in order to generate incomes that are astronomical by ordinary standards. Vast inequalities of wealth perpetuate ongoing inequalities of income; them that has, gets.

My *New Republic* colleague, Michael Kinsley, examined *Forbes* magazine's 1983 annual tally of the four hundred richest Americans. Weighing the details of how they got rich against George Gilder's claim that the social function of the rich is "fostering opportunities for the classes below them," Kinsley found that 204 of the 400 fortunes were substantially inherited; that another 45 were primarily based on lucky investments in natural resources or land, that another 22 were "paper entrepreneurs" who enhanced their own net worth (but not the nation's wealth) by manipulating financial assets; and that 14 more had built fortunes on — of all unproductive things — government contracts. Kinsley rapidly deflated the *Forbes* 400 to the *New Republic* 59: About one fortune in eight was actually built in Horatio Alger fashion.

Conversely, a good deal of innovation is accomplished by salaried people working in institutions, not entrepreneurs waiting for the opportunity to cash in big. One can point to Steven Jobs of Apple Computer, but one can also identify Dr. Jonas Salk, working on salary. Even in the for-profit sector, there are thousands of salaried engineers at Bell Labs, or at Toyota. Neither system of motivation has a monopoly on innovation.

When pressed, many neoclassical economists will concede that market-determined outcomes may not always be reasonable. Arthur Okun, in his discussion of "The Big Tradeoff," wrote: "In fact, most of the ardent supporters of the market reject the claim that distribution in accordance with marginal productivity is necessarily just distribution."

Rather, the inegalitarian typically falls back on the second aspect of the merit argument: that even if outcomes do not always reflect economic worth, tampering with them would deter effort and misallocate purchasing power. Even if not all wealth is necessarily earned, the wealthy remain the principal source of investment capital. Confiscate their wealth or tax it unreasonably and the "animal spirits" that supposedly animate capitalism will subside; the rich will just play golf. The redistributed wealth will be dissipated in consumption by lesser creatures who lack the refinement or the self-discipline to appreciate the rewards of patient accumulation and deferred gratification.

In traditional welfare economics, the justification for some redistribution is that there are many people whose need for an additional thousand dollars of income — by almost any standard — is plainly greater than the millionaire's "need" for an extra thousand. Again, the counterargument is entirely utilitarian: Do not be sentimental about even the "deserving poor," warns the libertarian, for redistribution pays a high price in incentive, efficiency, and growth.

But if neither personal reverses nor personal windfalls are entirely earned, then why should some redistribution destroy incentive? Who really thinks that people don't work as hard because they can look forward to social security, or because public education is free, or because some of their earnings are taxed? The hard practical question is one of degree: At what point do social benefits or high taxes begin to erode incentives? Concretely, how can policies be devised to minimize this risk?

Taxes

Virtually all of the studies of the effect of taxation upon effort conclude that taxation can have two opposite effects on work: An "income effect" — people actually work harder in order to maintain their pretax standard of living; and a "substitution effect" — people decide to substitute leisure for work. To this traditional analysis, one might add a third result: a tax-avoidance effect — when marginal tax rates are high and loopholes plentiful, people begin putting effort into sheltering their income from taxation rather than producing useful goods and services.

But the analysis is next to useless until one examines the details.

One could imagine a tax rate of, say, 95 percent that would surely depress the incentive to earn. However a tax rate of 40 percent might depress incentive — or enhance it — depending on the form of the tax, the legitimacy of the tax, the opportunities for sheltering the tax, the opportunities to earn, the uses to which the tax revenues are ultimately put, the particular society's norms about work and leisure, and a dozen other variables. At the other extreme, a low tax rate of, say, 5 percent would supposedly engender more efficiency than a 50 percent tax, because the prospect of keeping more of one's earnings would enhance the motivation to work and to save. But if pretax income, and hence purchasing power, are maldistributed, a tax rate of 5 percent could well diminish the efficient use of resources, and a much higher tax that redistributed demand could produce a more dynamic economy. There is no simple rule of thumb about taxes and economic efficiency. During World War II, tax rates and tax collections were at record high levels — and so was the rate of economic growth. One can imagine high taxes that retard efficiency, and low taxes that do the same.

Savings

Yet another efficiency cost of egalitarian income distribution is its supposed effect on savings. Along with the argument that high taxes must depress incentive, this was the principal appeal of the supply-side vogue. In this view, capital investment is the source of economic growth, and savings are the source of capital. If government taxes the income from capital excessively, investors will decide that spending is preferable to saving, the total rate of savings and investment will fall, and everyone will be worse off.

This argument can also be broken into several distinct fallacies. First, there are many ways to accumulate high national savings rates. Inducing the already-wealthy to save more is only one possible approach. Pension funds, which can represent savings on behalf of the nonrich, provide a good example of a device that enhances capital accumulation and broadens the distribution of wealth at the same time. Another example is homeownership subsidies for the nonrich. Public-sector savings — that is, budget surpluses — are yet another.

Second, there is no empirical evidence that overall savings rates must fall as the size of the public sector or the intensity of redistribution grows. As the nonrich become better off, their ability to save increases. Savings rates in Europe and Japan rose throughout the postwar period, while the public spending as a proportion of gross national product (GNP) rose, too. Savings rates in the United States have been remarkably constant for the past 35 years. The enormous "supply-side" tax cut of 1981 was supposed to boost savings and investment. But in fact, firms invest in new plant and equipment when they think they can sell more products. Not surprisingly, in the 1981–83 recession, capital investment dropped. It declined steadily for three straight years. The net savings rate declined, too. The big tax cut increased the federal deficit and the interest on the national debt — both of which soaked up a growing share of private saving. I will have more to say about the equity/efficiency aspect of savings, in Chapter 2.

A more subtle and seemingly plausible variant of the "savings" argument against distributive equity is the claim that the entitlement state produces an inflationary bias and therefore a disincentive to save generally. When inflation erodes the value of the currency, spending becomes a shrewder personal strategy than saving; *homo economicus* begins to consume more and save less. As more and more groups demand entitlements, the government fails to make choices, public deficits increase, which exacerbates the inflation and further depresses private thrift. Hence, a political economy that pursues egalitarian policies will pay a price in inflation, and eventually in lower real growth.

Again, the evidence contradicts the theory. Although the welfare state indeed has some built-in inflationary tendencies, they are not mechanical or universal. Consider the supposed inflationary impact of full employment. Some of the most expansive welfare states — West Germany, Austria, Norway — have enjoyed the West's lowest inflation rates. In practice, the so-called Phillips curve, which describes the tradeoff between inflation and unemployment, is almost as elusive as the Laffer curve.* Here as elsewhere, there is not one mechanistic tradeoff so much as many possible bargains, which in turn reflect institutional and political forces. Intriguingly, a compar-

---

*The Laffer curve, devised by Professor Arthur Laffer, held that lower tax rates in some cases could increase tax collections by stimulating economic growth. In practice, the 1981 tax cut led to unprecedented deficits.

ison of inflation-unemployment relationships in the major industrial nations shows that the best bargains occurred in nations where unemployment was *low*. Surprisingly enough, some of the most successful records of combining low unemployment and low inflation were made by countries with strong labor unions and powerful social democratic parties.

One mechanism that improves the terms of tradeoff between unemployment and inflation is a social bargain sometimes called an incomes policy: this means simply that average wage increases are politically bargained, equitably distributed, and held roughly to the rate of real growth in the economy. It turns out that unions, where they have substantial political legitimacy and influence, are often willing, if not eager, to trade the narrow goal of wage increases for the broader "solidarity" goals of full employment and comprehensive welfare protections. As their part of the bargain, they refrain from taking advantage of full employment to demand inflationary wage settlements. Paradoxically, therefore, strong unions, full employment, and wage restraint can be mutually reinforcing. This particular social bargain has enabled countries like West Germany and Austria, and to a lesser extent Norway and Sweden, to enjoy healthy inflation-employment outcomes, coupled with broad welfare entitlements and high savings rates as well.

Professor A. W. Phillips, in translating the unemployment and inflation data of many decades into a set of curves, looked at the issue mechanistically. As a neoclassical economist, he naturally reasoned that tight labor markets would increase labor's bargaining power and put upward pressure on wages; his graphs seemed to confirm the theory. He simply missed the practical possibility that institutional and political variables and a more sophisticated social contract could make a substantial difference in how inflationary tight labor markets had to be. In practice, the security afforded by full employment can be conducive to wage restraint.

Statism

Yet another basis for the claim that equality is bad for efficiency is the observation that the state is inherently less flexible than the market. This argument runs: To the extent that the state is the instrument of distributive justice, there will be efficiency costs. As a creature of formal rules and due process of law, the state operates according to rigid, bureaucratic norms; while the market, as a nimble and intuitive creature of invention, delights in breaking the mold. The more the state gets its clumsy oar in the market's way, the more it will slow down the boat: if you like the Post Office, you'll love socialism.

This claim, like the others, must be divided into its several strands. Let us first concede the obvious: no radical democrat should be too comfortable with a behemoth state as the sole instrument of social justice. None other than Karl Marx, in one of his more infelicitous phrases, called for the eventual "withering away of the state." Indeed, the early socialists were roused to indignation by the appalling effects of early capitalism on the traditional security of the individual. They hoped to restore community by means of voluntary, cooperative association, not to enlarge the state. The reality of twentieth-century communism mocks that vision. For an American radical democrat, the association of social justice with statism has to be troubling. Measures that promote social justice without expanding the domain of the state are always preferable to measures that enlarge it.

The association of equality with statism is not inevitable. Although it is often overlooked, a democratic polity pursues egalitarian policies in several distinct ways. Sometimes it "taxes and spends"; that is, it uses tax revenues to purchase goods (armaments, roads, factories) or services (education, health, child care), and in so doing it enlarges the state sector. But the welfare state also frequently influences economic distribution by rearranging money income within the private sector and by pursuing its older role as establisher of rules. In that capacity, the polity can have an effect on the distribution of private wealth and power, without necessarily enlarging the domain of the fisc. International comparison of the institutions of political economy reveals that democratic government often maximizes equality/efficiency bargains by functioning as a broker or allocator, rather than by absorbing private wealth into the public sector. For example, the government plays the broker role when it promotes incomes-policy bargaining.

American critics of welfare statism are often surprised to learn that countries like West Germany, with a much more comprehensive welfare state and a statistically "larger" public sector, have fewer government employees per capita than the United States does. The reason is that most of the welfare "state" is nothing more than a mechanism to channel tax revenues back to private consumers, not to spend them on public goods.

The biggest budget items of the modern welfare state do not enlarge the bureaucratic realm very much. Social security retirement exists as an item in the government budget only as an accounting convention. It simply represents income transferred from one set of citizens (workers), to another set (retirees); or, looked at another way, it is a setting-aside of private income during one phase of life (work) to be reclaimed in another (retirement), through the agency of the state.

Looking back at our own history, some of the most radically egalitarian interventions by the U.S. government on behalf of equality did not move resources into the state sector; they simply broadened their distribution within the private sector. The FHA programs of the 1930s and 1940s equalized the distribution of private wealth by making it easier for wage earners to own property wealth; they had no net cost to the public sector; incentives in public policy to encourage private pensions for blue-collar workers do the same.

The Homestead Acts of the nineteenth century, in fact, distributed wealth nominally owned by the government back to the private sector, *but with a deliberately egalitarian bias*. The legislation transferring government lands to private developers of railroads had the opposite distributive bias. Which policy was more "efficient"? Is the question even meaningful? Obviously, both policies stimulated growth, and growth produces dynamic gains. The distributive aspect was simply a political choice. It would be hard to argue that more efficient growth would have resulted had the government distributed land to big, aristocratic plantations instead of to yeoman farmers. On the other hand, one might well make the case that state-developed rail systems would have been no less efficient. State promotion of rural electrification co-ops versus privately owned utilities is a similar political choice with equality ramifications, but scant efficiency consequences or fiscal costs.

The political scientist Hugh Heclo rightly differentiates state programs to "spread wealth" — increase it and broaden its distribution at the same time — from programs that merely seek to redistribute existing wealth statically. Many economists tacitly assume that all egalitarian policies are of the latter sort.

The expansion of the polity as setter of rules or even as distributor of wealth need not expand the domain of the state as consumer of national income. In its rule-setting capacity, the egalitarian state can establish ground rules that improve the efficiency of the marketplace, either as explicit goals or as by-products. A well-known example is antitrust regulation. But for the antitrust laws, the Bell System would have gone on suppressing competition and innovation in the telecommunications field indefinitely. State regulation enhanced competition. A less obvious example is civil rights legislation. If we believe that natural talents are distributed without regard to race, then racial discrimination in hiring and promotion produces a less efficient use of manpower. It took state intervention — by rulemaking, not massive spending — to improve efficiency, as well as equality.

There are also countless examples of regulations that use marketlike mechanisms to create incentives to carry out private purposes. A good illustration is the federal regulation requiring airlines that overbook flights to compensate passengers with a free flight. This permits airlines to fly fuller than they otherwise might if airline companies were liable for damages for bumping confirmed passengers. But the spectacle of a flight attendant auctioning off a free flight is as pure an example of market efficiency as could be imagined. Passengers who must keep an appointment stay securely put. Passengers who can choose a couple of hours of leisure gain a windfall. There is a pure economic gain to efficiency, and one to fair play as well. But the fact that this particular market in free flights is the creature of a federal regulation makes it no less efficient, or inventive.

A careful comparison of welfare-state institutions suggests a surprising diversity in the actual relationships between equality and efficiency; between liberty and security; between state and market. Still, an egalitarian democrat must be uneasy about the central role of the State in the twentieth century as the agency of distributive justice. Preindustrial America was a unique social success (at least for white males) because little redistribution was necessary to combine liberty with equality, and security with opportunity. Seemingly, Jefferson's notion of a republic of small freeholders required scant interference by the state. Classical liberalism, which assumed no contradiction between liberal markets and liberal society, fitted the experience of preindustrial America perfectly. Given our national history, it is hardly surprising that Americans are more inclined to view the state as potential subverter of liberty than promoter of opportunity.

At the same time, however, one should not forget that even nine-teenth-century opportunity also relied on public subsidies — of education, of homesteads, and of public facilities. One should recall the legacy of economic conflicts between yeomen and money men going back at least as far as Jackson. Even America wasn't born into quite the innocent state of natural harmony that the laissez-faire vision implies. Pace the economists, it is possible to use statecraft to reconcile economic justice with economic growth and personal liberty. *Possible* — not easy.

THE KEYNESIAN INTERLUDE

Forty years ago, the equality/efficiency debate seemed all but settled intellectually. After the searing experience of the Great Depression, only a fool could argue that free markets were self-correcting. The appeal of totalitarianism demonstrated the fragility of political democracy that has been overwhelmed by economic insecurity. As the Depression obliterated the fiction of perfectly efficient markets, so World War II demonstrated simultaneously the possibility and the necessity of full employment. In the English-speaking democracies that were spared either occupation or home-grown dictatorship, the intellectual giants of economic discourse during the 1930s and 1940s were the practical egalitarians, Keynes, Beveridge, Tawney, Titmuss in Britain; Hopkins, Ickes, Eccles, Galbraith, Cohen, Berle, and countless others in the United States.

Keynes

The first of this book's several intellectual heroes must be John Maynard Keynes. Keynes wrote in a time like our own, when conventional economic prescriptions led to absurd practical outcomes. Although it is little remembered in the United States, England was in economic depression throughout the interwar period, not just after 1929. Between 1919 and 1939, unemployment dipped below 10 percent only once, in 1927. Throughout the 1920s, it averaged over 12 percent. An entire generation grew up experiencing the personal insecurity of high joblessness.

Keynes wrote as a humanist, not as a technician — though his technical virtuosity matched his ethical passion. Keynes's great contribution was to demonstrate once and for all that idleness is sheer economic and human waste. A liberal rather than a socialist, Keynes believed that gross inequality, episodic boom and bust, and the pain and waste of human idleness were not the inevitable hallmarks of capitalism. Today's born-again capitalists seem determined to prove him wrong.

In Keynes's day, as in our own, the resources of the economics profession were harnessed in the ideological service of the economic status quo. In the debate over public-works spending to relieve joblessness, most British economists subscribed to what came to be called the "Treasury View" — that unbalanced budgets would deepen the Depression. With millions out of work and output stagnant for want of effective purchasing power, the experts of that day counseled thrift as a solution to stagnation and wage reduction as a remedy for unemployment.

The Keynes of Economics 101 bears little resemblance to the man and his ideas. The radical Keynes, who understood that we could not maintain full employment as long as private owners of wealth remained responsible for allocating capital, is nowhere to be found. His radicalism has been denatured and appropriated into little more than a tactic to iron out business cycles. Maintain aggregate demand, and the idealized self-perfecting market is perfect once again. The so-called neoclassical synthesis, as propounded by the conservative Keynesians, is nothing but the old classical economics with the ingestion of as little Keynesianism as possible, an antitoxin to inoculate against further infection. In his famous textbook, Paul Samuelson, the leading American neoclassical "Keynesian," concludes his fiscal chapter with the sanguine observation that "appropriate fiscal and monetary policies can ensure that the economic environment can be such as to validate the verities" of classical theory. Keynes's great collaborator Joan Robinson appropriately terms this tradition Bastard Keynesianism.

Keynes, like Freud and Marx, deserves to be read in the original, not through the glosses of his lesser disciples. And what an original it is. Happily, Keynes wrote in English — I don't mean English as opposed to the German of Freud and Marx, but English as opposed to algebra. Keynes is an inspiration, not just because he proved that egalitarianism can be sound economics, but because he showed how political economy can be a fit subject for good, graceful prose. Re-reading Keynes in the age of Reagan and Thatcher is to appreciate anew his intellectual power and radicalism. In 1930, with the sheer delight of one who has discovered something so obvious once noticed that it is astonishing mankind missed the idea before, Keynes wrote:

> In the enforced idleness of millions, enough potential wealth is run-ning to waste to work wonders. Many millions of pounds' worth of goods could be produced each day by the workers and the plants which stand idle — and the workers would be the happier and the better for it. We ought to sit down to mend matters, in the mood of grave determination and the spirit of action at all costs, which we would have in a war . . .
>
> There are today many well wishers of their country who believe that the most useful thing which they and their neighbors can do to mend the situation is to save more than usual. If they refrain from spending a larger portion of their incomes than usual they believe they will have helped unemployment. If they are members of Town or County Councils they believe that their right course at such a time as this is to oppose expenditure on new amenities or new public works.
>
> Now, in certain circumstances all this would be quite right, but in the present circumstances, unluckily, it is quite wrong. It is utterly harmful and misguided — the very opposite of the truth. For the object of saving is to release labour for employment on producing capital goods such as houses, factories, roads, machines, and the like. But if there is a large unemployed surplus already available for such purposes, then the effect of saving is merely to add to this surplus and therefore to increase the number of the unemployed. Moreover, when a man is thrown out of work in this or any other way, his diminished spending power causes further unemployment amongst those who would have produced what he can no longer afford to buy . . .
>
> What we need now is not to button up our waistcoats tight, but be in a mood of expansion, of activity — to do things, to buy things, to make things. Surely all this is the most obvious common sense . . .

If the existing pattern of private savings was not automatically generating full employment, then there was nothing economically sacrosanct about it. In other words, wealth did not have to remain maldistributed in order to provide useful work. Indeed, excessive inequality harmed the cause of full production, because the rich were more easily able to horde their money while ordinary people spent it. As long as demand was kept full, the distribution of wealth was simply a political choice. One could argue about equality, but not on technical economic grounds. Keynes, as one French critic observed, was the "Freud of economics." Consumption was good for you; full employment was a mark of economic health. Inequality and parsimony, these were economic neuroses. "The patient does not need rest," Keynes declared. "He needs exercise."

In a depression, virtually anything that put people back to work and restored demand could fuel a recovery — even activities with scant inherent value. Long before World War II finally proved his point, Keynes wrote, "Pyramid-building, earthquakes, even wars may serve to increase wealth, if the education of our statesmen on the principles of the classical economics stands in the way of something better." How right he was. Groping for an illustration of a wholly absurd human activity to capture the ease with which government could prime the pumps if only it would, Keynes added,

> If the Treasury were to fill old bottles with bank-notes, bury them at suitable depths in disused coal-mines which are then filled up, top the surface with town rubbish, and leave it to private enterprise on well-tried principles of *laissez-faire* to dig the notes up again (the right to do so being obtained, of course, by tendering for leases of the note-bearing territory) there need be no more unemployment, and, with the help of the repercussions, the real income of the community, and its capital wealth also, would probably become a good deal greater than it actually is. It would, indeed, be more sensible to build houses and the like; but if there are political and practical difficulties in the way of this, the above would be better than nothing.

By 1936, Keynes had refined his brilliant intuitive conclusions and even rendered them in algebra for those who preferred that form of discourse. But Keynesianism was anything but "the most obvious common sense," for its implications were revolutionary. Full-blooded Keynesianism — substantial redistribution, social control over investment capital, and full employment — would transform power relationships utterly. Although the New Dealers in the United States had improvised their own ad hoc version of Keynesianism — "pump-priming" — neither Tory Britain nor more liberal America in the 1930s accepted the whole recipe.

Wartime Planning

Before peacetime Keynesianism was fully tried, war intervened. Even though much of the increased wartime production was of course quite literally blown up, unemployment in the United States melted from 14.6 percent in 1940 to below 2 percent in 1943. In three years, real output increased by 42 percent, or 14 percent per year — a growth rate that has been unequaled before or since.

World War II proved once and for all that organized planning in an industrial democracy could wipe out unemployment. The postwar challenge was to recreate a Keynesian equivalent of war, in peacetime. For a generation whose formative experience had been the Great Depression, that was no trivial revelation. After the Great Depression and the War, the generation then in power — liberals and social democrats alike — had experienced radically new fundamental lessons of political economy. Not only was unemployment an avoidable economic and human tragedy, but it was antithetical to the politics of social justice in subtle secondary ways. When high unemployment intruded, the "reserve army" phenomenon eroded decent wages; social income — which should be reserved for groups with particular needs such as the elderly, large families, and the handicapped — got consumed by the dole. The nonrich were easily divided into the still-working poor and the idle, and it became easy to blame the unemployed for their condition. In periods of high unemployment, workers turned into Luddites.

In the planning for the postwar period, the near-universal fear in England and America was that peace would bring with it renewed depression. High unemployment had followed World War I; it seemed inconceivable that the civilian economy could absorb ten million men in uniform, once the fevered pitch of wartime production slackened. In both Britain and America, planning for full employment became a central policy goal.

In America, where the War finally compelled the government involvement in the economy that the New Deal had never quite achieved, not only did the AFL and the CIO advocate postwar national planning, but major business groups worried about postwar depression did so as well. The Committee for Economic Development, founded in the summer of 1942, represented businessmen who no longer harbored ideological qualms about national planning; their concern was that planning exist in harmony with private industry, rather than as an alternative to it; their version paralleled what the French later called indicative planning — the government would collect data, anticipate market trends, perhaps even play some coordinating role in the allocation of private investment. Full employment was accepted as a central policy goal, even by the National Association of Manufacturers. For one brief moment, everyone was a real Keynesian.

In January 1944, in his State of the Union address, Franklin D. Roosevelt announced his "Economic Bill of Rights," which included the right to a job and to a minimum income. Just a year later, four senate liberals put the idea into legislative form, in the Full Employment Act of 1945. The original bill, authored by Democratic senators Robert F. Wagner of New York, James E. Murray of Montana, and Elbert Thomas of Utah, created the statutory right to a job and required a federal "investment and expenditure" program, sufficient "to assure a full employment of production."

During 1945, however, a major counterrevolution occurred. FDR died in April; instead of the predicted recession, the accumulated savings and the deferred wartime demand for consumer goods fueled an unexpected boom. Major segments of the business community reverted to their usual libertarian philosophy, with the New York Chamber of Commerce testifying in opposition to the bill, "An occasional depression is the price we pay for freedom." By the time the Employment Act of 1946 was signed by President Harry S Truman, the word *full* had been deleted, and the act was little more than a framework for setting macroeconomic policy. Full employment remained as an ideal, not as a concrete policy goal. The American welfare state existed as a patchwork of *ad hoc* programs, not as an entitlement to a job or to income. As Otis Graham, the historian of post-1933 planning, observed, the "Planning State" was truncated into a "Broker State."

In Britain, where the same intellectual transformation occurred, politics turned left after the War. As in America, the experience of wartime full employment, initially, had the same powerful effect on left and right alike. Unemployment seemed as unnecessary as it was indefensible. Moreover, the War was much closer to home in Britain;

just as there could be no atheists in foxholes, there were no aristocrats in bomb shelters. The common sacrifices of war brought home to the British middle class the unpleasant realities of gross social inequality.

Beveridge

The initial plans for a full-employment–welfare state were drawn up under Winston Churchill's war cabinet, a coalition government dominated by Conservatives. The drafting fell to William Beveridge, like Keynes a lifelong Liberal rather than a socialist. Beveridge's first report, written in 1942, laid out the blueprint for social insurance. It was very much in reformist tradition, conservative in its detail, but revolutionary in its vision. Beveridge was not concerned with whether the ownership of capital was ultimately private or social. But he wanted to make sure that nobody went without. He hoped to sweep away the prewar system of poor laws, means tests, and incomplete programs of welfare with a comprehensive structure of social security, sufficient to guarantee a mimimal standard of living as the right of a citizen. "Now, when the war is abolishing landmarks of every kind," Beveridge wrote, "is the time for using experience in a clear field. A revolutionary moment in the world's history is a time for revolutions, not for patching."

Two years later, in 1944, Beveridge issued his second report, *Full Employment in a Free Society,* in which he differentiated two distinct social ills, Want and Idleness. His earlier report, he now wrote, was a plan to free a British citizen from Want "when for any reason he cannot work and earn." The second, complementary report proposed as well "freedom from Idleness"; and Beveridge added, "Idleness is not the same as Want, but a separate evil, which men do not escape by having an income. They also must have the chance of rendering a useful service . . ."

After four intervening decades, Beveridge's second report remains the definitive exposition of why full employment must be the centerpiece of social citizenship. Without it, both the political logic and the fiscal viability of the welfare state fall apart. Paradoxically, Beveridge explained, a full-employment context enhances not only labor's bargaining power, but also labor's flexibility and efficiency. It makes substitution of capital for labor easier, not more difficult, for it assures that there will be new jobs to replace the old, even when the market temporarily has failed to create them. Beveridge utterly rejected the laissez-faire idea that slack in labor markets was a desirable condition. The labor market, he wrote,

> should always be a seller's market rather than a buyer's market. . . . The reason is that difficulty in selling labour has consequences of a different order of harmfulness from those associated with difficulty in buying labour. A person who has difficulty buying the labour that he needs suffers inconvenience or reduction of profits. A person who cannot sell his labour is in effect told that he is of no use. The first difficulty causes annoyance or loss. The other is a personal catastrophe.

Beveridge's logic is impeccable; and to a generation who had experienced the deep tragedy of depression, followed immediately by full employment in a planned wartime economy, there seemed no practical impediment to carrying the vision out. For Beveridge, social insurance against Want was necessary, but not sufficient. Unemployment remained a personal catastrophe,

> . . . even if an adequate income is provided by insurance or otherwise. Idleness, even on an income, corrupts; the feeling of not being wanted demoralizes. . . . As long as there is any long-term unemployment not due to personal deficiency, anybody who loses his job fears that he may be one of the unlucky ones who will not get another job quickly. The short-term unemployed do not know that they are short-term unemployed till their unemployment is over.

Conservatives, of course, would insist that the "inconvenience" of "loss of profits" is far more than the minor annoyance that Beveridge would have it be, but a major drag on economic efficiency, and hence a sin against the ultimate well-being of all. But Beveridge makes a powerful case that full employment is ultimately the best route to avoid the invidious necessity of having to trade off individual suffering for supposed social well-being. The conservatives have it exactly backwards. Growth is maximized when everybody is working and when the economy operates at full production. There are powerful secondary benefits to this logic, not the least of which is enthusiasm for technical innovation:

> Only if there is work for all is it fair to expect working people, individually and collectively in trade unions, to co-operate in making the most of all productive resources, including labour, and to forgo restrictionist practices. . . . [And further, Beveridge explained] Yet

another reason is the stimulus to technical advance that is given by shortage of labour. Where men are few, machines are used to save men for what men alone can do. Where labour is cheap it is often wasted on brainless, unassisted toil. The new lands of men are the homes of invention and business adventure in peace. Stimulus to labour saving of all kinds is one of the by-products of full employment in war.

As Beveridge so brilliantly explains, the logic of a full-employment context transforms the supposed equality/efficiency stand-off, in which the pain of unemployment and low wages for some must be traded off against the health of the economy as a whole. If the economy is kept at full employment, both society and worker gain from tight labor markets. Wages rise; employment security is a given. As new labor-saving processes are invented, drudgery is relieved, workers are able to shift to new opportunities, and society benefits from the productivity advances. Absent a full-employment context, of course, the market eventually shifts labor from one sector to another, too, but with far greater loss of output and social dislocation in the meantime. Wages decline; consumption falters. One has only to review the current debate about technological displacement to appreciate Beveridge's prescience. With unemployment averaging 10 percent throughout the industrial West, technology suddenly seems a menace again, and tenured $40,000-a-year economics professors are accusing $18,000-a-year factory workers of Luddism. How much less ambiguous a blessing technology would be against a background of full employment.

As a Liberal and as the nominal employee of a "grand coalition" Conservative-Liberal-Labour government, Beveridge was sanguine and even blasé about the prospect of socializing income without socializing capital. He wrote,

> The necessity of socialism, in order to secure full employment, has not yet been demonstrated. This implies no judgment on the general issue between socialism and capitalism, which remains for debate on other grounds. It does not mean that the problem of full employment and the problem of control of industry are in no way connected; they are connected in many ways. It means only a judgment that it would be possible to obtain full productive employment under conditions of private enterprise.

The logic of full employment also pushed Beveridge to implications beyond his Whig reformism. "The essential list of liberties," he could write in an aside that seems astonishingly casual in this age of the free-market redux, "does not include liberty of a citizen to own means of production and to employ other citizens in operating them at a wage. *Whether private ownership of means of production is a good economic device or not, it must be judged as a device*" [emphasis added]. Beveridge, of course, was right. The market system ultimately is a means, not an end. It stands or falls "as a device." And as a device even perfect markets produce imperfect human outcomes. That is why today's new laissez-faire ideologues struggle so mightily to imbue the crass business of getting and spending with transcendent virtues.

But how brave and simple the postwar world seemed in that resolute year 1944! Full employment would come, because it could come. A social safety net would be woven, because it was economically possible and socially just. Keynes provided the economic theory, Tawney the ethical rationale, and Beveridge the social machinery. Even the most fundamental, ideologically charged issue of all, ownership of the means of production (to coin a phrase!), was reduced to a mere tactical detail. If we can retain private industry, well, fine. If we need to socialize it, well, that's fine too.

These wonderful British wartime policy blueprints, in their innocence, considered everything but the necessary political underpinnings; they assumed the autonomy of public policy and the benign competence of technicians. They mistook the temporary wartime spirit of unity and sacrifice for a permanent social détente, an easy, bloodless victory over inequality. They erroneously assumed the benevolent neutrality of powerful business groups and wealthy individuals, who after all had more than a little to lose from a redistributive, full-employment state. The intellectual vision of the egalitarian technocrats seemed to have solved the ultimate social issue and retired class conflict. Full employment and growth would reinforce each other; social security would take care of society's unfortunates. All of this was not only justifiable as socially decent; it was good for business. Equality would not have to wait for the distant promise of growth. Equality would fuel growth. The design was sound enough. Only the politics were slippery.

WELFARE CAPITALISM

How different the world looks after forty years. Had they gone to sleep in the mid-1940s, Beveridge and Keynes might have awakened in the 1980s to find that much had not gone according to plan. The social sector of the economy was substantial, but the capitalist welfare state seemed in real danger of consuming the invisible hand that fed it. Economic growth, robust during the first two postwar decades, had faltered badly. In the industrial democracies, the public sector was consuming between 30 and 50 percent of the national income.

But the welfare state, however bloated, remained flawed and incomplete. Astonishingly, unemployment was running at levels above 10 percent — and many of the unemployed were either not voting at all, or voting conservative. The cost of maintaining the income supports in the face of slow growth and high idleness led to terrible deficits — as high as 15 percent of GNP in Europe's more comprehensive welfare states — deficits that could not possibly be sustained. Even in the United States, deficits were in excess of 6 percent of GNP, and that under a conservative administration.

Despite the large public sector, surprisingly little redistribution had taken place. Much as the radical critics of Keynes had warned in the 1930s, the costs of the welfare state were being borne by the middle class and the working poor. The social programs were becoming tatty, and losing their broad middle-class constituency. The class détente, the end of ideology heralded in the early flush of postwar growth, had collapsed. Ideology had returned in full force, borne on laissez-faire wings. A Keynesian might awake and say, with Prufrock, "That is not what I meant at all."

Overloads and Undercurrents

Despite the high fiscal cost, the promise of social citizenship remained only partly fulfilled. Alongside some truly universal programs, like social security retirement, a degrading, pre-Beveridge welfare state of poor laws and means tests remained, particularly in Britain and America. A family that slipped into the clutches of the AFDC system (Aid to Families with Dependent Children) was sure to encounter the indignity of pauperization, bed checks, and even demands for symbolic tribute in the form of dreary make-work reminiscent of the Dickensian workhouse. The same even applied to recipients of Medicaid and supplemental income security in old age.

The anomaly of safety-net entitlements amid persistently high unemployment created a new problem: the welfare trap. Once on the dole, families subsisted on a variety of means-tested benefits: AFDC, Medicaid, various free social services, food stamps, and perhaps public housing as well. If the family was able to regain some earned income, the social benefits declined apace; often the "tax" on earned income (in the form of benefit reductions) exceeded 100 percent. In America, the one advanced nation without universal health insurance, going off welfare meant losing Medicaid coverage. To break cleanly out of the poverty trap and improve one's real net income required a rate of pay more than twice the minimum wage, at a time when such jobs were seldom available to most people on welfare, least of all to the dependent mothers who made up the bulk of the caseload. Despite 10 percent unemployment, it became too easy to blame the poor for preferring the welfare existence.

Beveridge might have felt perversely vindicated: Without full employment, the whole welfare-state system fell apart — morally and politically, as well as fiscally. The necessary solidarity between the nonwealthy middle class, the working poor, and the needy came unglued; the costs of maintaining the idle produced insupportable taxes or damaging deficits.

The impasse of the advanced welfare state is multidimensional. Not only does the welfare state seem to encroach on the efficiency of markets, but the market keeps encroaching on state objectives, leaving the state to take the blame. The need to deal in or buy off private interests corrupts public purposes. In America, we build public housing by creating lucrative inducements to private developers, and then wax indignant at the public waste. The inducements, naturally, reflect the persistent influence of the same developers. A still-powerful market economy keeps trying to duplicate itself inside the nominally public sector. In the same manner, and for the same political reasons, we invite profit-motivated nursing-home operators to serve the elderly poor; we socialize the expense of medical care for the aged, but leave the provision of care to profit-maximizing market forces.

In a purely market transaction, the entrepreneur maximizes profits by minimizing costs; that is one of the authentic virtues of a market system. But in the United States, private entrepreneurs dependent on state reimbursements typically maximize their returns by *maximizing* costs. In effect, they are a lobby on behalf of inefficiency. This, of course, is not a necessary outcome. One could imagine a political system where doctors, private nursing-home operators, and housing developers had less political power to enforce a fiscal bargain damaging to the efficiency of the state. But that is not the political system we have. In many respects, the American mixed system of welfare capitalism marries the most inefficient aspects of the public sector to the most inefficient aspects of the private.

These contradictions are less extreme in the nations of Northern Europe, where there is ideological sufferance for public performance of public functions. Nonetheless, as we shall see, there are other fault lines where state and market mesh imperfectly, common to most of the industrial nations.

Redistribution Resisted

Throughout the industrial West, the welfare state has attempted to redistribute income to the needy, while leaving the market system essentially intact as the source of wealth. This particular compromise has its virtues, but it has made redistribution of income very costly and conducive to fiscal excesses. Although the details vary, the pattern is common to all of the advanced welfare states. The one notable exception to the rule is social security retirement, which pays disproportionately generous benefits to low-paid workers once they retire, and contributes significantly to the reduction of poverty among the elderly. The stubborn failure of all the public spending to accomplish much redistribution is a puzzle which will be addressed more fully in Chapter 5.

In most of the Western nations, the final distribution of private income in the late 1970s was little different from what it had been in the late 1940s. It is not substantially different after the application of taxing and spending than before. The technical explanation for this paradox lies on both sides of the tax and spending ledger.

As more income is distributed through the state, a progressive tax system becomes harder to maintain. When the state spends only 10 percent of total national income, most of that can be obtained from the rich. But when 50 percent of the GNP flows through the public sector, even 100 percent tax rates on rich people would not raise enough revenue; tax rates on the middle class and even the poor tend to rise steeply. For example in 1960, a British family with two thirds the average income paid no tax. Today, such a family pays 20 percent of its income to the government. Even the nominal elements of progressivity in the income tax are effectively washed out by tax shelters that benefit the affluent.

In the 1960s and 1970s, as the income tax reached top marginal rates of 80 and 90 percent which truly did begin to encroach on economic incentives, governments turned more and more to regressive payroll and consumption taxes. As a whole, most Western tax systems today are not redistributive, except at the very top and the very bottom, where they redistribute only slightly. Under the Thatcher and Reagan governments, tax incidence became substantially more regressive after 1980.

Interestingly, too, there is scant redistribution even on the spending side of the ledger, though there is some "leveling up" when truly universal social services are available. To a large extent, public spending tends to reflect, and often to reinforce, market-determined patterns of inequality. In the area of public education, for example, rich school districts with substantial property wealth are able to spend more money per pupil than poor districts can. In housing policy, the tax subsidy to the middle class via the mortgage interest deduction is worth about ten times the direct subsidy to the poor on public housing. Even in nonfederalist countries, where the ability to spend is less constrained by the tax base of local government, the same stubborn patterns persist.

The upper-middle class makes more use of free medical care because they have more sophistication and more leisure than the working poor. Subsidized mass transit and commuter rail services heavily benefit the already affluent. The upper-middle class takes disproportionate advantage of subsidized cultural activities. When federal law required local school districts to pay educational costs of "special needs" children with physical or mental handicaps, it was the suburban middle class that took disproportionate advantage of the entitlement. The affluent and the educated tend to send their children disproportionately to universities; where universities are state subsidized (in most nations) this represents yet one more redistribution from the general population to the already privileged. A very careful study by the English sociologist Julian Le Grand found that average expenditure by the British National Health Service per ill person was more or less equal across class lines, but since poor people suffer more ill health than do rich people, the intensiveness of medical care relative to need remained maldistributed in favor of the rich, by about two-to-one. Le Grand concluded that of all the British social service outlays, only rent subsidies and public housing expenditures represented net redistribution to the poor; all other outlays were either neutral, or pro-rich.

A defender of the National Health system might point out, of course, that poor people still got much more health care than they otherwise would have in the absence of the system, that leaving medical treatment to the vagaries of market-determined income would have produced far worse disparities; and therefore, that free health care nonetheless produced an important relative gain for the poor. And this observation goes to the heart of the political and fiscal paradox of the liberal welfare state: the principle of universal entitlement, though very costly fiscally, is necessary on both political and programmatic grounds.

To win broad popular support, social programs must be of high quality and must serve the middle class as well as the poor. It is axiomatic that "programs limited to the poor are poor programs." But when programs serve everybody, they accomplish little redistribution, and then tend to outrun their fiscal constraints. Further, the public expense of paying for them with broad-based taxes makes the tax system less redistributive as well. As Arthur Okun was wont to observe, the welfare state redistributes with a leaky bucket. To that extent, social programs are "inefficient" if the sole criterion of efficiency goal is economically measurable redistribution. But clearly, there are equity gains simply in having the poor and the nonpoor treated in the same hospitals, educated in the same school system, and subjected to the same rules when income supports may be necessary.

Not only is the "leak" of benefits to the nonpoor socially desirable; it is politically indispensable. Clearly, means-tested programs would target more income to the genuinely needy and therefore accomplish more redistribution, in the literal sense. As Christopher Jencks has written, "If we want to redistribute income, the most effective strategy is probably still to redistribute income." However, most forms of means testing, though administratively efficient, are politically doomed. Income-support programs narrowly targeted to the poor are notoriously unpopular politically, as well as destructive of social citizenship. Means-tested programs tend to be stigmatizing, invasive, and shabby around the edges, especially when times are hard and the fiscal mood is testy. One has only to consider the visual and procedural differences between a local welfare office and a local social security office to appreciate that the recipients of middle-class social entitlements are treated as citizens, while welfare clients are presumed chiselers until proven otherwise.

There *are* resolutions to these quandaries, to be addressed throughout this book. As we shall see in Chapter 6, the Northern European model of the welfare state manages to operate entitlement programs that serve entire populations according to need — the sick, the old, the jobless, and large families — without stigmatizing on the basis of need. Emphatically, the remedies do not lie in conventional equality/efficiency tradeoffs, or in a return to the primitive discipline of market consequences and private charity. They require a politics, as we shall see, which is difficult anywhere but most of all in the American context.

Ideological Consequences

By the mid 1970s, the entitlement state of Beveridge and Keynes was plainly coming a cropper. The fiscal arithmetic simply didn't work; the political bargain didn't work. Support for the tax burdens was evaporating, and the state as the agency of good works had consumed much of its political capital.

This state of affairs caused a grim sense of vindication at both ends of the ideological spectrum. For both laissez-faire conservatives and for the more dogmatic of the Marxists, it is no surprise that welfare capitalism cannot work; it is axiomatic.

For conservatives, the danger of open-ended entitlements in a political democracy is obvious enough. Consumers and providers of services alike become special-interest lobbyists for more money. Create a social program and you create an instant lobby. The roster of national associations of service providers is awesome. Politicians (except presumably those motivated by a stout laissez-faire conscience and a safe district) cannot resist pandering to the special interests; instead of making hard choices, they simply fund everybody. And, though few conservative critics bother to extend the analysis to point out a certain fearful symmetry, precisely the same dynamic operates on the tax side of the equation. Business groups, though seldom lobbyists for spending programs, want something from government, too: they want tax relief.

Thus, the lobby/entitlement-state wreaks fiscal calamity on both sides of the ledger. Some special interests successfully demand costly outlays; others successfully demand costly tax concessions. Politicians even-handedly respond to both. Dreadful deficits are the result. Government approaches bankruptcy, with hideous consequences for the broader economy. What opens Pandora's box, in the conservative view, is the principle of social entitlement. Politicians are weak mortals, with short-run horizons; they cannot resist bankrupting the state once private welfare becomes a legitimate public goal.

This view has more than a grain of truth, though it reflects a peculiarly American perspective. The tendency to fiscal ruin is far worse in a nonparliamentary and decentralized political system like our own that combines separation of legislative and executive powers, federalism, nonideological parties, and special-interest politics.

Interestingly enough, critics working in the neo-Marxist tradition have made many of the same points. In their view, the welfare state does not represent so much a concession to social justice wrested by democrats and trade unionists, as it does a quite rational device by owners of capital to make the system run more smoothly. Thus, public education serves capital by training and socializing workers; unemployment insurance, workmen's compensation, and subsidized retraining help market systems rationalize their work forces without sowing the seeds of open labor unrest. By the same token, social-welfare programs help to maintain harmony that would otherwise be undermined by the brutality of pure market dynamics; welfare outlays serve to pacify the reserve labor army.

The best known of the American Marxist welfare-state critics, James O'Connor, calls this function "legitimation" — state social outlays help win public acceptance of the capitalist economy; they serve to "legitimatize" it, without altering any of its fundamentals. We misunderstand the dynamics of the welfare state utterly, say the neo-Marxists, if we believe that its true "purpose" is redistribution.

The two most prominent American exponents of this view, Richard Cloward and Frances Fox Piven, argue persuasively that the apparent irrationalities of programs like Aid to Families with Dependent Children become much easier to fathom when they are understood as purposive.

Since, in the Marxian view, capitalism itself is a bundle of contradictions, it is hardly surprising that welfare capitalism produces fiscal contradictions. Because advanced capitalism keeps generating social catastrophes, the cost of maintaining social peace steadily increases. This will continue as long as ownership of productive wealth remains private, because the underlying relations of production have not changed. Deeper realities must corrupt ostensibly benign purposes.

This Marxist "functional" interpretation of the welfare state is provocative, but like all tautological analyses it also runs up against awkward evidence. How to explain trade unions? Were they just a capitalist device to maintain labor peace? And what about social security and health insurance? In their latest book, Cloward and Piven decided that most American social programs in fact represented real political gains after all, which should be defended at all costs. As Ian Gough, the British Marxist sociologist, observes teasingly,

> In the 1960s, radicals and Marxists were analyzing the welfare state as a repressive mechanism of social control: social work, the schools, housing departments, the probation service, social security agencies — all were seen as means of controlling and/or adapting rebellious and non-conforming groups in society to the needs of capitalism. Yet in the 1970s, these self-same people were rushing to defend the welfare state against "the cuts."

Which is it, Gough asks: Capitalist fraud or working class victory? This is not a question that need be resolved definitively. Surely, some social programs like social security and social medicine represent genuine gains for the have-nots, while others have as their primary goal social control. Many programs reflect both goals at once. This ambiguity indeed goes back to the English poor laws, where the charitable purpose of keeping people from starving collided with the concern that any relief above bare subsistence would encourage people to choose idleness over work. As Beveridge and Keynes might have pointed out, the dilemma is most acute when work is scarce. When work at decent wages is broadly available, the conflict subsides; for most people who can work prefer to work. When 10 million able people are involuntarily idle, the "truly needy" are rather harder to delimit. Unless one has a very mechanistic view of history, it should be clear that the welfare state is bogging down precisely because it is having difficulty serving multiple and often contradictory goals.

Welfare Capitalism Reconsidered

One needn't be a Marxist or a follower of Milton Friedman to agree that the welfare capitalism compromise has reached its fiscal limits. The essence of the postwar social democratic compromise was substantial socialization of income, but surprisingly little socialization of productive capital and individual fortunes. The dynamics of the market system and the concentrations of political power available to the wealthy were left untouched, except in three of four Western nations with very strong and cohesive labor movements. This bargain is desirable in theory, because it preserves the competitive discipline of the market, which serves as its main claim to social legitimacy, while ameliorating the market's unfortunate social side effects. Moreover, for those who believe that private property is a necessary bulwark of liberty, the social democratic compromise has the further virtue of leaving private property essentially intact.

But socializing income without socializing wealth indeed creates a tendency to "fiscal overload" because the market-determined distribution of income continues to recapitulate the gross maldistribution of private wealth. The more that the sphere of social citizenship is broadened, the more mightily the welfare state must labor to overcome this disparity, and at ever greater strain to itself and to the market system.

Moreover, there is an unfortunate feedback loop between maldistributed wealth and maldistributed power. In the political arena the owners of wealth are not exactly neutral spectators. Arthur Okun, with the political innocence that economists seem to cherish, could write, "There is no obvious and natural mechanism that conveys extra helpings of votes to the wealthy . . ." Okun conceded that some abuses existed, but he concluded that the remedy lay in "specific aids and sanctions rather than general efforts to curb bigness and wealth." In his own work addressing the political feedback problem, Charles Lindblom, though no more of a radical than Okun, disagrees. For

Lindblom, "the privileged position of business" in democratic capitalism introduces gross imbalances that are seldom fully calculated by political scientists *or* economists. "In short," Lindblom writes, "in any free enterprise system, a large category of major decisions is turned over to businessmen, large and small. They are taken off the agenda of government. Businessmen thus become a kind of public official and exercise what, on a broad view of their role, are public functions." And at another point, Lindblom comments, "In their pursuit of a definitive list of market shortcomings, economists do not include adverse effects of market systems on governments and politics. It is a blind spot in their analysis."

Lindblom, I think, has the better of the argument. The main obstacle to Okun-style reforms — "specific aids and sanctions" to keep money from corrupting the democratic process — is precisely the entrenched power of the rich, who would lose from permanent procedural reforms. The history of American democracy is one of episodic bursts of reform, which temporarily curb the political power of wealth, and longer periods of normalcy, in which the wealthy exercise immense political influence. The case for redistribution of wealth as a necessary concomitant to political democracy is persuasive to me, on grounds of efficiency as well as equity. Expanding on Lindblom, one might add another side effect of maldistributed wealth on welfare capitalism: the well-off do not have sufficient power to block social programs, but they have ample influence to attach conditions that raise their cost and blunt their effectiveness. The American health-care system is the most telling example. Government underwrites the cost of some medical care, but under terms heavily influenced by for-profit medicine.

Thus, particularly where the market ideology is strong and the offsetting influence of trade unions and social democratic parties is weak, the welfare-capitalism compromise is sufficient to leaven capitalism slightly but also to hobble it. Where I differ from both the Marxists and the free-market celebrants is that I do not believe this is an inevitable outcome. Egalitarianism need not come to a bad end.

Now that the postwar social democratic compromise has reached its fiscal and political limits, several alternative courses are possible. One is a return to laissez-faire, which has such strong ideological appeal at present. That would produce obvious costs to both economic performance and social justice, if history is any guide. Another is totalitarian socialism, with intolerable costs to personal liberty and to economic efficiency. But within the broad middle way, there are other approaches, which indeed maximize both efficiency and equal-ity and also preserve political democracy and personal freedom from either too much market or too much state. Despite the evident blem-ishes of the welfare state it is possible to glean some elements of a more hopeful course by looking at different bargains of political economy that already exist.

TOWARD BETTER BARGAINS

Since World War II, the United States has had one of the smallest public sectors and the slowest rate of public-sector expansion, com-bined with one of the widest gaps in income distribution, the least amount of national economic planning — and one of the lowest growth rates of any advanced industrial country. Other nations have man-aged to combine broader welfare protections with higher rates of savings and investment and more rapid growth, by blending different ingredients into a superior social bargain.

Sweden and Austria, for example, have refined and expanded the principles of Keynesianism. Sweden seeks to equalize the primary distribution of wage and salary income, so that there will be less need for redistribution after the fact. Sweden also relies heavily on an "active labor-market policy" to keep employment more or less stable throughout the swings in the business cycle. When unemploy-ment rises, the government pumps resources into a system of labor-market boards, which can subsidize the creation of jobs and the retraining of workers. This is the microeconomic counterpart of Keynesian macroeconomics. It enables Sweden to stay at or near full employment without overstimulating the whole economy.

By the same token, both Austria and Sweden have devised centrally bargained income policies to keep wage increases closely aligned to the real rate of growth of the economy. They can thus operate full-employment societies without triggering unacceptable inflation. Aus-tria relies heavily on centralized economic planning; Sweden does not. Sweden has largely socialized its supply of savings through a funded national pension system. Austria achieves a high rate of sav-ings by running a government budget surplus and by encouraging corporate profits. The structure of wages looks markedly different in Sweden and America. A Swedish corporate executive earns only two or three times the wage of a production worker; a doctor perhaps twice that of a nurse. A waitress not much less than a skilled machinist. But this supposed "distortion" of market signals doesn't seem to do much damage; for the strong purchasing power provided by a full-employment/high-wage society more than makes up for the affront to theory.

During most of the postwar period, Sweden and Austria managed to combine superior growth rates (Sweden's in the last decade has been about the same as ours; Austria's is still far higher), with far more egalitarian distributions of income. While U.S. unemployment rates have soared into double digits and American economists now define full employment as 6–7 percent joblessness, Sweden and Austria have kept their unemployment rate below 3 percent most of the time.

Some of the elements of Swedish and Austrian Keynesianism have often been proposed in the United States. Many economists have looked longingly at the successful incomes policy and the comprehensive labor-market boards. But in the United States there is neither the ideological commitment to egalitarian outcomes nor the cohesive, ideologically motivated labor movement necessary to broker compliance and to assure that such policies would advance social equality as well as social discipline.

The two top economic performers of the postwar era, West Germany and Japan, have some characteristics in common, but other clear divergences. The Japanese social bargain involves a great deal of government planning and brokering, a very egalitarian distribution of primary income, low corporate net profits, and surprisingly high corporate taxes. In fact, Japan's tax system has a higher reliance on taxation of capital than any other major nation. Japan achieves a good deal of social security with a relatively small public sector, through corporate paternalism. In recent years, however, Japan's public spending as a fraction of GNP has approached American levels, and its nonmilitary public spending now equals ours. The West German social bargain includes a far larger public sector than the United States or Japan, a fairly egalitarian income distribution, and a modest degree of coordinated economic planning, with the key planning role performed by big private banks. In both West Germany and Japan, banks are the primary source of investment capital. Both nations tend to have far more stable monetary policies, with lower real interest rates and hence lower costs of capital to industry. The West Germany tax system is effectively more redistributive than ours, with a more progressive income tax and fewer tax loopholes. Japan and West Germany have a more nearly equal income distribution than the United States, both before and after taxes, as well as much higher rates of capital investment and growth.

Britain, on the other hand, has a public sector, an overall tax load, and a final income distribution very comparable to West Germany's, but the worst record of recent economic performance of any advanced country. These comparisons are always difficult because they violate the economist's disclaimer, *ceteris paribus*. In comparing the economies of different nations, other things are never equal. The fractious British labor movement bears no resemblance to the well-mannered but nonetheless powerful West German labor movement. For West German workers, an incomes policy is a reasonable social bargain. For British unionists, it is a capitalist plot. Econometrics doesn't help us understand the difference. An understanding of political history and social context does.

At worst, comparisons of international economic performance levels and social bargains suggest that growth does not necessarily thrive on inequality. The reality is that a variety of bargains are possible, and that other industrial nations have optimized growth and equity objectives far better than the United States has. Equality and efficiency are not a "big tradeoff," so much as many possible bargains, some of which do not require a sacrifice of either goal at the expense of the other.

The comparisons also challenge the claim that burgeoning government necessarily crowds out productive investment. In West Germany and France, Austria and Norway, which enjoyed far better records of economic growth than the United States did, the public sector surpassed 30 percent of GNP in the early 1950s — on the eve of a sustained economic boom. Their public sectors three decades ago were bigger than the American public sector today. It is also significant that all of the major industrial economies began showing the effects of global slowdown in the mid-1970s, regardless of their particular social bargains.

The very best economic performers seem to have these characteristics in common: an effective system for converting savings to productive investment; a well-trained and diligent work force; and social institutions that provide personal security and opportunity and minimize class discord. It is astounding that one could expect gross inequalities of wealth and income to foster any of these conditions.

Within a relatively short time, *capital formation* has entered the lexicon of "good" words — not quite equal to Home and Mother, but still a policy goal few would disagree with.

— Charls Walker, Chairman
American Council for Capital Formation, 1980

2

CAPITAL

NOTHING IS MORE POWERFUL than an idea whose time has come because it happens to serve the self-interest of immensely powerful people. At the center of the resurgence of laissez-faire economics is the claim that the supply of capital is the key determinant of economic growth. Since savings is the source of investment and investment is the source of growth, rewarding the process of capital accumulation is deemed paramount. In a capitalist economy, presumably, the prime source of capital is capitalists. Therefore, the contention that taxation and redistribution must be bad for capital formation enjoys a certain appeal to common sense. Where the Keynesian paradox held that redistribution is good for producers, the supply-side paradox holds that inequality is good for everyone.

In the more extreme fever of supply-side economics, some theorists, such as the economist Arthur Laffer, went so far as to claim that incentive effects on suppliers of capital are so potent that lower tax rates will actually increase tax collections, so efficiently will they stimulate investment and economic growth. That claim was never accepted by most economists, and it stands quite discredited by events, notably by President Reagan's $200 billion supply-side deficit. A more modest version of the supply-side idea, however, retains a quite tenacious hold on the popular imagination.

Buried in the argument lies a series of fallacies that merit careful dissection. The central fallacy is the assumption that since the rich are the people with riches, redistributing some of those riches will necessarily leave society with less wealth to invest. But that, of course, depends on how the rich would spend their riches if left alone, and how the laissez-faire pattern of investment compares with one that obtains after redistribution takes place. A related mistake, raised pointedly by Thorstein Veblen against the supply-side sybarites of his day, is the presumption that financial holdings necessarily equal productive investment. The rich have no rival at innovative consumption. More surprisingly, the most important single source of capital is no longer private capitalists. It is pension funds, which represent the deferred wages and future nest eggs of wage earners.

In reality, capital supply is only one of many determinants of growth. The others include aggregate demand, technological dynamism, and the productivity of the work force. Pioneering work by the economist Edward Denison disaggregated the sources of productivity growth and found that the skills and educational levels of workers, money allocated to research and development, and a variety of other factors were more important than capital supply. And although there is indeed a relationship between capital supply and growth, it is not at all clear that a less equal distribution of wealth enhances the accumulation of capital or its useful investment.

I will suggest in this chapter that a much broader distribution of wealth and income than the one we now have is fully compatible with high rates of savings, investment, and growth, even within a system that continues to rely substantially on market signals to allocate investment. Before pursuing that discussion, however, the recent ideological arrival of the "capital-formation" cause is worth a moment's reflection.

It is more than a little ironic that "capital accumulation," once a rather tendentious Marxian view of a supposed capitalist obsession, should have become — of all things — Wall Street's own *slogan*. Worry about capital supply first entered the American policy debate only about a decade ago. In the 1974–75 recession, federal tax receipts fell well below projections, leaving a deficit in the then-astronomical range of $50 billion. William Simon, President Gerald Ford's Treasury Secretary, sounded the alarm that government borrowing was "crowding-out" more productive uses of capital by private capital markets. Subsequently, capital formation was appropriated as a rallying cry by business groups resisting demands by tax reformers for higher taxes on capital gains. The so-called supply-side school associated with Arthur Laffer never represented more than a tiny fraction of economists and was essentially just a more outlandish version of the mainstream business claims. But the supply-siders popularized the capital-supply worries of Wall Street and imbued them with a democratic flavor since they offered a rationale that rewards to the rich would unlock new prosperity and growth for all.

With Ronald Reagan's election, the capital-supply school of economics came fully of age. Interestingly, the ideological watershed came not in 1980 but in 1978. Until that year, public opinion was generally on the side of more tax reform. Rich people did not enjoy any special approbation. On the contrary, there was indignation that loopholes were enabling the wealthy to avoid paying tax rates anywhere near the nominal tax schedule. Tax-reform legislation passed Congress in 1969 and again in 1976, and was signed into law by Republican presidents. In the 1976 campaign, President Jimmy Carter had called the tax code a "disgrace to the human race," and had pledged further closing of loopholes.

In 1978 the business lobbies geared up to defeat President Carter's anticipated tax-reform package. The shrewdest of these was the American Council for Capital Formation, a small tax-cutting lobby that had begun life with a less transcendent but more candid name, the American Council on Capital Gains and Estate Taxation. Under the leadership of Charls Walker, a former Treasury official who is probably Washington's best-connected lobbyist, the council mounted an extensive campaign to convince public opinion that low taxes on the wealthy are the key to broad prosperity. At about the same time, several authors published works celebrating the social virtue of the rich.

In mid-1978, Carter's tax experts took a head count and decided they lacked the votes for a major tax-reform offensive. Taxpayer revolts were echoing through the hinterlands. The business lobbies found themselves all dressed up with no place to go. By the end of the legislative year, the ideological mood had shifted radically. Adam

Smith was back in fashion and the wealthy enjoyed new legitimacy. Happily, their function was no longer seen as just their own enrichment, but society's. The newly respectable supply-side doctrine explained why the wealthy advanced the well-being of society more efficiently by keeping wealth rather than sharing it. The business press enthusiastically warmed to the theme of capital formation, and Congress soon passed legislation to *cut* capital gains taxes.

The capital-formation movement found itself on a roll. In 1979, the momentum for further tax reduction expressed itself in two rival proposals: The populist Kemp-Roth bill called for an across-the-board cut in personal income-tax rates. The business-backed Steiger-Hansen bill proposed a liberalization of corporate depreciation allowances known as "10–5–3,"* which translated to an annual $50-billion cut in corporate income taxes. The two proposals were seemingly incompatible, because taken together they sacrificed so much revenue that the Treasury would be awash in red ink. However, when Ronald Reagan was elected President riding the supply-side wave, he characteristically declined to play favorites. Mr. Reagan split the difference: in 1981 he signed *both* tax cuts, and then some.

In the various debates over tax policy and capital formation during the late 1970s and early 1980s, liberals found themselves drawn inexorably into conservative logic. They, too, "believed in the market." They, too, wanted American industry to recover and regain a competitive position in the world economy. If industry needed capital and capital required savings and savings required higher rates of return, then the obvious remedy was something akin to the Reagan tax program. In the congressional debates over the supply-side tax cuts Democrats virtually outbid Republicans to design the more lavish package of business tax cuts and other tax preferences to stimulate personal savings. The bipartisan influence of the business PACs (political action committees) and the prospect of campaign contributions was undoubtedly at work, but so was something even more forceful: the power of a reigning ideology.

Much as the critics warned, the supply-side medicine did not work miracles. The real function of the tax cuts served a double-barreled ideological purpose. It starved government for revenues, which served

*The term *10–5–3* refers to the depreciable lives of capital assets: 10 years for structures, 5 years for most machines, 3 years for vehicles.

the crusade against the public sector. And it shifted the distribution of taxes away from the rich. What it did *not* do was promote capital supply. The overall personal savings rate has actually declined, from an average of 7 percent in the 1970s to about 5.5 percent under Reagan. The affluent 6 percent of the public fortunate enough to *have* capital gains is enjoying substantially lower tax rates. "Business savings" — profits — are up; but for the economy as a whole the big public deficit, which consumes capital, has more than canceled out any increases in private savings.

Investment declined sharply between 1980 and 1983, as it predictably does during a recession. It recovered only when consumer spending revived, after the Federal Reserve Board took its heavy foot off the money hose. When recovery came, it was a demand-side recovery fueled by the antithesis of Reaganomics — a $200-billion deficit and newly loosened money. Increased capital investment only came later, when businesses saw the resumption of consumer demand. Rewarding the well-to-do with lower taxes, in short, did not have its advertised effect. Wider inequality failed to improve economic efficiency. To appreciate why the plan failed, one needs to sort out the multiple meanings of the beguiling phrase *capital formation*.

SAVINGS AND DISTRIBUTION

In formal economic analysis, the supply of savings equals the difference between total income and total consumption in the national economy. By definition, only money that is saved can be left over to be invested. At the simplest textbook level, when one citizen puts aside some savings in the bank, it constitutes capital for him to invest or for the bank to lend out elsewhere. If nobody saves, there will be no money to invest. Just as savings are the precondition of investment, it also follows quite logically that a nation's rate of productive investment is a prime determinant of its rate of economic growth. It is investment that finances new capital equipment, and thus productive innovation. An economy, of course, can also grow by making people work longer hours, but the preferred form of growth rests on technological advances — growth that represents additional output for the same human input. Therefore growth requires the creative application of capital. On these fundamentals, conservatives, liberals, and socialists have no dispute.

The dispute arises over the relationship between the rate at which the economy *as a whole* accumulates savings and the necessary rewards to a *private* saver/investor, in a system where wealth is distributed very unequally. In other words, to what extent must existing inequalities of wealth be tolerated or widened, in order to maximize the accumulation and productive investment of capital?

The issue of capital supply is thus a nearly perfect proxy for the broader equity/efficiency dilemma. If you want growth, say the capital-formation theorists, you must have high savings and investment. To coax out capital, you must reward capitalists. Once you accept the premise of that analysis, the obvious remedy seems to follow logically: lower corporate-income tax rates; liberalize depreciation schedules; cut capital-gains taxes; and reduce marginal tax rates on high personal incomes — exactly the Reagan program. The program has multiple distributive consequences: Reducing taxes on investment income disproportionately helps the well-to-do, since financial investments are highly concentrated. As rich people get more lenient tax treatment, the nonrich pick up a growing share of the total tax bill. To the extent that total tax revenues drop, there is also a distributive consequence as the public sector shrinks and the poor receive relatively less money from public income transfers.

In this respect, supply-side economics is only a slight exaggeration of market economics. If individual holders of wealth are the principal source of investment capital, then they must be assured adequate returns for the risk they bear, or capital supply will dry up. If taxation aimed at redistribution lowers the effective return to capital, wealthy people will stop investing and growth will cease. Distributive goals indeed seem in direct conflict with growth goals. Redistribution seems sweet, but it is poison. Inequity is nothing but the handmaiden of incentive.

Mistaken Identities

One can begin to challenge this perverse logic by untangling the several different meanings of the terms *savings* and *investment*. Economists define *savings* as equaling "investment," but the real story is in the fine print. In the debate over tax and spending policy, as Veblen would have appreciated, the catch phrase *capital formation* is used polemically to mean, at once, increased *personal* savings, increased *national* savings, increased *financial* investment, and increased *productive* investment, as if these goals were necessarily identical. But at a given time, personal savings may be dropping while pension-fund savings are rising (which in fact is the recent history). Or total private savings may be rising but being absorbed by large public-sector deficits, which equal "dissavings" (also recent history). This case of mistaken analytical identity opens the way to untold confusion of ends with means and to a quite cavalier and avoidable sacrifice of distributive goals.

Although economists teach that savings and investment must equate, the two are not identical; nor are they undifferentiated. On the *investment* side of the equation, financial investment is not tantamount to productive investment. Capital may be pouring in and out of the commodities exchanges, tax-sheltered real estate, limited partnerships, old issues of gold stocks, and pre-Columbian art without adding one whit to productive investment and economic growth. Additional quantities of savings make possible productive investment, but additional savings in no way guarantee that productive investment will occur.

By the same token, the *savings* side of the equation is made up of several distinct components — personal household savings, corporate profits, net additions to collective pools of savings like pension funds and life insurance company reserves, and the annual surplus or deficit in the national budget. Each of these components reflects gross savings, minus withdrawals, or borrowings, in that sector. If for example the nation's pension funds take in $40 billion in contributions and pay out $35 billion in benefits, they have contributed net additions to national savings in the amount of $5 billion. If private households save a total of $100 billion, but borrow $110 billion to finance mortgages, consumer loans, and MasterCard purchases, then the household sector has depleted other sources of savings by $10 billion, and functions as a net "dissaver" — that is, it consumes savings from other sectors.

Maximizing *personal* savings may conceivably require some toleration of income inequality, since rich people by definition have more discretionary income and therefore have a higher propensity to save. Even here, however, it is not entirely obvious why a more egalitarian income structure would fail to raise the savings propensities of the nonrich, and produce the same ultimate savings rate, or even a superior one. But even conceding, for the sake of argument, the point that some income inequality may be conducive to *personal* savings, there are many forms of *collective* savings (pension funds, national budget surpluses) that do not depend on income inequality at all.

The laissez-faire school also depends on a blithe and unsupported assumption that *public investment* is something other than investment. But let us compare two different routes to the same investment, a new power plant. In the first case, an investment banking house sells a billion dollars' worth of bonds, tapping the pool of private savings. That finances construction of the new generators for a private electrical utility company. In the second case, let us assume that government raises taxes by a billion dollars and builds the plant. In both cases, money is spent and jobs are created; the economy has invested a billion dollars and now has that much more electrical capacity. The difference, however, is that in the first case the increased investment requires tapping a billion dollars' worth of private savings; and a supply-sider could argue that without available savings the plant might not have been built or that interest costs would have been higher. But in the second case, the plant gets built just the same. One can argue whether public power or private power is more "efficient" in an administrative sense (I happen to prefer public power), but that is an entirely separate argument. Via the public route, investment is financed with taxation rather than savings. Public investment can also rely on savings, as it does when a government investment agency sells bonds. But if we are intellectually consistent about it, public capital formation is just as potent a source of productivity enhancement as private. The efficiency case for the private sector rests elsewhere.

Inequality with Inefficiency

The Reagan program that eventually passed the Congress increased the return to savings and investment by lowering taxes — on corporate profits, on high personal incomes, on capital gains, and on income set aside as savings. Inflation, higher social security taxes, and reductions in social transfers more than wiped out the slight nominal income tax reductions for the nonrich. In general, people earning less than $30,000 lost from the Reagan tax program. According to the Congressional Budget Office, the combined effect of the 1983–1985 Reagan tax and budget changes was to decrease the disposable income of households earning less than $10,000 by $17 billion, while giving $55 billion in tax benefits to those with incomes over $80,000. A study by two Urban Institute economists, Frank Levy and Richard C. Michel, calculated that among the poorest one fifth of families, average disposable income fell by fully 9.4 percent between 1979 and 1984. Some of the decline was the result of the recession, but most of it was caused by the increased tax burden (mainly payroll taxes) and the loss in social benefits that resulted from the Reagan program.

Many of the particular tax preferences that lowered the tax load on the well-off produced a near-perfect marriage of inequality with inefficiency. The "savings incentives" actually reduced revenues more than they increased savings. For example, in the 1981 tax bill, two of the popular tax devices to promote private savings were the tax-exempt "All-Savers Certificate" and the tax-deferred Individual Retirement Account (IRA). Both of these permit a deduction against taxable income for money put aside as savings. The cash value of the tax deduction rises with your tax bracket.

One gimmick long advocated by the savings bank lobby, the "All-Savers Certificate," paid the saver a below-market interest rate that was tax exempt. While a regular savings certificate might be paying 12 percent, an all-savers paid about 9 percent. This saved the bank money, and for savers in high tax brackets, the tax savings more than made up for the lower nominal interest. In practice, only savers in the 30 percent tax bracket or above came out ahead.

For the same reason, tax-deferred Individual Retirement Accounts are primarily useful to the well-to-do. Under the Reagan program, IRAs were liberalized. The program now permits an individual to put up to $2000 of his or her annual income into a long-term blocked savings account earmarked for retirement and to pay no income tax on the current income that is set aside. According to the U.S. Treasury Department 57 percent of eligible individuals with incomes over

$50,000 took advantage of the IRA tax shelter; only 9 percent of those with incomes below $20,000 did so.

The IRA and All-Savers tax preferences thus made the income tax that much less redistributive, at a cost to income equality. But what of the efficiency effects? If these tax subsidies truly coaxed out more savings, perhaps the tradeoff was worthwhile. Though no precise statistics are available, it became apparent that only a small fraction of IRA savings or "All Savers" deposits represented genuinely "new" savings.

In the case of IRAs, many wealthy people simply transferred the maximum amount, $2000, from one savings account to another in order to qualify it for the tax deduction, or put $2000 that they would have saved anyway into a tax-sheltered Individual Retirement Account. If the average tax bracket of people making use of IRAs is 35 percent and only 10 percent of IRA savings are really "new savings," then the Treasury gives up 35 cents of revenue in order to increase the household savings supply by 10 cents. The program actually decreases the total supply of savings in the economy because the loss to the Treasury exceeds the net addition to private savings. The program saved the affluent billions in reduced taxes and cost the Treasury billions in lost tax revenues, but it is not at all clear that any increase in net savings resulted. According to a study by the Federal Reserve Bank of New York, virtually none of the money put into IRAs represented "new" savings that would not have occurred anyway.

Thus, even by supply-side lights, a severe sacrifice of distributive equity did not enhance economic efficiency — and probably harmed it, if our test is the supply-side litmus of financial capital formation. After enactment of the Reagan tax program, personal savings increased slightly, but all the tax cuts added up to a huge federal deficit. And a *deficit,* by definition, equals *dissavings.* Business did not step up its rate of investment, for the very practical reason that in a recession fewer customers were available to buy the merchandise. The incentive to invest depends not just on the theoretical after-tax return (supply) but on whether there is purchasing power in the economy to consume the product (demand). In fact, according to the U.S. Commerce Department, capital spending measured in constant (1972) dollars actually declined from $159 billion in 1981, to $150 billion in 1982, and declined further to $144 billion in 1983.

SAVINGS AND GROWTH

If the supply-side analysis of the problem is flawed and the remedy perverse, the concern about "capital formation" is nonetheless valid. To grow, an economy indeed requires productive investment of capital. It is not surprising — indeed it is axiomatic — that the countries with high rates of savings and investment are those that have experienced rapid economic growth. But there are many ways of accumulating savings.

Collective Savings

The conservative analysis has as its paradigm the individual, profit-maximizing *homo economicus,* rationally weighing whether to consume or to save his last dollar of income. In theory, if the rewards are sufficiently great, he will choose to save and invest rather than consume, and — hosannas! — the economy will grow. Even this assumption, which is probably true at the extremes (a 20 percent real rate of return on passbook savings would undoubtedly increase personal thrift), is surprisingly inapplicable within the usual range of interest rates on personal savings. Household savings rates are not very well correlated with interest rates. People have multiple motivations to save or spend, only one of which is yield. For example, personal savings rates often rise during recessions when real interest rates are low, because people are nervous. Statistically, household savings rates have remained remarkably stable over the past several decades.

Moreover, the assumption of the hyperrational individual saver altogether ignores the growing importance of collective private savings (pension funds, annuities, and life-insurance savings). The savings behavior of the institutional saver is not at all like that of the personal saver. And if there is some scant argument that redistributive taxation retards individual savings, the argument vanishes in the case of collective savings.

Pension-fund savings, for example, operate by automatically deducting a predetermined share of wages, often matched by employer contributions, and placing the funds in a collective capital pool. Once the money is set aside, the pension fund operates the same as any other investor — perhaps a bit more prudently because of the added "fiduciary" responsibility of managing somebody else's money. But pension funds do not depend on wealthy individuals with substantial discretionary income in order to amass savings. With collective savings such as pension funds, the relationship between equality and efficiency is transformed. Inequality ceases to be a necessary precondition of enhanced capital accumulation. On the contrary, pension funds serve to accumulate wealth on behalf of the relatively non-wealthy. They function to *equalize* the distribution of capital, even as they increase its formation.

Further, pension funds are *blocked, long-term* savings. In most cases, you can't capriciously withdraw the principal, as in the case of a passbook-savings account or a block of shares. So from the perspective of the economy as a whole, which depends on stable pools of long-term savings, pension-fund savings are ideal.

But in real economic terms are collective savings a perfect substitute for individual savings? Are they as good for economic growth? This is another of those questions that must be settled by evidence, not assumption. In the national capital markets of the modern industrial economy, it turns out that more and more capital is supplied by institutional investors — giant pension funds and life-insurance companies — to be invested in or lent to well-established enterprises. Between 1940 and 1980, the holdings of private pension funds grew from $2.4 billion to over $400 billion. Public and private pensions together own between a third and a half of the value of stocks on the New York Stock Exchange. From the perspective of a General Motors or an AT&T, it matters not at all whether the purchaser of a block of GM stock or a telephone bond happens to be an individual millionaire or a pension fund representing 1000 wage earners. A dollar of capital is a dollar of capital.

It is true that pension funds, as fiduciaries, tend to be rather cautious investors. But so for that matter do bank trust departments investing the fortunes of individual wealthy widows. Most of the demands on the nation's organized capital markets are from stable, institutional customers — not rugged entrepreneurs. Telephone and utility bonds, Fannie Mae (Federal National Mortgage Association), stock issues by Fortune 500 companies, state and municipal borrowings — these do quite well tapping institutional capital markets; they do not require wealthy individual risk takers. No small investor ever got rich on telephone bonds. Even if we concede the rather romantic role ascribed to the lone entrepreneur, genuine venture capitalism consumes only a tiny fraction of the annual flows of capital markets. Whatever is retarding innovative entrepreneurship, it isn't a scarcity of aggregate savings.

Characteristically, this distinction has been conveniently ignored in the capital-formation literature. One looks in vain for the capital-formation lobby to espouse special tax favoritism only for venture capital or to limit special capital-gains treatment to new issues of stock. Instead, the capital-formation lobby fought for, and got, across-the-board cuts in capital-gains taxes and across-the-board liberalization of depreciation allowances. Passive investors, whose greatest entrepreneurial risk was the risk of cutting a finger while clipping coupons, managed to wrap themselves in the popular banner of capital formation, and to reap the same tax concessions as the most daring venture capitalist.

Savings and Debt

A second fallacy in the usual formulation of savings and investment is to ignore the key role of debt in the supply of capital. In conventional national income accounting, the term *net savings* describes gross savings minus capital consumption. In other words, if the economy saves $100 billion, but scraps outmoded capital equipment worth $25 billion, the effective rate of disposable savings is only $75 billion. Fair enough. However there is another key distinction between gross and net savings that frequently is overlooked, namely the difference between gross and net savings by households.

In the debates about the failure of American households to save, the statistic that gets the publicity is the low fraction of disposable household income put aside as savings. But that figure is highly misleading, for it represents total household savings minus total household borrowing. It turns out that America's *gross* rate of household savings is not significantly different from that of many European countries. But because of the unlimited tax favoritism for consumer borrowing and the unlimited tax deductibility of mortgage interest, the American household sector in most years consumes nearly all of what it manages to save. One family's savings simply serve to finance another family's tax-subsidized consumption and tax-sheltered housing. The bottom line translates this, misleadingly, as a low household-savings rate. Thus, household savings, which have been as much as 10 percent of household disposable income, are not a significant source of industrial investment in the United States. This contrasts radically with West Germany and Japan, where *consumer borrowing is not tax deductible,* and where less than 25 percent of gross household savings go to finance consumer borrowing.

A very detailed study by the British economists J. C. Carrington and G. T. Edwards contrasted household savings and borrowing in several countries. In one typical year, 1972, the gross savings rates of West German, British, and American households were very similar. The Germans saved 9.11 percent of their Gross Domestic Product; the British, 9.95; and the Americans, 10.65. But while the German households borrowed less than 1 percent, the Americans borrowed 7.34 percent and the British 8.05 percent, leaving West Germany with a far higher rate of *net* household savings.

Thus, as Carrington and Edwards suggest, substantial German household savings are available to finance productive investment, while American household savings pour into tax-deductible consumer and mortgage credit. Interestingly, West Germany does offer a tax-incentive for owner-occupied housing, but the tax writeoff is based on the total value of the house, where in America it is proportional to the money *borrowed.*

Moreover, while regulations in the United States have artificially depressed the interest rate banks may pay small savers, the German government subsidizes small savers (government savings premiums are limited to moderate-income families), and the true, inflation-adjusted interest rate on small savings has remained positive while America's lagged behind inflation consistently between 1975 and 1982. Not surprisingly, the financial strategy of the typical German family includes substantial savings, while the American household relies instead on tax-favored consumer debt and heavily mortgaged homeownership. German thrift may have something to do with cultural predisposition, but in this case culture is reinforced by consistent public policy. If anything, given the disastrous inflation of the Weimar era, it has been a remarkable policy accomplishment to induce the prudent Germans to keep their wealth in financial assets at all.

As long as tax incentives favor excessive borrowing by households, additional tax incentives intended to promote a higher rate of gross household saving are unlikely to be an efficient form of savings inducement. As the "All-Savers Certificate" and IRA record showed, an inefficient tax preference designed to enhance savings may actually depress the national savings rate as a whole, because a tax expenditure deprives the Treasury of revenue, which increases the national deficit. This in turn requires the public sector to borrow from the available pool of private savings — which depresses the economy's total rate of savings.

Consider the equity/efficiency consequences of tax-favored borrowing to finance consumption. The equity effects are quite plain: being able to deduct interest payments from taxable income has value to the taxpayer depending on the taxpayer's marginal-income tax bracket. A low-income taxpayer in the 10 percent bracket saves only 10 percent of his interest costs in avoided tax. But for a high-income taxpayer in the 50 percent bracket, the government in effect pays 50 percent of the interest cost every time he borrows to finance consumption. Thus, this form of tax favoritism disproportionately benefits the well-to-do, and widens income inequality. It gives the rich man a tax-subsidized consumption "discount" worth five times that of the poor man's discount. The efficiency consequences are also plain. The tax inducement to finance consumption through borrowing uses up savings that otherwise might go to finance investment.

Housing and Savings

Housing provides the most striking example of how inefficiency can reinforce inequality. In the United States (and in Sweden, interestingly enough) the tax laws provide extremely liberal treatment for housing. Homeowners pay no tax on the imputed income they enjoy from living in their own house even though it is also a capital investment. If they sell the house for a profit, they pay no capital-gains tax on the transaction as long as they plow the proceeds into a more expensive house. Mortgage interest is, of course, tax deductible. And the owner of investment property can reap fictitious "depreciation" deductions, which have the effect of reducing other taxable income, even though the value of the property may actually be appreciating. The result of all this tax favoritism is that capital pours into real estate, especially during an inflationary period when other financial assets may not be holding their value. The effect is to fuel housing speculation, drive up prices, and to disproportionately help rich people to lower their tax bills. This has the perverse consequence of pricing housing beyond the means of poorer people, and at the same time it soaks up savings that might better be used elsewhere.

During the 1970s, many homeowners increased their net worth many times over, solely because they happened to own houses in advance of the great housing inflation. Many such families put aside less in the way of real savings than they otherwise might have, because their appreciating house was accumulating paper net worth on their behalf. And hundreds of billions of dollars of other people's savings were borrowed against homes whose prices had conveniently appreciated, in order to finance consumption. Meanwhile, nonhomeowners found houses terribly hard to afford. Those who did manage to buy a house found themselves struggling to make the monthly payments; they had less left over at the end of the month to save. If the goal is to enhance savings supply, the policy managed to make the rich richer and the poor poorer and to deplete the supply of savings in the bargain. In the case of tax-subsidized borrowing, the supposed tradeoff between equality and efficiency is precisely transformed. Inequality and inefficiency — far from being opposites — are working the same side of the street.

A comparison between the U.S. and Canadian savings rates suggests the influence of tax-sheltered mortgage deductions on savings rates. Prior to 1974, Canadian and U.S. personal savings rates were both rising steadily, though the U.S. rate was slightly higher. After 1973, however, the U.S. personal savings began falling sharply, while the Canadian rate continued to rise. By 1981, the U.S. rate was about 6 percent, while the Canadian rate had risen to 13 percent. There are two main explanations for the disparity. Canadian tax policy in the mid-1970s began giving tax advantages for private savings. However, a careful study by the Canadian economist Gregory Jump found that at most one fourth of the difference was explained by the tax favoritism. The more potent explanation is the fact that the United

States gives significantly more generous incentives for "housing savings." U.S. mortgage interest is tax deductible, while Canadian is not. When the real interest rate is low and the rate of inflation is low, as in the 1950s and 1960s, the mortgage-interest deduction is a nice extra, but not a major influence on savings and investment patterns. In a period like the late 1970s, however, it becomes a potent incentive indeed.

From 1975 to 1979, the inflation rate averaged over 10 percent, while mortgages hovered around 9 percent. Housing prices were inflating at 15–20 percent a year. For someone in the 33 percent tax bracket, a mortgage with a nominal interest rate of 9 percent meant 6 percent after taxes — or four points below the rate of inflation. Moreover, borrowing mortgage money at this negative interest rate could produce a capital gain of better than 100 percent a year on the investor's down payment. Housing in the 1970s meant tax-sheltered windfall. No wonder U.S. capital poured out of financial savings and into housing savings! To add to the disparity, U.S. mortgages during the 1970s were typically at a fixed interest rate, while Canadian mortgages have their interest rates adjusted every five years.

Lately, some neoclassical economists have come round to the point of view that "we oversubsidize housing" — we give housing too many tax breaks and thereby distort the allocation of capital. That conclusion is true, but far too sweeping. All too characteristically, it ignores the distributive distortion. In reality, we don't oversubsidize "housing"; we oversubsidize *rich people's housing*. From the point of view of a young family looking at $1000 monthly payments as the ticket of admission to their first house, housing is not oversubsidized at all. From the perspective of a millionaire contemplating whether to trade in a tax-sheltered $400,000 house for a tax-sheltered $600,000 house and enjoy a tax-free capital gain, housing is nicely subsidized indeed. We could cap the tax subsidy, or limit it to first-time homeownership, and we would enhance both equity and efficiency.

Capital Shortage?

A third rather dubious premise in the conservative formulation is the claim that what ails the American economy is primarily a capital shortage. No matter how one defines *savings*, the supply of savings has been surprisingly uniform during the postwar era. In the 1948 to 1964 period, savings by individuals averaged 8.4 percent of GNP. Between 1965 and 1972, the rate rose to an average of 9.6 percent. In the post-OPEC years 1973 to 1980, the savings rate actually rose to 9.9 percent. The gross national savings rate has been even more constant, averaging just under 16 percent consistently since World War II, and dropping below 15 percent only twice in the past three decades (the recession years of 1958 and 1975). Moreover, the rate of nonresidential fixed investment (the best proxy for "productive" investment), has also remained quite steady and actually increased somewhat during the 1970s.

Perhaps a case can be made that the rate of productive investment should be increased even further. Since 1973, the quadrupling of the price of energy has rendered a whole generation of capital plant and equipment obsolete. The great increase in the labor force since 1970 requires more capital just to keep the ratio of capital to labor constant. Workers become more productive only when they have more productive tools to work with. There is also evidence that the competitive pressure of foreign trade shortens the useful life of technology and calls for intensified investment. And it is true that the United States continues to save and invest a smaller fraction of GNP than comparable nations (although when one counts "housing savings" — the equity in owner-occupied housing — as a form of savings, most of the disparity disappears). Since our rather exaggerated reliance on housing as a substitute for financial savings is substantially an artifact of the U.S. tax code, however, it makes little sense to pile on a new set of equity-destroying tax incentives for the sole purpose of overcoming the present equity-destroying tax provisions that steer speculative capital into housing. Thus, the emphasis on the after-tax rewards to private savings and investment as the key to America's savings supply is at best highly exaggerated. We would do better to consider such factors as the structure of capital markets and their efficiency at channeling savings to productive investment; the tax laws that encourage the depletion of savings pools to finance consumption; and the relative impact of public-sector deficits. In short, we may have a "capital-supply" problem, but it is minor. We have a bigger capital-allocation problem. And even if we do choose to increase our overall savings rate, we need not sacrifice distributive goals.

HOW DIFFERENT NATIONS SAVE
(OR, THE WEALTH OF NATIONS)

A comparison of savings rates and income distribution among different nations makes clear the opportunities to reconcile high savings with broader material equality. Savings rates among advanced industrial nations differ widely. The total share of net savings as a fraction of gross domestic product varies from a low of about 8

Average Net Savings Ratios

Country	Period	Average National Savings Rate	Net Household Savings Rate
Japan	1965–79	25.1	20.8
Switzerland	1960–79	20.8	12.4
Netherlands	1960–79	18.7	14.1
Austria	1964–79	18.1	8.8
West Germany	1960–79	18.0	15.5
Australia	1960–79	17.5	12.0
New Zealand	1971–79	17.2	NA
Greece	1960–79	16.9	14.0
France	1960–80	15.9	12.9
Italy	1960–79	15.9	21.8
Spain	1964–79	15.5	10.0
Denmark	1966–79	15.3	NA
Norway	1962–79	14.7	13.7
Portugal	1960–76	14.7	13.4
Belgium	1960–79	14.6	14.9
Sweden	1960–79	14.5	4.9
Finland	1960–79	13.9	5.5
Ireland	1960–74	12.1	NA
Canada	1960–79	11.8	7.5
United Kingdom	1960–79	10.3	6.5
United States	1960–79	8.2	7.0
AVERAGE		15.7	11.2

Source: Peter Sturm and Derek Blades, "International Differences and Trend Changes in Savings Ratios," OECD study (Paris: OECD, 1981).

percent in the United States to a high of 25 percent in Japan. The composition of savings also varies substantially. (Savings, let us recall, includes household savings, corporate savings, collective private savings, and government savings.) In Italy, for example, net savings averaged about 15.9 percent of GDP in the 1960 to 1979 period, slightly above the median for OECD nations. But Italy's household savings ratio — 21.8 percent of income — was actually superior even to the Japanese rate; Italy, however, soaked up a substantial portion of its household savings through a huge public-sector deficit. On balance, Italy was left with a reasonably favorable supply of savings and despite high inflation and a chaotic economy, a fairly robust growth rate as well.

It may surprise American readers to learn that many nations that are rather socialist by U.S. standards enjoy substantially higher savings ratios than ours. France and West Germany, both with large public sectors and expensive welfare outlays, each has national savings rates above the OECD average. Several of Europe's more advanced welfare states, far from viewing the State as a rival claimant for the pool of available capital, use the State to increase the national capital supply. Austria, with a very high total tax load and a very influential trade-union movement, enjoys a finely tuned economy that managed to ride out the recession of the early 1980s with low inflation and low unemployment. The Austrians typically run a public-sector surplus. Thanks to that surplus, although the Austrian household savings rate is almost as low as the U.S. rate, the overall savings rate is close to that of the Japanese. The Austrians also have a sophisticated government capital-investment budget.

Sweden

The Swedes employ yet another formula. During the first three postwar decades, until the post-1973 worldwide economic slump, Sweden normally ran a public-sector budget surplus, which added to net savings supply. The Swedish economist Gösta Rehn recognized as early as 1951, however, that the Swedish program of aggressive income redistribution would eventually mean that neither business self-financing nor traditional capitalist private savings, nor a modest state budget surplus, would be adequate to supply Sweden's capital needs.

Rather than sacrifice equity goals in the name of capital formation, the Swedish Social Democrats devised what might be called a supply-side economics of the left. "If you rely entirely on traditional private capital to solve the capital formation problem, you have to accept much more inequality than we can possibly tolerate," says Anna Hedborg, a senior economist with the Swedish Trade Union Confederation, the LO. In Sweden, socialization of savings has come to be viewed as necessary on grounds of both income distribution and maximum capital formation for productive investment. It is Sweden's way of reconciling the equity/efficiency dilemma, at least with respect to capital supply.

Socialization of savings also avoids the clumsier and more bureaucratic course of nationalizing industry. In the first phase of this strategy the Swedes designed a supplementary national pension system that substantially increased the supply of savings in the public sector. Other major Western social security pension systems are financed essentially as transfer systems in which current tax receipts are just sufficient to finance current payout obligations, plus a small cushion of reserves. Sweden, however, designed its system to accumulate a large pool of capital, on the model of a *funded* private pension plan. The Swedish system deliberately sets the tax rate sufficiently high so that a large capital pool is created. That capital pool is then available to be invested, and the return on the investment pays a portion of current pension benefits.

By the early 1970s, Sweden's supplementary National Pension Fund had become the most important source of savings, overtaking both household savings and corporate earnings. Fund reserves have been as high as half of GNP. Translated to American proportions, that would equal a socialized capital pool of two trillion dollars! Conventionally, most Americans understand Keynesianism to mean the use of taxation and debt to finance government consumption. But the ingenious Swedish Keynesians use taxation to finance savings.

Just as Gösta Rehn predicted, the Swedish *personal* savings rate has declined — in part because of high marginal taxes on income and in part because Sweden shares many of America's perverse tax incentives that stimulate borrowing to finance high-income consumption. But thanks to Sweden's unique system of socialized savings, the overall savings rate has held fairly constant. Today, more than half of the annual addition to Swedish savings is supplied by social security savings. Thus, despite Sweden's egalitarian income-distribution policies and its admittedly rather low rate of *net personal* savings (much of which is explained by heavy household borrowing), Sweden's national savings rate is only a shade below the OECD average, and nearly twice that of the United States.

The availability of socialized savings also provides secondary distributive benefits. For one thing, it has enabled Sweden to hold to its course of maintaining nearly full employment in the face of worldwide recession. Since the mid-1970s, Sweden has accomplished this feat only by running large government budgetary deficits. But the large pool of socialized savings gives Swedish fiscal policy the option of relying on big deficits without bankrupting the economy.

Here, a comparison with neighboring Denmark is instructive. Like the Swedes, the Danes have responded to recession by running a deficit in the area of 12–15 percent of GNP. But Denmark, which has no comparable system of socialized savings, must fund its entire deficit by paying crushing interest rates to the private Danish capital market and by borrowing abroad. By 1981, the strategy had ceased to be viable, and the Danish economy had slipped into a severe fiscal crisis; the ruling coalition of left parties headed by the Social Democrats, though they retained a majority in Parliament, simply gave up and handed over the reigns of government to the first Danish Conservative Party prime minister to hold office since 1901, to carry out the inevitable austerity program. Sweden, on the other hand, has been able to fund about half of its current budgetary deficit by tapping its pool of socialized capital, which reduces the effective public-sector deficit to a more manageable 6–7 percent of GNP.

Promoting Savings

There is a dense technical literature that has built elaborate econometric models attempting to account for the wide national variations in savings rates. There is also a comparative literature describing concrete differences in institutions intended to promote savings. The evidence offers small comfort to those who predict that distributive equity is the enemy of high rates of savings.

Equal-income distribution, if anything, correlates positively with high national savings rates. Japan, where the bottom 20 percent of the population has a larger share of national income than in any

OECD nation except possibly Sweden, is the top saver. While the capital-formation lobby can perhaps take some comfort from Japan's relatively small public sector, the European champion savers include West Germany, Austria, and the Netherlands, all with explicit programs of income redistribution and very large public sectors.

The explanation for the wide variations in savings rates tends to be found, rather, in institutional differences: demographics, policies aimed at small savers, tax treatment of borrowing, structure of capital markets, down payments required for homeownership, lump-sum payroll bonuses, the design of national pension systems as savers or dissavers, and the overall effect of the state budgetary surplus or deficit. Corporate retained earnings (profits), which loom very large in the capital-formation literature as a source of savings, nowhere account for more than 30 percent of the annual increment to national savings supply. The implication of this is of fundamental importance for the debate about entrepreneurial reward, for it suggests that national economies can and do save and invest very effectively, despite relatively modest corporate profits.

As it turns out, corporate savings are a very small fraction of total savings in the nations with the highest savings rates: Japan and West Germany. Among nations with high savings rates, only socialist (!) Austria relies on corporate earnings for more than 20 percent of its total savings supply. The United States, United Kingdom, and Canada, with the three lowest national savings rates in the OECD, have the heaviest dependence on corporate profits to supply savings.

Japanese Savings

The Japanese case warrants special attention, since it underscores the importance of institutions, and not just private calculations of return. Most Japanese observers ascribe significance to the Japanese custom of paying workers large, lump-sum bonuses, which may equal several months' wages. Traditionally, a large portion of these sums is plowed into savings. A second factor promoting a high savings rate is Japan's relatively underdeveloped pension system. Until very recently, many Japanese workers had no pension coverage at all, and those who did could expect their pensions to be quite modest. Absent social provision for retirement, Japanese workers relied more heavily on private savings. In the past decade, however, that is changing. Japanese pensions now exceed the OECD average, and interestingly, there is no corresponding drop in the personal savings rate. In explaining this, some economists have reasoned that as people become more aware of planning for retirement, the desire increases not to have living standards fall after one retires. Third, the Japanese tax system does not reward consumer borrowing; housing is expensive and requires high down payments. Fourth, the Japanese government usually runs a tight fiscal policy (small deficits) and a loose monetary policy (low real interest rates). Government, therefore, is not a big dissaver.

A final factor in the high Japanese savings rate is demography. Japan has a relatively small population under age 20, which means that middle-aged Japanese at the peak of their earning power have a smaller child-rearing expense than their OECD counterparts and more discretionary income to save. Even more striking, the ratio of retired people to working people in Japan is by far the lowest of any advanced country. In Japan, fully 49 percent of people over age 65 are in the labor force, more than double the average OECD rate. While one might assume that this longer working life would depress the inducement to save for retirement, it seems to have just the opposite effect when one considers the economy as a whole. Apparently, with older people continuing to work, *dissavings* by the elderly is less of a factor than elsewhere (that is, old people don't need to draw down their savings accounts), and this contributes to Japan's high overall national savings rate.

Taken together, all of these factors enable Japan to reconcile a very high rate of savings with a fairly egalitarian income distribution. The favorite remedy of the American supply-siders — high after-tax yields on private savings — is not part of the picture.

In general, most economists believe that rapid economic growth correlates with high national savings ratios. When people's real income is rising, they feel able to put aside more savings. Japan certainly seems to bear that out. During the 1950s, when Japan was a much poorer society, savings as a fraction of personal income never exceeded 16 percent. Since 1970, however, as the Japanese affluent society blossomed, savings rates have hovered around 25 percent. It is not at all surprising that contemporary Japan, as the fastest-growing of the industrial nations, should have a high savings rate. But the relatively low Japanese savings rate during the 1950s calls into question the usual assumption about cause and effect. The relationship between growth and savings seems to be a dynamic one. High savings rates are as much the consequence of rapid growth as the cause.

Promoting Small Savings

Another important factor that has positive equity results, and at worst, neutral efficiency results, is the systematic promotion of small savings. Japan is one of several nations that give special tax treatment or direct subsidies to encourage the nonwealthy to accumulate savings. The Japanese "Maruyu" (tax-exempt small savings) program exempts interest earnings from taxation up to a maximum total asset value of three times annual income. Thus, a Japanese family with $20,000 annual earnings pays no tax on the interest earnings of up to $60,000 in savings.

West Germany employs a savings-premium system. Moderate income households may set aside savings in a blocked long-term account in order to accumulate capital for the down payment on a home. When the account matures, the government will match a portion of the savings with a cash subsidy. The savings account is also tax exempt. These two subsidies taken together produce a positive interest rate equal to about 20 percent.

Under the quite similar French system, which was expanded under Mitterrand, a saver agrees to a five-year blocked savings account in order to save for a down payment. The bank pays a tax-free interest rate of 9 percent, which includes a government subsidy. At the end of the five-year term, the saver can qualify for both a cash subsidy and a low-interest mortgage loan. On balance, these programs may not substantially increase the national savings rate; the subsidy is, of course, a cost to the public treasury. But they do help the nonrich to get into the habit of setting aside regular savings, and their positive distributive effect is double barreled. Not only are the nonrich helped to accumulate financial savings; they are also helped to become homeowners. Since homeownership accounts for most of the net worth of most wage earners throughout the industrialized West, creating homeownership opportunity is a major contribution to a less unequal distribution of wealth.

SOCIAL SECURITY AND SAVINGS

The effect of national social security systems on private savings and on national savings rates has been a cause célèbre in the economics journals. Professor Martin Feldstein of Harvard University, President Reagan's chief economic advisor, devoted much of his early econometric work to "proving" that social security was depressing the national savings rate. In one famous and controversial journal article anticipating supply-side economics, Feldstein calculated that social security was depressing the national savings rate so seriously as to depress the gross national product by precisely 19 percent a year. In other words, were it not for social security, the American economy would have grown by an additional two trillion dollars over the past four years.

By the early 1980s, a number of events conspired that seemed to prove the conservative critics right. The fiscal pressure on the social security system suddenly intensified. Despite an increase in payroll taxes enacted only in 1978, social security payouts were exceeding revenues by over a billion dollars a month. Trust-fund reserves were depleted. Retirement-fund accounts were borrowing, first from each other, then from Medicare accounts. The social security crisis prompted a spate of near-hysterical popular and scholarly journal articles echoing Feldstein's Cassandra warning and adding several new ones. Social security was "heading for a crash," warned the investment banker Peter G. Peterson in a widely noticed article in the liberal *New York Review of Books*. Not only was social security depressing the national savings rate, the deficits in the social security accounts were widening the public-sector deficit generally, which in turn forced the Federal Reserve System to apply the monetary brakes, thus wrecking prospects of a recovery. By the year 2050, Peterson gravely reported, the social security accounts would have an accumulated deficit of over $21 *trillion*. To close that deficit, payroll taxes would have to rise to an astronomical 44 percent of income. Social security claims were in danger of bankrupting not just the social security system itself, but the entire economy.

Peterson proposed to cut benefits sharply and raise the retirement age. Other conservative critics, following Feldstein's own suggestion, went further. The ultimate solution, wrote Peter Ferrara of the White

House staff, was to privatize social security. If social security were replaced with an expanded system of tax-subsidized individual retirement accounts, argued Ferrara, the national savings rate would soar and so would economic growth. This shift, admittedly, would have distributive consequences. Social security, as presently structured, is highly redistributive. A low-income wage earner gets back from social security a much higher fraction of his final paycheck than a high-income wage earner. In this manner, social security has substantially reduced poverty in old age. That gain, of course, would be sacrificed if social security were privatized, but such are the costs of economic progress.

Interestingly enough, although Feldstein and Ferrara were both part of the Reagan White House, Congress and the President rejected the more extreme counsels and acted to shore up the present social security system. In reality, social security's fiscal crunch was the result of four trends, two foreseen and two unforeseen. The most easily predicted of these was the aging of the population. As life spans lengthened, the claims on social security increased. Moreover, only after one full generation had paid into the social security system all of its working life was the system "mature." Workers who retired in, say, 1955, did not qualify for the maximum possible benefit, because they had been contributing for only twenty years (since the system's founding in 1935). As a result, social security payouts during its early years were nicely depressed, and social security seemed a bargain. These two demographic realities were anticipated. Indeed, the system's designers foresaw the need for periodic tax increases to bring the system in line with changing worker-to-retiree ratios. In 1935, the President's Committee on Income Security projected that social security would require one third of its financing from general revenues by about 1965.

Two other shifts, however, were not anticipated. First, the indexing of social security adopted in 1972 tied social security benefit adjustments to the rate of inflation. This meant that social security payouts were tied to prices, while social security financing was based on wages. As long as the economy grew in real terms and wages continued to grow faster than prices, social security would remain solvent. After 1973, however, this assumption fell apart. Between 1973 and 1981, the real purchasing power of wages fell by 16 percent. In one year alone, 1980, prices (hence social security checks) went up by 14.3 percent, while wages (and social security tax collections) went up by only 8.3 percent. This second unforeseen change, namely the slowdown in real growth, interacted disastrously with the indexation formula. If social security benefits had been pegged to wages rather than prices, there would have been no fiscal crisis. But with prices outstripping wages, social security soon went into the red and pensioners (hitherto described as "people on fixed incomes") were now the only Americans with a real hedge against inflation.

In early 1983, Congress, in one of its finest hours, acted to repair social security's finances, rather than abandon its goals. Indexation was tied to wages, rather than to prices. Taxes were raised slightly to replenish reserves; and the retirement age was ordered gradually increased to age 68, to reflect longer life spans. Even with this change, the average social security pensioner who retires in the year 2010 will live many more years on a pension than did his shorter-lived grandfather who retired in 1950. Interestingly enough, in the congressional deliberations about how to save social security, the concern about social security's supposed effect on savings was not taken seriously, and the proposals for privatization stayed in the closet. President Reagan, with his sure instinct for a popular program, kept both Feldstein and Ferrara far away from the social security debate.

Funding Social Security

The conservative critique of social security as a depressant of private savings commits one elementary error of logic. It confuses the issue of whether pensions should be in the public sector with the issue of whether a retirement system should be financed by a pool of capital. If social security depresses savings rates, it is only because it is unfunded.

Whether to provide for retirement privately or socially is a political choice. One value of socializing a pension program is that it makes it possible for the nonrich to retire, and thereby opens up jobs for the working-age population. In 1935, when the unemployment rate was over 20 percent, that was a prime motivation behind the original system. Second, a socialized retirement system is a key part of the so-called social safety net. Poverty in old age has been substantially reduced, thanks to social security.

Whether to *fund* a retirement system is another issue entirely.

Feldstein's critique is accurate only to the extent that social security — *as presently structured in the United States* — operates on a pay-as-you-go system. Payroll taxes flow in and pension benefits flow out. There is no big pool of accumulated capital as in the Swedish system or as in a U.S. private pension fund. This is by design. When Congress passed the Social Security Act in 1935, the intent was not to socialize savings. (However, Congress did provide for substantially larger capital reserves than the system now has. At one point during the 1950s, earnings from capital reserves were sufficient to pay about 20 percent of current payouts. In 1972, Congress optimistically projected future economic growth based on the boom years of the 1960s; it proclaimed that social security was "overfunded," and promptly raised pension rates and deferred a planned payroll-tax increase. A decade later it had to reverse course to save the system from insolvency.)

Therefore, social security, *as presently structured,* does reduce a savings rate below what it would be if social security were a funded system. This results because social security, as a pay-as-you-go system, creates a spurious form of "savings." From the perspective of a wage earner contemplating retirement, an $800-a-month pension from the government is equal to the income on $96,000 of accumulated savings (assuming a 10 percent rate of return). But from a macroeconomic perspective, that $96,000 does not exist. It is a mirage. The pensioner's retirement is provided not by the earnings on a pool of invested capital, but by payroll taxes on current wage earners. This outcome, however, is not the inevitable result of a socialized retirement system, as Feldstein would have it; it is only the result of the decision not to have a funded system. The structure of social security pension systems throughout the industrial West (except for Sweden) is a good example of the welfare state's habit of trying to socialize income without socializing capital.

Moreover, in practice, social security's anticipated depressant effect on private savings is apparently offset by other factors. Feldstein's assumption is that since social security benefits substitute for personal resources, people — rationally! — would set aside more income for their retirement if social security didn't exist. That at least makes intuitive sense, but historical data cast some doubt on the assertion. Retirement is, after all, a fairly recent innovation. Before World War II most working people didn't retire at all. They worked until they were too old to work, and then their families took care of them. Most nonrich failed to accumulate substantial savings for retirement, because they couldn't afford to. In practice, despite steadily increasing real social security benefits, the U.S. national savings rate has been quite constant, both before and after the introduction of the social security retirement system. As noted in the Japanese case, the most plausible explanation for this paradox is that as people live longer and become more deliberate about planning for their old age, and as living standards have risen, it becomes clear that social security pensions are not adequate to maintain purchasing power, and people become more aware of the need to supplement them with private resources. It was also disclosed, almost a decade after Feldstein's first technical paper on social security and savings, that his original equations contained a serious technical error, and that once the error was corrected, it led to the dubious finding that social security somehow *increased* the national savings rate — which creates grave doubts about the assumptions buried in Feldstein's original equations. Such are the perils of econometrics.

Nonetheless, it is axiomatic that an *unfunded* national retirement system, other things being equal, must produce a lower national savings rate than a funded one. To the extent that social security pension systems create fictitious private savings, the problem is not that the system exists in the public sector or even that it redistributes, but rather, that it lacks a pool of capital to finance the payouts. The remedy, as the Swedes noticed nearly thirty years ago, is not to privatize the system, but to fund it. This would require increasing annual tax contributions to social security slightly, so that the system would gradually build up a capital surplus.

With a funded national pension system, there is no equity/efficiency problem in maximizing the supply of savings. In macroeconomic terms, the effect of a funded pension system on savings supply is identical whether the fund exists in the public sector or in the private. If contributions exceed payouts by, say, $10 billion, then $10 billion has been added to the aggregate savings supply.

If we not only are serious about our concern for savings supply but also wish to enhance distributive equity (or at least not worsen it), then increasing the pool of collective savings is the obvious solution, either by funding the public social security system or by broadening the private pension system. In 1981, the net addition to private pension fund reserves was over $43 billion, representing some 40 percent of the net increase in private financial savings. Under U.S. tax law, neither the employer nor the employee pays income taxes on contributions to pension fund reserves. In 1981, this "tax expenditure" cost the federal treasury an estimated $23.6 billion. Note, however, that this subsidy equaled only about half the net addition to pension savings. So, compared to other tax schemes intended to promote individual savings, stimulating pension-fund savings is a relatively efficient tax expenditure. Distributively, pension-fund savings compare favorably with individual savings. They are tilted slightly upward since they are earnings related; a middle-income wage earner will have more pension savings accumulated on his behalf than a low-income worker, who may have none at all. But the overall distribution of pension savings is less skewed to very well-to-do individuals than are private holdings of wealth.

From an equity perspective, private pensions as a source of savings are preferable to purely individual wealth, which tends to be grossly concentrated. However, a nationwide, socialized pension system such as social security is superior to purely private pension systems, because the latter are tied to the individual's job. Most private pension systems require a certain minimum tenure of employment, typically five years, before pension rights are locked in or "vested," whereas social security account credits follow the individual wage earner from job to job. Social security savings, unlike private pension savings, are not only collective, but public. Their distributive pattern reflects market allocations of income only to the extent that the polity chooses it to.

In practice, social security savings are highly redistributive. A worker who earned the minimum wage all his life will collect a social security check equal to about 52 percent of his wage; a worker who earned the maximum wage subject to social security taxes (currently $37,500), will collect only 31 percent of that. Social security is financed by a regressive payroll tax, but of course it need not be. Subsidizing social security from general treasury revenue would make it more progressive in its incidence. As presently designed, social security is a regressive program as it impacts workers, but a very redistributive program as it affects retirees. Mainly due to social security, the percentage of elderly poor has been reduced to slightly less than the percentage of poor people in the population as a whole. Social security provides for about 39 percent of the total money income of the elderly, but 76 percent of the income of the elderly poor.

Whether the social security system should function as a net saver or a net dissaver is also a political choice. As noted, Sweden is the only nation that has deliberately designed its national social pension system as part of a social democratic strategy of capital formation. Significantly, Sweden's decision to fund its social security pension system, and thus to socialize a substantial portion of its savings supply, was anything but a technical fix. It was a deeply political step, and it was widely recognized as such. Swedish conservatives resisted the move; they warned that this approach would turn Sweden into an "Eastern European country." The national debate during the late 1950s over whether to create a funded national pension system was fierce. It moved Sweden a big step closer to socialized capital markets; before the plan was finally enacted, the ruling Social Democrats fought an election (successfully) on the issue.

On the whole, the strategy has worked. Sweden has maintained a moderately high national savings rate in the face of declining personal savings. At the same time, the high inflation and slow economic growth of the 1970s have eroded the capital value of the pension funds. About 72 percent of the total capital funds have been invested in bonds, with the largest amount going to finance housing and local government obligations. Unfortunately, money invested during the 1960s was locked into long-term fixed-rate bonds, whose real interest rate turned negative as inflation rates rose. From 1974 to 1976, the real rate of return on pension funds was −2.5 percent. As a consequence, the capital funds have contributed a declining share of pension payouts. Since 1976, there have been several years when pension payouts have substantially exceeded the funds' net income. In 1981, social security tax receipts enjoyed a slight surplus over payout obligations. Revenue amounting to 24.7 billion SKr was collected, of which 1.6 billion went to capital surplus, and the rest to pension payouts.

The Swedes have rejected the temptation to use their national pension system as a kind of public development bank. Rather, they recently created a separate system of "wage-earner funds" as a kind of super profit-sharing system, which both broadens the distribution of productive wealth and increases the rate of capital formation (see Chapter 6). Of the accumulated pension-fund capital, only about

4 percent has been invested in stocks through a special "fourth fund." The vast bulk of the capital remains in local and national government bonds. This has two effects. It finances public obligations largely with public savings, which frees private capital markets for productive investment. It also lowers the cost of capital to the public sector, although in effect this lowers the rate of return on pension savings and could be considered a kind of advance tax on pensioners.

A strong case can be made, on both equity and efficiency grounds, that the United States should fund at least a portion of the social security pension system. This would admittedly require a slight increase in the tax rate in the short run, but the added accumulation of capital would head off the need for further tax increases in the long run as the population keeps aging. There is no reason why we need to keep financing social security through regressive payroll taxation. Increased revenues could be provided either by an income tax surcharge or by subjecting the entire payroll to taxation, and not just the income of wages below $37,500. This would substantially improve the progressivity of the social security tax base.

Moreover, social security should be taken out of the federal budget. Social security pensions are transfers, not government outlays. Not counting social security, the public sector spends a smaller fraction of national income now than it did in 1960. If social security were designed to gradually build up a pool of capital, it would run an annual surplus. This should be credited to social security's own accounts, as social security savings, not as government savings. As social security is gradually funded, it would also make sense to send each citizen an accounting once a year to show how much social security savings has been accumulated on his or her behalf, and the pension benefit earned to date.

KEYNES SAVES

When supply-side economics was in vogue, it was fashionable to chastise Keynes and the Keynesians for stressing demand to the exclusion of capital supply. Whoever believes that cannot possibly have read Keynes. It is true, of course, that Keynes was writing during the Great Depression, when conservatives were calling upon workers to lower their wages and government to reduce its spending, as solutions to unemployment. It was Keynes's great insight to recognize that when total purchasing power ("aggregate demand") is deeply depressed, it is no remedy at all to drive demand down still further by promoting thrift.

But Keynes was acutely cognizant of the problems of capital supply, not the least of which are its distributive dimensions and the arguable efficiency of market allocation of investment. On the one hand, Keynes recognized, excess savings by definition reduces spending and hence the demand for goods; too little demand causes unemployment. On the other hand, it takes investment to create jobs and investment requires savings: "Employment can only increase," he wrote, "with an increase in investment."

Keynes, however, was among the first to observe that one individual's savings do not necessarily increase aggregate investment by the same amount, least of all do they necessarily lead to productive investment. "There is no clear evidence from experience," he wrote, "that the investment policy which is most socially advantageous coincides with that which is most profitable." And again, in a famous passage, "When the capital development of a country becomes the by-product of the activities of a casino, the job is likely to be ill-done."

For Keynes, the insight that aggregate demand was all important removed one of the central social defenses of gross inequality of wealth. People are dissuaded from supporting greater progress toward economic equality, he wrote, "by the belief that the growth of capital demands upon the strength of the motive towards individual saving and that for a large portion of this growth we are dependent on the savings of the rich out of their superfluity."

Keynes offered two ways out of this box: a demand route and a supply route. First, the new emphasis on full employment and aggregate demand reduced the need to tolerate gross inequality in the name of maximizing capital formation. When the economy is not at full employment, he suggested, "the growth of capital depends not at all on a low propensity to consume, but is, on the contrary, held back by it." In this context, "the abstinence of the rich" is bad for the economy, and the redistribution of purchasing power to those with a greater propensity to consume is beneficial. Thus, concludes Keynes triumphantly, "One of the chief social justifications of wealth is, therefore, removed."

But Keynes also offers a supply side. Once the economy is at full employment, he suggested, there is indeed a danger that the savings rates will be too low. In that circumstance, he wrote (anticipating the Swedish invention of social security savings), "it will still be possible for communal saving through the agency of the State to be maintained at a level which will allow the growth of capital up to a point where it ceases to be scarce."

As early as 1926, in his famous essay "The End of Laissez Faire," Keynes wrote that

> some coordinated act of intelligent judgement is required as to the scale on which it is desirable that the community as a whole should save . . . and whether the present organization of the investment market distributes savings along the most nationally productive channels. I do not think that these matters should be left entirely to the chances of private judgement and private profits, as they are at present.

Later, as an advisor to the Chancellor of the Exchequer, Keynes was to suggest a highly concrete plan for socialized savings in his 1940 pamphlet, "How to Pay for the War." Keynes recognized that reliance on voluntary savings in the amount necessary to finance World War II would require government to offer high real interest rates, which would surely be inflationary. Instead, he proposed a graduated system of deferred wages. Beyond a subsistence level of income, all wage earners would be required to take a percentage of their paychecks as blocked savings. The "tax" rate would be graduated; the rich would save the highest percentage of their income. This form of forced savings would be both distributively equitable — moderate-income people would be exempt — and efficient: It would lower government's borrowing costs, and hence inflation. The plan was not carried out quite the way Keynes envisioned. But the wartime experience in both Britain and the United States suggested that huge private savings rates can finance large public-sector deficits and lead to noninflationary growth at unparalleled rates of 10–15 percent annually.

In the concluding chapter of his *General Theory,* Keynes the supply-sider offers yet another ingenious rationale for socialized savings — one that has entirely eluded the contemporary debate about capital formation. Under a pure market system, high interest rates are required to coax out savings. The higher the yield, the greater the incentive the private citizen has to save rather than to consume. But high interest rates for savers translate into high interest *costs* for investors, when what the economy needs to grow is low interest *costs*.

Socialized savings, in contrast, can live with relatively lower interest yields, since they are not driven by yields. This is precisely the Swedish experience. Keynes, in his supply-side incarnation, recognized that an abundance of capital at very low real interest rates was conducive to economic growth. But unlike today's supply-siders, he was shrewd enough to appreciate that very high interest rates on private savings constituted a poor way of reaching that goal.

Low real interest rates were also the main goal in the financial system that Keynes proposed for the postwar period. As one of the architects of the Bretton Woods system, Keynes recognized that economic recovery depended on an abundance of capital at interest rates that were both relatively low and relatively predictable. American influence at the Bretton Woods conference ultimately created a somewhat more market-oriented system than Keynes wanted, but full liberalization of international currency movements did not come until the post-1973 era of "flexible exchange rates." As Keynes would have been the first to appreciate, one result of this system has been increasing instability of currency values, and higher true interest rates. In the 1980s, the deregulation and unification of financial markets, another cherished goal of free-market liberals, has also added to interest costs. For Keynes, long-term planning — by both corporations and governments — required a modicum of stability. When laissez-faire creates instability, the move to a freer market can be something less than pure gain. In order to achieve interest rates that were both low and stable, Keynes recognized that the worldwide financial order was far too important to leave to the vagaries of markets. As we shall see in Chapter 3, he had rather the same view of international trade.

Not surprisingly, the countries that have enjoyed high growth rates are usually those with low real interest rates. Throughout the postwar boom, the real interest rate in West Germany barely fluctuated from a range of 3–4 percent. According to one study, the real cost of capital is nearly four times greater in the United States than in Japan, where a loose monetary policy keeps interest rates down, and where coordinated industrial policymaking permits firms to get most of their capital from loans rather than equity investors.

Savings and Capital Markets

Although it is rarely acknowledged in the American debate, structural differences in national capital markets have immense influence over both capital supply and end use. In the Anglo-Saxon countries, as Carrington and Edwards so persuasively document, household savings flow mainly to finance household consumption. However, other nations, for example, West Germany and Japan, use household savings primarily to finance industrial investment, largely with banks as intermediaries. The banking system collects savings from households and lends them to corporations.

In the United States, the United Kingdom, and Canada, commercial banks are far less involved in either the financing or the management of business firms, and companies rely largely on retained earnings and equity issues to provide investment capital. But in much of continental Europe and in Japan, debt finance is the overwhelming source of investment capital for industry. During the 1970s, for example, the ratio of debt to equity fluctuated between 50 and 60 percent in both the United States and the United Kingdom. In West Germany, the ratio of debt to equity was almost 100 percent. In France it approached 150 percent, in Sweden it exceeded 175 percent, and in booming Japan, the ratio rose from 229 percent in 1970 to over 350 percent by 1977. As Japan has grown wealthier, its stock market has finally become more important as a source of equity capital, but Japanese firms remain among the world's most highly leveraged. In fast-growing industries, it is not unusual to see debts of 500 percent or even 1000 percent of equity.

It is more than a bit ironic that Japan lately has begun to give in to pressures from the United States to "liberalize" its capital markets. In practice, this means that Japanese savings institutions will pay higher interest rates to domestic savers and allow the yen to trade freely in international markets. Linking the yen to the global market — at a time when real interest rates are very high and unstable — will almost surely raise interest costs domestically in Japan.

Greater reliance on debt finance has interesting implications for the relationship between efficiency and equality. In neoclassical economics and in its supply-side mutation, the individual entrepreneur risking his own money is all important. Traditionally, especially in the British and American literature, equity capital is esteemed on the ground that it frees the firm to take risks. Investors, if they choose, can forgo the fleeting pleasure of current returns in favor of reinvesting profits, in the hope that the firm will grow. According to this view, heavy leveraging is bad because it produces a thin cushion for the bad years, and the risk of either bankruptcy on the one hand, or excess entrepreneurial caution on the other.

The dynamism of the highly leveraged Japanese economy, however, leads to a rather different conclusion. Apparently, debt financing also has its virtues. It can liberate management from the tyranny of the short-term balance sheet and lead to more reasoned planning for long-term growth. Moreover, in the case of a rapidly growing firm, greater debt financing increases the capacity of the firm to expand, notwithstanding the constraints of its own stream of retained earnings and the limited patience of its investors. The Japanese, West German, and French experience also suggests that greater reliance on debt finance brings into being a constructive role for development-oriented financial institutions, whether public or private, which can create new centers of expertise in the dark art of development finance and help produce the "patient finance" that industry needs. Heavy leveraging, of course, also involves government planning, for it is the Japanese government's role as backstop that allows banks to permit high debt-to-equity ratios.

To be sure, greater bank involvement in industry is a mixed blessing. There would be little political support in the United States for bank domination of industry on the German model. Even in West Germany, notwithstanding that nation's successful record of industrial growth, excessive bank involvement in industry and the relative scarcity of "risk-bearing capital" are hotly debated concerns.

Nonetheless, the European and Japanese experience does suggest that, at the very least, economies that rely more heavily on debt finance to provide investment capital can do as well as the United States, with its heavy reliance on equity and retained earnings. And that finding has very significant implications for the equality/efficiency debate.

For if debt finance is an equally good — or better — source of investment capital, then one central justification for tolerating extremes of individual wealth has disappeared. When financial intermediaries (banks, pension funds, life-insurance companies) are providing the financing, it doesn't matter whether the ultimate source is the savings of one wealthy individual or the savings of a thousand wage earners. Moreover, the need to demonstrate high current profits to attract investors is moderated, too.

Investment

As noted, it may well be that the problem is less on the "savings" side of the equation and more on the "investment" side. Private, profit-maximizing investors often fail to invest capital in a manner consistent with the long-term health of their own industries, let alone that of their employees and local communities. There is now an extensive business school literature documenting the rise of "paper entrepreneurship" and industry's habit of investing capital to maximize short-term yield. If the owners of capital are squandering it, or investing it for speculative return, then much of the capital-supply issue is a red herring.

A good case in point is the American steel industry. While it is often argued that the American steel industry fell into technological obsolescence because of a failure to invest, the surprising reality is that during the booming 1960s and early 1970s, American steel makers actually out-invested their Japanese counterparts by about 20 percent for each ton of steel produced. Unfortunately, most of the American industry's investment went for new capacity based on old, outmoded technologies. As international competition from more efficient foreign producers intensified during the mid-1970s, the return on that investment dropped. American steelmakers, who now desperately needed to invest more capital in modernization, calculated that from their private, profit-maximizing point of view, steel was simply a bad investment. In recent years, steel has produced a return on equity of less than 5 percent. Steelmakers could do better than that by putting their money in the bank, or by buying an oil company (as U.S. Steel in fact did). Thus, though the American economy as a whole badly needs a modern, competitive steel industry, private profit-maximizing investors using short-run market criteria simply cannot get us from here to there.

*   *   *

This chapter has treated the issue of capital accumulation, not capital allocation. The two issues are logically separable. One could imagine a system in which the accumulation of capital were substantially socialized, but the allocation of capital remains left mostly to market forces. Sweden, where savings are largely collectivized but there is little public ownership of industry and surprisingly little national government investment banking, is close to that model. One could also imagine a system where accumulation of savings is largely private, but capital investment decisions are heavily influenced by public planners. That pretty well describes Japan.

In the debate about equality, efficiency, and capital supply, it is possible to pursue distributive goals in the *accumulation* of capital — that is, savings — without worrying about the investment side of the ledger at all. As we have seen, inefficient tax incentives, such as the Reagan program, squander the national supply of savings; they harness inequality to inefficiency. Collective savings mechanisms and measures to broaden wealth creation can improve both equality and efficiency.

The desirability of national economic planning, in the sense of planned capital allocation, is a separate issue entirely. The case for selective government planning to allocate investment capital, admittedly, is mixed. In some societies, notably Japan and France, government planning has worked fairly well. It would be very hard to prove that the French and Japanese economies would have grown faster if French "indicative planning" of the period between 1947 and 1981 had never been invented or if Japan's famous Ministry of International Trade and Industry had not played its key role.

I have little respect for the argument that markets by definition optimize outcomes and hence planning cannot work. Real world markets are not very much like textbook markets. Resources are seldom at full capacity; investors never have perfect knowledge or foresight; markets are not in mathematical equilibrium. At the same time, successful public planning depends on appropriate institutions. Of the three relatively successful models of economic planning in a political democracy — the *dirigiste* tradition of France, the highly centralized and paternalistic economy of Japan, and the benevolent "left-corporatism" of Sweden, none is particularly well suited to the United States.

The case for a degree of economic planning, American style, rests on three other grounds. First, when unemployment is high and resources are idle, the theoretical claim that markets optimize the pattern of capital investment is not worth very much. During World War II, the United States grew at a rate of better than 13 percent a year because government was investing massively in armaments and in new technologies. At that rate of growth, we could afford to "waste" some capital. "Optimal" capital allocation by the market in a climate of high unemployment and slow growth accomplishes little; if investors look for market signals indicating where to invest, the market will tell them not to invest at all, for nobody is buying their products. Government investment often represents an improvement on no investment.

Second, we already have substantial government planning in the United States. We just fail to acknowledge it as such. Whenever the tax code creates a preference for real estate over steel, whenever the Justice Department decides to prohibit collaborative industrial research on antitrust grounds, whenever NASA or the Pentagon decides to procure and subsidize a particular technology, whenever Congress legislates subsidized credit to stimulate investment in synthetic fuels, exports, or tobacco — that is economic planning. That is the government superseding market forces.

Third, and perhaps more urgent, economic planning is being forced on America, like it or not, by the practical pressures of world trade. We are engaging in planning, and we might as well plan competently; otherwise, once again, the sacrifice of efficiency and equality march hand in hand, to a laissez-faire beat. The intertwined issues of trade and capital allocation will be the subject of Chapter 3.

> I was brought up, like most Englishmen, to respect free trade not only as an economic doctrine which a rational and instructed person could not doubt, but almost as a part of the moral law. I regarded ordinary departures from it as being at the same time an imbecility and an outrage . . . It is astonishing what a bundle of obsolete habiliments one's mind drags round even after the centre of consciousness has been shifted.
>
> — John Maynard Keynes

3

TRADE

IN THE FIRMAMENT of American ideological convictions, no star burns brighter than free trade. Our conviction about free trade represents ideology reinforced by three decades of self-interest. During the post-war Pax Americana, the free-trade regime plainly served American interests. As the world's premier producer, we could commend the virtues of free trade to our allies the way the biggest kid on the block calls for a fair fight. Today, the ideal of free trade remains resolutely bipartisan; it is the elevation of the free-market philosophy to a global scale.

If the success of the 1950s and 1960s proved to moderate Keynesians that demand management coupled with a mild welfare state "worked" domestically, it also proved to champions of free trade that market economics still reigned internationally. Among orthodox economists, one can find bitter disputes between Keynesians and monetarists, but one must look far and wide to find one who challenges the universal benefits of free trade.

The recent debate over free trade offers an instructive study of the way entrenched ideology denies changing self-interest. By the late 1970s, American interests were no longer served unequivocally by the free-trade regime. Europe and Japan had recovered from World

War II; U.S. technology was easily transplanted to Third-World countries with extremely low wage rates. No longer did free trade mean cheap prices of imported raw materials and effortless exports of American manufactured goods. Instead, it meant that in industry after industry, foreign producers were making deep inroads into American domestic markets, driving American companies out of business and American workers onto the unemployment rolls.

In this new world of stiff foreign competition, the injured industries and their trade unions were not slow to clamor for relief; intellectual revisionism came much more uneasily and hesitantly. The early demands for protection were purely defensive and as a national economic strategy, largely indefensible. Nonetheless, farmers, textile manufacturers, automakers, and steel companies did get partial shelter from import competition, through an *ad hoc* assortment of subterfuges, of which more below.

From the point of a pure free trader, *any* toleration of departure from the principle opens the way to abuse. One can find plenty of cases that seem to justify that argument — oversubsidized "loser" industries that ideally should be phased out in favor of more dynamic ones. Protection of excess capacity in steel or in autos seems to be a dead-weight economic loss. But in the real world, there are so many affronts to the pure theory of free trade that the practical policy question has long since changed. It is no longer *whether* to manage trade, but to manage it according to which criteria and to what degree. As the different faces of industrial policy suggest, protection can be a refuge to shelter losers — or to incubate new progeny. There is no guarantee that economic planning will always be used wisely— just as there is no guarantee that "free trade" won't lead to worldwide excess capacity and a competition to batter down wages. But these issues need to be debated at the level of practical policy, and not unreal theory.

Lately, a more systematic critique of the free-trade ideology has gathered force. Characteristically, it has developed almost entirely outside the economic profession. The critics (including this writer) argued that as long as other countries were succeeding by neomercantilist methods, the "free-trade versus protection" debate was an unproductive misstatement of the practical alternatives. If the Japanese were making steel more productively, it didn't necessarily mean that the Japanese therefore had an immutable comparative advantage in steel and that American industry had better find something else to do. It only meant that Japanese steelmakers, at least in the 1970s, had been rather cleverer than American steelmakers.

Does America *need* a steel industry? That question should be addressed unsentimentally and, above all, knowledgeably. If a steel industry is deemed essential, then a number of measures to restore the industry to productivity are possible and desirable. Some of these are conventionally "market" remedies and some are conventionally "protectionist"; but the labels and the free-trade ideal have ceased to be useful as practical criteria for policy. In this chapter, I shall do my best to explain why.

To both of these challenges — the self-serving demands of the injured industries and the more dispassionate intellectual challenge to the free-trade ideal — the orthodox response was fierce. To be a protectionist, of any stripe, is still considered the mark of an economic illiterate. As trade unions have wrestled with sickening declines of employment in America's basic industries and as moderately liberal policy intellectuals have considered how trade policy might connect to industrial policy, The Rising Tide of Protectionism has become an easy lecture for editorialists.

"Protectionism," warned *The New York Times* in a stern editorial denouncing domestic content legislation sponsored by the United Automobile Workers, "might mean a few jobs for American autoworkers, but it would depress the living standards of hundreds of millions of consumers and workers, here and abroad." The bill has become a lightning rod for antiprotection indignation. Editorial opposition runs all the way from the *Wall Street Journal* to the *Village Voice*, which managed to brand the UAW as racist for wishing to keep automaking jobs in the United States.

In principle, free trade is another area where short-run concern for equity, however well-intentioned, clashes with everyone's long-run interest in efficient use of resources. According to the free-trade orthodoxy, measures to protect the U.S. auto, steel, or textile industries and their wage earners only frustrate the emerging comparative advantage held by foreign producers like Japan, Korea, and Brazil. Protectionism, in this view, is nothing but a self-serving demand by loser industries, overpaid workers, and their political toadies to fence out superior imported goods. If Toyota makes a better car, who are we to keep it from American consumers? Protection denies

American citizens the benefits of more efficient, cheaper products; it shelters declining industries that need the discipline of competition, and it retards the transition of the economy to new industries where our natural comparative advantage lies. It will raise prices, hold back economic progress, deny poor nations the fruits of their own energies; it will court stagnation, retaliation, and deeper worldwide recession.

TRADE ACCORDING TO RICARDO

The free-trade orthodoxy has its roots, of course, in classical economic thought. Its assumptions deserve to be carefully tested against the realities of the contemporary world economy. For the classical economists, free trade had multiple virtues. Adam Smith pointed to the efficiencies of specialization, the tonic of wider competition, the benefits of broader consumer choice. Two generations after Smith, the English economist David Ricardo refined the argument. As Ricardo explained it in 1817, if Portugal is more efficient at making wine and England is superior at manufacturing cloth, then it would be absurd for each nation to make both products. Far better for each to do what it does best, and to trade the excess. Moreover, Ricardo added, even if a country is absolutely less efficient than its trading partners at everything, it still makes sense for that country to specialize in producing that at which it is relatively less inefficient, and to gain from the superior relative efficiencies of its trading partners. And even a country that is more efficient than its partners gains by concentrating activity on what it does best; if you happen to be a superior writer *and* a superior typist, it still makes sense to hire a typist to leave yourself more time to write. Add some algebra, and you have the theory of trade as it continues to be taught today.

Since Ricardo, economists have analogized the benefits of trade to the benefits of technology. Both are about the closest that one gets in economics to the elusive "free lunch." In the same manner, both provide more output for the same input. If my word processor allows me to write twice as quickly as my old Underwood, I am suddenly twice as productive. If the Koreans can sell the same pair of trousers at half the price, my budget for trousers suddenly has doubled in purchasing power. Trade, like technology, promotes efficiency; barriers to trade, like Luddism, retard it.

In this century, the economists Eli F. Heckscher and Bertil Ohlin added the further suggestion that as costs of capital and access to technology tend to equalize worldwide, actual trade patterns will increasingly reflect natural comparative advantages. For example, it is not surprising that the United States exports farm products and capital goods, because we have plentiful, relatively cheap land, and a relatively advanced labor force. Nor is it surprising (or alarming) that mass-production processes, even sophisticated ones like microelectronics, should shift to Third-World countries, for their comparative advantage is in cheap labor.

Thus, in theory, the economically sound way to deal with the Japanese challenge is simply to buy their entire cornucopia — the cheaper the better. If they are superior at making autos, TVs, tape recorders, cameras, steel, machine tools, baseball gloves, semiconductors, computers, and other arguably oriental products, it is irrational to shelter our own benighted industries. Far more sensible to buy their goods, let the bracing tonic of competition shake America from its torpor, and wait for the market to reveal our niche in the international division of labor.

This formulation, unfortunately, is based on multiple theoretical fallacies. Consequently, it miscasts the practical choices. As a theory, it ignores key characteristics of the modern world economy: technological dynamism and state influence. It describes a static world; it denies the possibility that competitive advantage can be created. Second, Ricardian economics presumes that the economy is operating at full-employment and full-capacity utilization. It overlooks the possibility that trade itself might have feedback effects that cause an economy to slip below full production and full employment. It fails to measure the efficiency gains of trade against the efficiency losses in output. Finally, it tends to confuse description with prescription. Free trade is presented as both a description of what is and a recommendation of what produces the best outcomes. But if we assume, by definition, that more free trade is better, we are at a loss to know how to proceed when a successful international player flourishes by defying the norms of free trade.

Ricardo in Wonderland

Consider the practical consequences of the assumption that technology is static and governments passive. Ricardo, as embellished by Heckscher-Ohlin, assumes that a nation's comparative advantage will be *revealed* by its patterns of exports, based on what economists call "factor endowments" — the nation's natural advantages of climate, minerals, location, arable land, or plentiful labor. But the theory does not fit a world of learning curves, technological dynamism, economies of scale, declining unit costs, and targeted industrial policies. In 1954, Edwin O. Reischauer, one of America's eminent students of Japan (and later Ambassador to Tokyo), wrote:

> Japan's situation is basically similar to England's, but infinitely worse. She is far less richly endowed with the vital resources of coal and iron . . . She is far less industrialized . . . She has no overseas empire to aid her . . . and she has almost twice the population to support on meager resources.

Most observers analyzing Japan of the 1950s in the tradition of Ricardo, concluded with Professor Reischauer that she was naturally suited (doomed) to an export regime of cheap, labor-intensive products. Poor Japan!

Increasingly, comparative advantage today is not "revealed" by natural factor endowments and market forces; it is created by governments pursuing neomercantilist strategies. Even where governments do not deliberately target commercial industries, they have immense influence over where capital flows. If Boeing got a big head start on the 707 from multibillion-dollar military contracts to develop an air force transport, is that a sin against free trade? If Europe, in order to get a foothold on the civil aviation market, responds with subsidized loans to the Airbus, is that worse? If the Japanese counter by demanding coproduction agreements, requiring assembly of portions of the McDonnell-Douglas F-15 and the Boeing 767 in Japan, doesn't that distort markets?

Of course. But the planes fly. All of these are sinners against Ricardo, and it is hard to judge which sinner is the worst. By free-trade lights, the Airbus A-300 is a tainted product, because it was produced by subsidized capital. But, as it turns out, the A-300 is the most fuel-efficient plane of its generation. And it stimulated Boeing to accelerate production of its own fuel-efficient wide-body jet. Were it not for the "distortion" of capital flows and the "protectionism" of the Airbus consortium, Boeing would have dominated world markets indefinitely and the A-300 never would have flown at all. Nor is it a foregone conclusion that the subsidized capital that launched Airbus would have been better used elsewhere by the market.

Looking around the industrialized world, one can see countless offenses against the free-trade ideal, which nonetheless lead to positive-sum economic gains. According to free-trade orthodoxy, protectionism can perhaps help the protectionist country for a time, but only at the expense of the rest of the world, and ultimately at the expense of economic efficiency. In practice, however, some protectionism has served to incubate real technological breakthroughs that benefit everyone. Japan's system of public-capital allocation, research subsidies, sheltered domestic markets, and market-sharing cartels is an unequivocal violation of free-trade norms. But it has produced technological gains that benefit the Japanese and the entire world. Free-market notions of optimality may have been transgressed, but the Hondas and Sonys and steel mills are superior products nonetheless. The economists who compare the absolute gains of trade to the gains of technology tend to overlook the paradoxical link between the two: Technological advance often thrives in sheltered and subsidized markets, which defy free trade. Japan gains because its aggressive mercantilism has moved it up the product ladder; the world gains from the technological advances. Moreover, Japan acquires a comparative advantage in skilled labor thanks to the industry it developed. Conventional economics has the cause and effect backwards. It is not a productive work force that leads to the industrial dynamism, but the industrial base that allows an advanced work force to mature.

KEYNESIAN TRADE

The free-trade ideal also creates a second, quite distinct, practical dilemma: a Keynesian one. Ricardian free trade, as noted, begins with the assumption that all resources are productively deployed. The equations assume that the economy is at or very near full employment. But today's global economy is not unlike that of the 1930s.

All the industrial countries are suffering high unemployment; globally, there is excess capacity in most industries. As more and more countries seek to produce advanced products for Western consumer markets, overcapacity worsens. It is reminiscent of the 1930s in the sense that the *world economy is not able to consume all that it produces.*

Writing those words in the present tense feels anachronistic; for that condition was supposed to have been consigned to economic history. Keynesian demand management, in theory, solved the problem of overcapacity and underconsumption. But the heightened game of world trade — in conditions of easily transferred technology and the entry of new, low-wage players — recreates Keynesian problems of overproduction and excess capacity, which cannot be solved by one government's pursuing Keynesian demand-management policies in isolation.

Consider the steel industry. Steel is a "high-value-added" industry, meaning that it produces a relatively high-value output for each hour of labor input. A Nigerian carving figurines adds perhaps $1000 to Nigerian GNP in a year. A Nigerian working in a steel mill may add that much in a day. Not surprisingly, the development experts have urged Third-World countries to shift to higher value-added industries whenever feasible. As it happens, the self-interest of Nigeria coincides with that of Western exporters of technology and capital goods, who are happy to sell the steel mill. Similarly, the desire of, say, the Philippines to shift from exports of mahogany to exports of computers coincides with the self-interest of the Atari company, which paid its assemblers $5 an hour in Los Angeles, but only $1 in Manila.

Steel and Veal

The overcapacity problem arises because each producer tries to enter an established industry at the expense of all existing producers. And while there is a productivity gain because the heightened competition produces technical breakthroughs and lowers costs, there are also losses. To pursue the case of steel, one loss is that everybody except the newest, most advanced entrant is now producing at a lower fraction of total capacity. Very expensive capital equipment sits idle much of the time, which lowers productivity. Much still-viable capital equipment is phased out prematurely. The heightened competition also lowers profit margins, which means that the return on capital is depressed, which in turn depresses the market incentive to invest and discourages market-motivated producers from staying in the game.

In theory, the system is self-regulating: the increased personal income created by the new advanced production in the Third-World location enhances worldwide demand for the product — Nigeria as a member of the steelmaking club is now a bigger customer for steel (and other products) — and the market ought to reach a new "equilibrium" at a higher total level of output. But in practice, at least for a long transition period, much Third-World production of advanced consumer products is intended for First-World markets. Korea was making color televisions when there was no color TV broadcasting in Korea. Few home computers are consumed in the Philippines. Nigeria's income from steel production may add little to global demand, because Nigeria is pursuing a supply-side strategy and plowing the proceeds into investment. In short, whether the income generated by enhanced Third-World production is sufficient to soak up that increased production is another of those troubling issues that must be settled by evidence, not theory. By worldwide standards, wages of Third-World producers of advanced products are still very low — too low to turn them into Western-style mass consumers. And the evidence indeed suggests that Third-World production has outstripped Third-World domestic demand.

In this kind of world economy, each individual national producer reacts in much the same way an individual farmer does during a depression. Although the economy as a whole suffers from overproduction, it is still in the interest of each individual farmer to maximize his individual output. The price of wheat may be a miserable $2.00 a bushel, but farmer Jones who has fixed costs to amortize still does better producing 2000 bushels than 1000. In fact, in conditions of mass overproduction, he will do better lowering his price to $1.90 if that's what it takes to unload his crop.

Precisely the same dynamic operates in the steel industry. With high fixed costs, each individual producer aims to maximize production and lower price, despite worldwide overcapacity. In fact, it is even rational for a new entrant to minimize profits and perhaps to price his product below his cost for a time, in order to attract market share from established producers.

The difference between *national* overproduction in agriculture and global overproduction in steel (or computers or semiconductors) is also highly instructive. In the case of farm products in one country, it is possible for the State to structure markets and create a system of rewards and punishments to stabilize prices and limit production. This is of course not free, in either sense of the word. It transgresses laissez-faire, and it incurs costs. The price support system sometimes seems jerrybuilt, and mistakes are sometimes made. But in order to induce farmers to keep producing and to invest in farm machinery, the State has had to offer them some assurance of stable, predictable markets. Even in Ricardian America, agriculture is almost totally protected from imports. And on the whole, managed markets in agriculture have been a vast improvement over pre-1914 market anarchy.

In the same fashion, macroeconomic demand-management techniques at the level of the nation-state represented an advance for industrial producers over the previous system of wild, periodic swings of boom and bust, as the market failed to consume what was produced. But within the new global, free-trade economy, effective policies to stabilize demand are very difficult as a matter of practice, because national borders are no longer barriers to flows of capital and commodities. Moreover, interfering with global flows of commerce is of course ideologically impermissible, for that would violate the norms of free trade.

Competitive Ruin

Domestically, even relatively conservative, market-oriented economists have allowed a Keynesian Exception to the general doctrine that markets always optimize outcomes. It is acknowledged that market economies have an unfortunate tendency to degenerate into episodes of boom and bust, and that government meddling to manage aggregate demand may in fact be an improvement upon the invisible hand.

No such Exception, however, is permitted in trade doctrine, even though the dilemmas of worldwide overproduction, underconsumption, and competitive deflation are quintessentially Keynesian. Because free-trade theory assumes that the economy is operating at full employment, most economists just take it for granted that when a

Japanese supplier of, say, steel, displaces a U.S. supplier, the displaced American capital and labor will find some more useful application. "Suppose," said one prominent trade economist, speaking at an international conference,

> that in one year one million workers move from a declining sector to an expanding sector, doubling their productivity. This is a shift of one percent of the total labor force . . . Doubling productivity for one percent of the labor force would add one percent to the growth rate of productivity.

But suppose instead that unemployment is at 10 percent and industrial capacity use is at 75 percent. And suppose that most of the million workers displaced by import competition move not to a more productive industry, but to the fast-food business or to the unemployment rolls. During a period of high unemployment, this is surely the more realistic supposition. Research by economists Bennett Harrison and Barry Bluestone found that of 674,000 workers displaced from industrial jobs in New England between 1958 and 1975, just 18,000, or 3 percent, found jobs in high technology, and 106,000 (18 percent) ended up in service and retail jobs, generally at lower wages. Nothing in the free-trade model guarantees that workers in one economy displaced by trade will necessarily be reemployed at more productive occupations. Indeed, steel and autos, two "declining" sectors, typically have far higher value-added per worker, and in turn far higher wages, than the average jobs in the economy.

Just fifty years ago, Keynes himself predicted how the pressures of anarchical trade could interfere with the ability of one national economy to stabilize and maximize its own production. Given the system's propensity to underconsume what it could produce, blind reliance on market forces made no more sense to Keynes as a principle of foreign commerce than as an ideal of domestic economics.

In a widely reprinted 1933 essay titled "National Self-Sufficiency," Keynes wrote:

> Most modern processes of mass production can be performed in most countries and climates with almost equal efficiency . . .
> National self-sufficiency is to be considered, not as an ideal in itself, but as directed to the creation of an environment in which other ideals can be safely and conveniently pursued.

The "other ideals" Keynes had in mind were, of course, full employment and maximum production at decent wages. To the extent that open trade restored the primacy of the market via the back door, Keynes mistrusted it. He concluded, not without some reluctance, "Economic internationalism embracing the free movement of capital and loanable funds as well as of traded goods may condemn my own country for a generation to come to a much lower degree of material prosperity than could be attained under a different system."

For Keynes, it was not at all clear that the putative gains of totally open trade necessarily justified the loss of national autonomy with which to pursue the strategic goal of full production. It was exactly the same conclusion reached intuitively by American leaders during our period of high-tariff industrialization in the mid- and late-nineteenth century, and by Japanese leaders after World War II.

Today, nearly half of world trade is conducted between units of multinational corporations. Just as Keynes foresaw, most basic products (steel, plastics, microprocessors, textiles, machine tools) can be produced almost anywhere, but by labor forces with vastly differing wages. And this raises another Keynesian dilemma: the tendency of open trade to depress wages.

Open trade under corporate auspices in an era of mobile capital and portable technology creates strong competitive pressures to reduce labor costs. In a world where technology and capital are highly transferable, there is a real risk that comparative advantage comes to be defined as whose labor force will work for the lowest wage. The postwar Keynesian social contract in the Western democracies— full employment, a costly welfare state, rising real wages — suddenly comes unglued. "High labor costs" (people's jobs!) are again seen as a luxury which "we" cannot afford if we are to remain competitive.

In such a world, it is literally possible for industries to grow more productive while the national economy grows poorer. How can that be? The factors left out of the Ricardian equation are falling real wages and idle capacity. If America's autos (or steel tubes or machine tools) are manufactured more productively than a decade ago, but less productively than in Japan (or Korea or Brazil), and if we practice what we preach about open trade, then a growing share of U.S. purchasing power will go to provide jobs overseas. Even if American technology is twice as efficient, foreign producers can compensate by paying their workers one fourth the wage, which will increase pressures on American producers to lower their own pay scales. A growing share of American capital and labor will lie idle. American manufacturers, detecting soft markets and falling profits, will decline to invest. Steelmakers will buy oil companies. Consumer access to superior foreign products will not necessarily compensate for the decline in real income and the idle resources. Nor is there any guarantee that the new industrial countries will necessarily use their burgeoning income from American sales to buy American capital equipment (or computers or even coal), for they are all striving to develop their own advanced, diversified economies.

Against this background of tidal change in the global economy, the conventional reverence for free trade as an ideal or as a policy guide is just not very helpful. In a world of mercantilism where none of the practical alternatives resembles pure free trade, attachment to the ideal has a series of perverse consequences. It suggests that we are helpless to repair our own economy in the face of new, "revealed" foreign comparative advantages, save by increasing the rewards to capital and punishing labor. It implies that we can enrich ourselves as a society only by lowering our wages — another convenient implication for owners of capital. And, as we shall see, our reverence for free trade assures that the form of protectionism that we do get is purely defensive, which fails to bring about constructive changes in the protected industry.

Almost any form of industrial policy requires subsidies and marketing strategies aimed at domestic industries, which by definition are departures from the free-trade ideal. If these are ruled out as ideologically impermissible, then we deny ourselves an indispensable tool for restoring a full-production economy.

The seductive fallacy in the free-trade ideology is to project our own enthusiasm for the ideal onto the actual world economy. Since free trade is defined as the optimum, it is assumed that successful exporters must be playing by the rules and that we are fools not to defer to their Ricardian superiority. So canny a critic of political economy as Michael Kinsley could write, "Very few American workers have lost their jobs because of unfair foreign trade practices, and it is demagogic . . . to suggest otherwise." But what, exactly, is an unfair trade practice? By free-trade lights, unfair trade practices are pervasive. In late 1982, the European Community (EC) filed a complaint alleging that the entire Japanese industrial system is one great unfair trade practice! Almost any national strategy of economic planning must run afoul of the canons of free trade.

THE FREE-TRADE REGIME

To the extent that the rules of liberal trade are codified, they repose in the General Agreement on Tariffs and Trade. The GATT is one of those multilateral institutions created in the American image just after World War II — a splendid historical moment when America's self-interest seemed to coincide with altruistic international purposes. Wartime strictures had shattered normal trade relations, which had already been eroded by the high tariffs of the 1930s. A restoration of commerce was widely agreed to be indispensable for European recovery.

The basic GATT treaty, ratified in 1947, requires that all member nations get the same tariff treatment and that tariffs, in theory at least, are the only permissible form of barrier. Governments are supposed to treat foreign goods exactly the same as they do domestic ones: no subsidies, tax preferences, cheap loans to home industries; no quotas, preferential procurement, or inspection gimmickry to exclude imported products. Nor can producers sell below cost (dumping) in foreign markets.

The GATT regime also commits members to progressive, multilateral tariff reduction. Since 1947, there have been seven "rounds" of multilateral negotiations under GATT auspices, which have sharply reduced prevailing tariffs. In the last series of talks, the so-called Tokyo Round, American diplomats pressed unsuccessfully for reductions in what U.S. negotiators like to call "nontariff barriers"— subsidies, preferential procurement, and the like. Not surprisingly, this campaign failed. For, what we consider nontariff barriers are the essence of other nations' economic development strategies.

Even the original GATT system represented an uneasy compromise between the ideal of pure free trade and the exigencies of practical politics. As originally envisioned by its American sponsors, the postwar free-trade regime was to include not just a GATT, but an International Trade Organization (ITO) to bring about and supervise the system of liberal trade. At the 1948 Havana Conference on Trade and Employment, representatives from the major Western nations agreed on a comprehensive ITO code, prohibiting all forms of discrimination in trade relationships. But the code proved too great a threat to the economic autonomy of several European nations (who saw a more active role for the state in economic development), and the ITO Act was never ratified.

By default, the GATT became the international umbrella organization setting trade norms. From the outset, however, the GATT tolerated numerous deviations from the ideal. Preferential trade zones such as the British Commonwealth were allowed; new customs unions such as the European Common Market were permitted to maintain relatively high tariff walls around the union, so long as they were making progress toward trade liberalization within. "Escape clauses" were permitted, allowing nations to levy duties on imports that caused substantial injury to domestic industries. And instead of prohibiting subsidies, low-interest export credits, preferred procurement arrangements, etcetera, such industrial targeting policies were made the subject of case-by-case negotiation. A government could retaliate if it wished, but such retaliation invited further retaliation.

Interestingly enough, even the American sponsors did not want pure free trade. Agriculture was kept out of the GATT system, not for any sound theoretical reason, but because American agriculture was and remains a protected sector. A free-trade regime in agriculture simply did not serve America's self-interest. At the insistence of American negotiators, primary products were excluded from GATT rules, and the United States continues to have a patchwork of unilateral and "voluntary" quotas on farm products. Later, as advanced industrial nations felt pressure from cheap textile imports in the 1950s, textiles were also removed from the GATT regime.

Even as the champion of the GATT system, the United States has freely ignored it when American interests were at stake. While professing to support the GATT regime, both conservative and liberal U.S. administrations have negotiated "voluntary" quotas known as orderly marketing agreements restricting imports of textiles, steel, automobiles, shoes, and numerous lesser products. Although we rail against tax subsidies used by foreign governments, for over a decade we refused to modify the 1971 Domestic International Sales Corporation (DISC) Act, which gives tax advantages to U.S. exporters. From the European perspective, military contracts serve as a vast subsidy to the U.S. aerospace and electronics industries.

GATT also lacks an enforcement mechanism. It is more of a standing diplomatic conference than a policeman. If an alleged treaty violation is confirmed by an official GATT study panel, the complaining country has the right to impose countervailing duties. But despite the pseudolegalistic flavor of the GATT apparatus, decisions to retaliate are invariably decided on diplomatic, not legal, grounds. For example, when the European Airbus consortium cracked the U.S. market with a billion-dollar sale to Eastern Airlines, the deal included subsidized loans far below prevailing commercial rates, a clear violation of GATT rules. After much hand-wringing, the United States — torn between alienating Boeing or alienating Eastern and half of Europe — did nothing.

In the nearly forty years of the postwar free-trade regime, trade has moved in two distinctly opposite directions. On the one hand, explicit trade barriers — tariffs — have been reduced and other restrictions liberalized. At the same time, most nations have devised all sorts of measures that violate the free-trade ideal, which are good for their own economic development. Some of these amount to pure protectionism of the beggar-my-neighbor variety; others stimulate real economic growth and create positive-sum gains. Unfortunately, the Ricardian paradigm is useless to differentiate between the two.

Japan, Inc., Meets Ricardo

In classical free-trade theory, the only permissible candidate for temporary protection is the "infant industry." Even in Ricardian terms, a nation with a potential comparative advantage in something might justifiably need a respite to gain a toehold against competitors. In the nineteenth century, when technologies developed slowly and natural factor endowments loomed larger, the infant industry exception could remain an exception. Today however, Japan and its imitators, not unreasonably, treat *every emerging technology* as an infant industry. Japan uses a highly sheltered domestic market as a laboratory or — to shift the metaphor — as a shield behind which to launch one export success after another.

By the free-market test, Japan should be paying a heavy price for its blatant protectionism as its capital is misallocated, its consumers are denied the benefit of superior imported goods, and its industry stagnates. Weep not for Japan. The details of the Japanese industrial system have been amply described elsewhere, but the essence is worth recapitulating as a litmus for free-trade theory.

The Japanese government, in close collaboration with industry, targets sectors for development. The favorite straw man of the neo-laissez-faire school is the claim that government can't possibly have enough acumen to "pick winners"; the metaphor suggests a gambler playing the horses or the stock market. But the Japanese government doesn't *pick* winners; it creates them. It lends subsidized capital through the Japan Development Bank, which signals private bankers to let funds flow. In Japan most government research and development funds are aimed at commercial applications, while in America government R&D spending is about 70 percent military. Where our government offers tax-depreciation allowances and other tax subsidies to all businesses according to a formula (at a cost estimated to reach $87 billion in fiscal year 1985), Japan taxes ordinary business profits at stiff rates and saves its subsidies for targeted ventures. Japan tends to the demand side as well as to the supply side. The government subsidizes the purchase of emerging technologies to create domestic markets for new Japanese industries; and it sometimes buys back outdated capital to stimulate markets for newer capital goods. The Japanese government also waives antimonopoly laws to allow for joint development of new products and organizes "recession cartels" to negotiate reduction in capacity when overcapacity is a problem. And far from defying the useful discipline of the market, the Ministry of International Trade and Industry (MITI) encourages fierce domestic competition before winnowing down the field to a few export champions.

The famed MITI has of course made its share of mistakes. There are numerous examples of schemes that went awry and of persistent entrepreneurs who succeeded over MITI's objections. Japan debunkers conclude that MITI's influence is exaggerated. Japan enthusiasts observe that MITI's light hand underscores that this is a system of consensus-brokering, not industrial czarship. My purpose in invoking Japan is not to suggest that Japanese industrial strategy should (or could) be imported to the United States, for there are aspects that are ill-suited to our own institutions or are plainly repugnant.

But Japan does suggest that norms other than Ricardian ones can achieve prosperity. Only the most diehard ideologue would deny that, on the whole, industrial targeting has served Japan well. For nearly thirty years, MITI has pursued this same essential strategy, keeping foreign borrowers out of cheap Japanese capital markets, letting in foreign investors only on very restricted terms, moving Japan up the product ladder from cheap and labor-intensive goods in the 1950s to autos and steel in the 1960s, to consumer electronics in the 1970s, and to nearly every advanced technology by the 1980s.

Free-trade purists and neoprotectionists alike can readily agree that America should bargain harder for reciprocal access to Japanese markets. But that would solve only a small part of the "Japan Problem." The other elements of Japan's brilliantly successful mercantilism — the subsidized loans, the cartels, the incubation of supply with state-seeded demand — simply constitute a fundamentally different strategy of economic development, which happens to be attractive to much of the world. It is not likely to be banished from international commerce by American appeals to the GATT or to the sainted memory of David Ricardo.

Defining Away Japan

The palpable success of the Japanese model and the worldwide rush to emulate it create both an ideological crisis for the free-trade regime and a practical crisis for American economic policymakers. Ideologically, the Japanese success compels Ricardians either to revise their theory or to insist that flourishing Japan, despite appearances, is nonetheless playing by Ricardian rules if we just look hard enough. Reinterpreting the facts has proven less arduous than questioning the theory (economists are nothing if not inventive). Despite a conclusive body of evidence by students of Japanese institutions documenting Japan's system of mercantilism, it has become fashionable in free-trade circles to insist that Japan really doesn't protect after all. William Cline of the prestigious Institute for International Economics observes that some foreign producers do compete effectively in Japanese markets ("For example, Coca-Cola is the largest selling soft drink in Japan, Schick is number one in the razor market . . . "), and concludes, "there is little systematic, empirical evidence that Japan protects its market substantially more than the United States does its own." In fact, the scholarly and diplomatic evidence documenting Japanese protectionism is overwhelming.

Cline bases his astonishing assertion on econometric work by the University of Michigan economist Gary Saxonhouse, who argues that given Japan's geographic remoteness, its paucity of natural resources, and its diligent labor force, its huge trade surplus in manufactured goods is only natural. Since the market, by definition, optimizes outcomes, Japan's deliberate industrial policy must be of little consequence. Saxonhouse writes,

> No other advanced industrialized economy combines such poor natural resources at such a great distance from its major trading partners. It is these distinctive characteristics and not, for example, an industrial policy . . . which gives Japan a robust comparative advantage in so many manufactured products.

For Saxonhouse, this means that even Japan's famed labor discipline is a relatively minor factor:

> It is the natural resource wealth of the United States and the natural resource poverty of Japan, far more than the real or imagined differences in the motivation of factory workers in the two countries which explains relative Japanese success in so many manufacturing lines.

Seemingly, a poor resource base is the key to a comparative advantage in industrial goods. By this test, Britain should be thriving and arid Turkey soaring. To nail down his case, Saxonhouse adds several pages of algebra using a general equilibrium model of trade. His model reveals that only in precisely 4.3 percent of her total trade are Japanese protectionist practices statistically significant — less than many other countries. Japanese mercantilism disappears, through the alchemy of algebra.

A more subtle variant of this argument is to concede that perhaps Japan does protect, but that it doesn't make any difference. If the state, by definition, cannot outguess the market, then it only follows logically that mercantilism cannot improve outcomes. Japan's remarkable rise to pre-eminence in steel was not related to the government's deliberate strategy of steering cheap capital to steel, subsidizing steelmaking applications engineering, or creating a domestic market for Japanese steel producers, insists Paul R. Krugman, a senior staff economist at the Reagan Council of Economic Advisors. If Japan was destined to have a comparative advantage in steel, it all would have happened anyway; if not, efforts to create one would have been futile. Krugman writes:

> By the early 1960s, the Japanese steel industry would have had a comparative advantage over the U.S. industry even if the Japanese government had kept hands off. The same technological "book of blueprints" was available to both countries; access to raw materials was no longer a crucial factor; and labor costs were much higher in the U.S. Capital was becoming steadily more available in Japan, thanks to a high saving rate. Quite independent of industrial targeting, Japan was gaining a comparative advantage in steel, while the U.S. was losing one.

This form of logical reasoning will be familiar to students of Voltaire's *Candide*. By definition, the existing outcome must be the natural one and hence the best possible one, for if it could have been better it would have been better. Human intervention, by definition, is impotent to improve things; meddling can only worsen them. Such is the perfection of the natural order. The power of this method is that it reliably disposes of evidence. The logic is relentless: no evidence could persuade Krugman that targeting policy in fact did help Japan gain a comparative advantage in steel, for that possibility has been ruled out by the premise. The same tautological method has equally good results for Marxists seeking to corroborate the labor theory of value, fundamentalists endeavoring to disprove Darwin, or racists wishing to confirm the superiority of Aryans.

Conventional economic analysis ignores the possibility that a *created* comparative advantage, attained in conditions of other-than-perfect competition, can lead to a cumulative advantage that will simply drive potential competitors out of business. In the primitive textbook model of perfect competition, a monopolistic advantage will be short-lived, because other prospective producers will notice the super-normal profits, enter the market, and force the monopoly producer to lower his costs. However, this neat picture fails utterly to capture the actual world of global trade. Nowhere is it guaranteed that the United States (or France or Britain) will regain the advantage that they once had as makers of steel or automobiles; and nowhere is it guaranteed that the goods that we manufacture as substitutes for auto production will be as good for our economy.

A number of economists have noticed that in a world of imperfect competition a producer might indeed gain an insuperable lead over prospective rivals — and these economists include such respectable fellows as Alfred Marshall, Leon Walras, Gunnar Myrdal, and Nicholas Kaldor, among others. Myrdal called the tendency of success to breed further success and failure to beget more failure the "principle of circular and cumulative causation." But this recognition has passed largely from the view of mainstream American economists, who insist that maximum competition from Japan, Korea, et al., must be good for American industry, even if Japan and Korea are far more mercantilist than we. By definition, if we are driven out of steel and auto production, there must be a very good reason for it, somewhere in the natural order of things.

If the successful mercantilism of much of the developing world had only created a crisis for Ricardian theory, the logical contortions would discomfit neoclassical economists, amuse journalists, and be of little wider consequence. But unlike crises in the theory of, say, literary deconstructionism, whopping fallacies in economic theory have real consequences.

The Japanese not only sin against our theory of market economics, but they convert sin into productive virtue. By our own highest standards of economic success, they must be doing something right. Thus, their very success creates a terrible conundrum for American trade policy, which is still deeply wedded to the ideology of free trade and believes that only [market] virtue can triumph. As Professors John Zysman and Steven Cohen of the University of California observed in a thoughtful 1982 paper for the Congressional Joint Economic Committee, America as the main defender of the liberal GATT philosophy now faces an acute dilemma: "How to sustain the open trade system and promote the competitive position of American industry" *at the same time.*

TRADE AND INDUSTRIAL POLICY

Because American policymakers believe so fervently in markets, we tend to shun any kind of intervention until an industry is in very deep trouble. Then, reacting to short-run and guilt-ridden political pressure, we give it the sort of purely defensive protection that free traders quite rightly condemn; we build it half a bridge.

There is no better example of the lethal combination of *ad hoc* protectionism plus market-capitalism-as-usual than the steel industry. In most of the world, steel is not a product that conforms to the principles of free trade. *Nowhere* does steel production earn a market rate of return. Major industrial nations promote their steel industries because they consider steel a central link in an advanced economy.

As Europe rebuilt its steel capacity after World War II, the American industry became partially dependent on protection from imports, initially through unofficial quotas. The American steel industry is oligopolistic. It was slow to modernize. Major U.S. firms invested heavily in new steelmaking capacity during the 1960s, using outmoded technologies. By the mid-1970s, world demand for steel was leveling off — just as aggressive new producers like Japan, Korea, and Brazil were flooding world markets with cheap, state-of-the-art steel.

Under the GATT rules, individual firms damaged by subsidized imports may seek legal remedies, or they may ask their governments to find diplomatic ones. As the Carter administration took office in 1977, American steel producers were pursuing antidumping suits. The new administration had a better idea, one that seemed more consistent with neighborly economic relations. Carter officials devised a "trigger-price mechanism," a floor price for steel entering U.S. markets. The trigger price was the actual cost of steel produced in the world's most modern (Japanese) mills. Producers selling at below the trigger price were presumed to be dumping. The trigger price was supposed to hold imports to a moderate level and to accelerate the pressure on U.S. producers to become more competitive. But no sooner did American steelmakers withdraw their antidumping suits than imports began creeping up again, and U.S. producers again filed antidumping charges.

Planning Blind 1: Carter and Steel

Caught between its diplomatic defense of free trade, its ideological faith in markets, and its practical need to salvage and modernize the domestic steel industry, the Carter administration groped toward a minimalist industrial policy for steel. In 1979, officials created a kind of near beer called the Steel Tripartite Advisory Committee, made up of representatives of industry, labor, and government. The Steel Tripartite was supposed to come up with a strategy. The eventual recommendations included more protection from imports, a "stretchout" of costly environmental regulations, and new tax incentives.

The Steel Tripartite Committee readily agreed that the industry needed $4.7 billion for modernization during the 1980–84 period, and that insufficient funds would be available from profits, new borrowings, and new sales of stock. But the committee could not reach agreement on where the additional capital might come from or what tradeoffs might be reasonable in exchange for further official import limitations or waivers of environmental rules. In the committee's report, government representatives and industry representatives disagreed on the wisdom of further tax subsidies. Steel-industry officials backed the 10-5-3 tax-depreciation bill, which promised big tax breaks. Carter administration officials opposed it. In the end, the administration did support legislation softening environmental controls on steel.

What the Tripartite steel policy could not include was adequate capital or an enforceable commitment to modernize the steel industry. The U.S. government does not have at its disposal discretionary subsidized loan funds or equity capital or procurement commitments as tools to be used in an industrial restructuring; under the free-market dogma, tax concessions are the only legitimate form of capital subsidy, and they are a blunt tool indeed. By market standards, massive retooling of the steel industry was not a rational course, because the return on steel investment was well below prevailing yields on other investments. Even at the 90 percent capacity utilization that the Steel Tripartite Committee assumed (which turned out to be wishful thinking in light of what followed), steel was only barely profitable.

Government officials had neither the ideological mandate, the policy tools, nor the knowledge to devise a long-term strategic investment plan for steel. The only real *quo* they had to offer in exchange for the industry's inadequate *quid* was more import protection. Interviews with several officials involved in the Carter administration's stillborn industrial policy revealed a dawning awareness that they were caught in an ideological twilight zone — neither pure laissez-faire nor coherent planning — but possibly the worst mixture of both.

According to Alan W. Wolff, formerly a deputy to U.S. Trade Representative Robert Strauss, "We make policy in profound ignorance of how the rest of the world functions. The assumption is that the entire world operates in our own image. We refuse to adopt affirmative industrial policies because we don't like protection, but we end up with the protection anyway."

Robert Herzstein, the Commerce Department's assistant secretary in charge of trade, was surprised to find how little competence the government had to evaluate the industries it was dealing with. He recalled, "I repeatedly had the experience, in autos or aerospace or aluminum, where some issue would come up and I would ask, 'Who knows anything about this industry?' And the staff would invariably say, 'We'll call up the industry and have them send somebody over to brief us.' "

Government's institutional ignorance proved a critical weakness in its efforts to negotiate a restructuring of the steel industry. "We would sit around and talk about rods versus plate versus specialty steel, and none of us in government had any knowledge of how the steel industry actually operates," said C. Fred Bergsten, a free trader who served as the Treasury's top trade official under Carter. "There has never been a government study of what size and shape steel industry the country needs. The country has groped towards an industrial policy, ass-backwards, driven by the pressures of trade. If we're going to go down this road, we should do it right, rather than just preserving the status quo."

That view, of course, was heresy to most of the Carter people (even Bergsten states it gingerly, as a hypothetical case). Industrial planning is even clearer heresy to the Reagan administration. The saga of the steel negotiations has an intriguing epilogue. Upon taking office, the Reagan administration quickly ended the government's mild flirtation with industrial policy. U.S. Steel again pressed its antidumping case; it also purchased Marathon Oil. In 1982, with the steel industry operating at below 50 percent of capacity, the free-trade Reagan administration negotiated a new round of tough import quotas on basic steel. In 1983, barely a month after the Williamsburg economic summit where America's allies were made to pledge allegiance to free trade, the administration extended the quotas to specialty steel. There were no commitments by the steel industry about restructuring, no explicit design for which segments of the industry could remain competitive, no jointly agreed-upon targets for domestic production. Intriguingly enough, in August 1983, after giving the industry substantial protection, Commerce Secretary Malcolm Baldridge quietly divulged plans to revive the steel tripartite. Officials vehemently denied that this was anything like planning, for the Reagan administration believes in markets.

As the steel case suggests, trade policy and industrial policy are closely linked. In order to pursue a successful industrial policy, it is necessary both to supersede domestic market allocations of capital and to limit the privileges of laissez-faire enjoyed by some foreign products — even superior ones — that may be the fruits of somebody else's industrial policy. From a Ricardian standpoint, of course, both industrial targeting and limits on imports are equally illegitimate, as transgressions against the wisdom of the market.

The issue has ceased to be whether to protect or not to protect. Rather, the practical choice is whether to engage in some protectionism in the context of strategic plans to keep our economy at full employment and improve our industries — or merely to protect defensively, as free traders in public office have been so quick to do.

Planning Blind 2: Reagan and Motorcycles

Another recent case not nearly so well known as steel suggests why most trade-policy issues are really industrial-policy issues. In July 1983, the Reagan administration agreed to give an unprecedented dose of protection to the Harley-Davidson company, America's last producer of motorcycles. This was one of the very few cases where tariffs were raised on imports, not because of a finding of dumping, but simply because the American producer was able to show injury. In an earlier (1980) case, the domestic auto industry sought higher tariffs on imported cars, but U.S. tariff officials held that most of the distress in domestic sales was the result of the recession, not import competition.

Harley's injuries were severe indeed. By 1982, it was selling fewer than 35,000 big bikes a year, less than half its traditional market and well below its break-even point. Japanese producers, who had entered the U.S. market in the 1960s with sleek cycles in the 250–600cc range, were now driving Harley out of the upper end of the market as well. Under U.S. law, injury cases are filed with an agency

called the International Trade Commission. (The name is a characteristic euphemism; this is a domestic agency that used to answer to
the more descriptive name, The Tariff Commission.)

The commission determines whether injury has occurred and who
or what is to blame. It recommends a remedy, which must be finally
approved or modified by the White House. In this case, the commission recommended an increase in tariffs on Japanese heavy motorcycles from 4.4 percent to 49.4 percent, and the White House
concurred. The tariff surcharge will gradually be reduced over a
period of five years, during which time Harley is supposed to revive.

Why was this remedy chosen? Harley-Davidson in its complaint
to the commission filed extensive plans for restructuring. The company contended that it was well along in the process of developing
a new engine and redesigning its line of heavy motorcycles, that its
new line could effectively compete in the open market with Japanese
products, but that it desperately needed to retain its market share in
order to stay viable and raise adequate capital in the interim.

The U.S. government doesn't really have any experts on the motorcycle industry. But the officials of the Commerce Department, the
U.S. Trade Representative's Office, and the International Trade Commission, who reviewed the case, were all impressed. "They clearly
did have a strategy for becoming competitive," recalled David Morrissey of the Trade Representative's office. "They were reducing their
break-even point; their new engine was using state-of-the-art technology." So the ITC's remedy was based on the company's own
projections of when it could reasonably expect to become competitive
again. Trade officials will scrutinize company finances periodically
throughout the four-year period of protection.

In this case, like it or not, the Reagan administration was engaging
in a cardinal sin: economic planning. Whether the Japanese had
subsidized their domestic motorcycle industry was not at issue. As
far as this case was concerned, the Japanese were following the rules
of market economics. They were driving the last remaining U.S.
producer out of business mainly on the basis of a superior product.
But that was not considered an acceptable outcome. So U.S. trade
officials, forced to adjudicate a trade-injury case, found themselves
making seat-of-the-pants industrial policy. Officials managed to fa-
miliarize themselves with the motorcycle business and with the investment plans of the Harley-Davidson company, at about the same

level of sophistication as a stock analyst in a brokerage house who functions as the gatekeeper to private capital markets. The automotive specialist at E.F. Hutton may not know how to change a piston ring, but he can read a balance sheet. Likewise the motorcycle man at the Commerce Department.

Officials, in short, were presuming to outguess the market. The market was telling Harley to go make something else. But officials after some careful study concluded that Harley might survive as a strong competitor after all, given a little import relief and restructuring. The U.S. government was playing the role of MITI — but with one hand tied behind its back.

The difference between our de facto industrial policy and theirs is that the United States does not admit to *having* an industrial policy. There is no mandate to consider whether the country needs a motorcycle industry. There is no mandate to look into the value of linkages between, say, motorcycle production and metallurgy or machine-tool building. Nor is there an array of policy tools, save trade restrictions and perhaps some special-interest tax favoritism. Officials could decide whether Harley's own plans were plausible and weigh their conclusions against the predictable diplomatic outcry if tariffs were raised. But they did not have the option of offering Harley, say, subsidized loans; or directing the Pentagon and the fifty state police departments to buy a given number of Harley-Davidson motorcycles during the life of the restructuring plan; or subsidizing applied research into the high-stress metallurgy needed to accelerate production of Harley's new engine — as part of a restructuring package.

What a self-defeating limbo for public policy! The *practice* of free trade certainly has been abandoned, and for sound reasons. But the ideology lives on. And, as the motorcycle case illustrates, the force of the ideology is no longer sufficient to keep us loyal to the conduct of free trade, but it remains just powerful enough to deny us the tools of competent planning. It is rather like the teen-age girl who becomes pregnant because her moral scruples lead her to forgo birth control, but not sex.

To some defenders of the Ricardian regime, steel and motorcycles are nothing but declining smokestack industries. If developing nations have an emerging comparative advantage in such products as steel, by definition this cannot be the result of superior statecraft (which cannot exist); it is only the market's way of telling us that it is time for the United States to specialize in something else, where our own presumed comparative advantage in high technology can be maximized.

This conclusion is dubious on several grounds. First, it defines an entirely spurious category of industry: "high technology." In reality, of course, old smokestack industries can be reborn as both consumers and suppliers of high-technology products. A modern motorcycle, like a modern steel mill, is a high-technology good. A textile mill, which used low technology in 1950, uses high technology today.

Planning Blind 3: High Technology

Ominously enough, precisely the same mercantilist strategies that are driving American producers out of traditional industries are operating in advanced technology fields as well. For example, the basic building block of advanced computer electronics is semiconductors. They were invented in America, thanks in large measure to the steady subsidy of big defense contracts — that is to say, government-created demand. Since the late 1970s, Japan has adroitly leapfrogged over the last generation of semiconductor technology, and now has over half of the U.S. domestic market in advanced random-access memories.

The Japanese accomplished that feat via the usual methods. They targeted semiconductors as a strategic sector. They kept out direct U.S. investment, while insisting that American producers wishing to sell in the Japanese market share their technology with Japan. Texas Instruments, for example, was permitted to set up a joint venture with Sony, but it had to limit its market share to 10 percent, and license its patents to Sony, Hitachi, Toshiba, NEC, and Mitsubishi. In the early 1960s, MITI organized a consortium of Japanese producers into the Japan Electronic Computer Company, which received low-interest loans from the Japan Development Bank. The two industries were developed in tandem, for computers were the prime market for the infant semiconductor industry.

A similar linchpin industry is machine tools, another old-line business rapidly being transformed into a high-tech field. The future belongs to computerized "numerically controlled" machine tools, which can be reprogrammed to perform a variety of industrial tasks — and another natural target of MITI. In 1976, Japanese suppliers held just 3.7 percent of the American market for numerically controlled machine tools. By 1982, the figure had risen to nearly 60 percent. Numerically controlled ("NC") machine tools were invented in America and also in response to government demand, in this case an air force requirement for extremely precise machining tolerances. But other than the implicit planning of Pentagon contracts, the United States has no industrial policy for machine tools. And unlike the Harley-Davidson case, there is no disposition on the part of the Reagan administration to protect machine tools, even though that industry is far more strategic than heavy motorcycles.

The absence of a clear policy for machine tools was made clear in the recent Houdaille case. Houdaille Industries is a Florida-based maker of computer-controlled machine tools and machining centers. Its market has been heavily invaded by Japanese competitors, benefiting from MITI's targeting strategy. In 1982, Houdaille's President Philip O'Reilly, casting about for redress, stumbled on a little-noticed provision of U.S. trade law. Under an obscure section of the 1971 tax act, the President of the United States has the discretion to disqualify purchasers of a foreign product from taking the 10 percent investment tax credit, if he finds that the foreign product was marketed in violation of trade norms.

O'Reilly and his lawyers set out to document that the Japanese machine-tool industry systematically benefited from subsidies and targeted marketing that would be illegal in the United States. The investigation, conducted by the prominent Washington law firm of Covington and Burling, eventually cost Houdaille a million dollars. It produced one of the most intimate pictures of Japanese industrial strategy yet available in English.

MITI began by ordering marginal producers out of the Japanese machine-tool industry. The remaining big producers then got exemptions from Japanese antitrust laws. The venture got the usual R&D help and the preferential low-interest loans. The Japanese also devised an ingenious subsidy to help domestic manufacturers of consumer products to become *customers* for the new computerized machine tools. Several hundred million dollars in revenues from the popular parimutuel sports of motorcycle and bicycle racing are funneled to municipal research centers for the application of advanced machine-tool technology.

A lawyer for Houdaille, Richard Copaken, actually videotaped

Japanese officials proudly describing the process. On Copaken's tape, the officials recount one typical story: A Tokyo watch manufacturer finds that he could eventually save money producing watch parts with NC machine tools, but that the start-up costs are prohibitive. At no charge to the watch company, the municipal center's engineers design software, test it, refine it, and use it to produce custom, prototype watch parts. The watch company then purchases a state-of-the-art NC machining center, with the custom-designed computer program ready to go. The machining center, needless to say, is made in Japan.

A smiling official explains to Copaken's videotape recorder, "These manufacturers cannot afford to do this work themselves and still make a profit. So our center does this work for them."

"This work," certainly, is a strategic subsidy, and a particularly ingenious one. The Japanese government does not paddle upstream against the market, but uses the engine of public subsidy to forge downstream faster: MITI does not tell makers of NC machining centers what to design, or how to design it. Nor does it force anybody to buy their product. Rather, it accelerates the mass marketing of this important capital good by subsidizing the weakest link in the market for it — the application software.

Lawyer Copaken returned to Washington very pleased with his smoking gun. For a few weeks in 1982, officials all over the Capital were viewing private screenings of Copaken's home movie, and expressing amazement that the Japanese had openly admitted such a subsidy — on tape. But despite the prima facie case that the Japanese government was subsidizing a key high-tech export industry, the Reagan administration decided against giving any relief to Houdaille. The administration had no disposition to devise an industrial plan for the American machine-tool industry, and it had higher priority issues to negotiate with the Japanese.

While the Houdaille case was pending, Japanese Prime Minister Yasuhiro Nakasone visited Washington. High on the American agenda were Agriculture Department desires that the Japanese open their markets to American oranges and beef, and Pentagon wishes that Japan accelerate its rearmament. Machine tools were not a major issue. In their defense against the Houdaille petition, lawyers for the Japanese employed a wonderfully nervy argument. Restriction of the investment tax credit to American machine tools, they warned, would violate the GATT.

The bitter, high-level dispute within the Reagan administration over the Houdaille case was finally resolved after Prime Minister Nakasone personally persuaded President Reagan not to protect Houdaille. By all accounts, Nakasone appealed to both America's diplomatic interests and its oft-repeated defense of the free-market system. That the Japanese machine-tool industry was something other than the creature of free markets was politely overlooked.

MANAGED TRADE

The argument that we should let "the market" ease us out of declining industries is unconvincing, because the very same nonmarket pressures are operating right across the industrial spectrum. It is also arrogant, even a little racist, to assume that mercantilist Asian countries, having learned to apply Western technologies to make mass-production goods at low wages, will be content to leave the most advanced technologies to the United States. And the argument that blames overpaid U.S. labor for our diminishing comparative advantage also collapses when one understands that semiskilled labor in several Asian nations is producing for American markets at wages of less than a dollar an hour. The world's most advanced steel mill, in Nigeria, pays its skilled labor about $200 a month, and it has long waiting lists of job applicants. Who really thinks that we should lower American wages to that level in order to compete? Given American living standards and living costs, the option is unthinkable.

In theory, other nations' willingness to exploit their own work forces to provide American consumers with good, cheap products offers a deal we shouldn't refuse. The fallacy in that logic is to measure the costs and benefits of trade only in terms of each isolated trade transaction — the old Ricardian assumption that the economy as a whole would be at full employment. But as we have seen from the Japanese case, when foreign, state-led competition drives American producers out of industry after industry, the costs to the economy as a whole can easily outweigh the benefits. As Professor Wolfgang

Hager, a consultant to the European Community, has written, "The cheap [imported] shirt is paid for several times: once at the counter, then again in unemployment benefits. Secondary losses include input industries·[such as] machinery, fibers, chemicals for dyeing, and finishing products."

Weaving Stability

As it happens, Hager's metaphor, the textile industry, is a fairly successful example of managed trade, which combines a measure of protection with substantial modernization. Textiles, by the common consent of the industrial nations, have been removed from the GATT regime in favor of an international market-sharing agreement.

U.S. production of raw cotton has long been almost totally protected. Except for a token import quota amounting to less than one percent of mill consumption of raw cotton, all cotton used in American mills is grown domestically. This quota was necessary to complement the domestic farm policy of price supports: if U.S. farmers are to be guaranteed a certain return on their crop, then it logically follows that the domestic price will be above the world price, and domestic cotton farmers will require shelter from open imports. Since raw cotton is the main ingredient in cotton cloth, it also follows that totally free trade in finished cotton goods would undermine the farm policy of supporting raw cotton prices — apparel makers would simply buy cheaper foreign cloth, or consumers would switch to cheaper foreign finished goods. (By extension, one might observe that a wage regime that involves holding U.S. wages above the worldwide "free-market equilibrium wage" will also necessitate some protection from open trade.)

In the mid-1950s, the American textile industry began suffering insurmountable competition from very low-wage Asian imports. The United States first imposed quotas on imports of cotton fibers, through a series of bilateral negotiations. In the early 1960s, a multilateral "long-term agreement" on cotton fibers was negotiated with other major textile producers. In 1973, broadened to cover woolens and synthetics, it became known as the Multi-Fiber Arrangement. This regime effectively shelters the textile industries of Europe and the United States from runaway import penetration. Under MFA, import growth was limited to an average of 6 percent per year. Exports from one country may grow faster, but only at the expense of other exporting countries.

The consequences of this, in theory, should have been stagnation. But the result has been just the opposite. The predictability afforded by import limitation, and a climate of cooperation with the two major labor unions, encouraged the American textile industry to invest heavily in development of advanced technology. Interestingly, modernization was also stimulated by another nemesis of market economics: health and safety regulation. The cotton dust standard of the Occupational Safety and Health Administration (OSHA) devised to protect workers from byssinosis (white lung disease) served to accelerate rapid investment in cleaner, more efficient weaving and spinning machinery.

During the 1960s and 1970s, the average annual productivity growth in textiles was about twice the U.S. industrial average, second only to electronics. According to a study done for the Common Market, productivity in the most efficient American weaving operations is 130,000 stitches per worker per hour — twice as high as in France, and three times the productivity level in Britain. Thanks to this high level of productivity, textiles, surprisingly enough, have remained an export winner for the United States. In most recent years, net exports have exceeded imports.

Again, in theory, the American consumer pays the bill when the domestic market is sheltered from open foreign competition. It is possible to perform some algebraic manipulations in the spirit of Ricardo and show that textile prices would have been lower in the absence of protection. One such computation places the "cost" of each protected textile job at several hundred thousand dollars.

But these static calculations are useless as policy guides; for they leave out the several benefits: the spur to innovation, and the long-term value of maintaining a textile industry in the United States. Beyond the jobs, the benefits also include the contribution to GNP, to the balance of payments, and to the farmers who grow cotton, as well as the plain fact that investing in this generation's technology is the ticket of admission to the next.

In fact, textile "protectionism" led neither to stagnation nor to spiraling prices. Thanks to steady gains in productivity, textile prices have risen at only about half the average rate of the producer price index, both before and after the introduction of the Multi-Fiber Arrangement. Protection did not produce high-priced stagnation, in part because the domestic industry is highly competitive. The top five manufacturers have less than 20 percent of the market. The industry still operates under a 1968 Federal Trade Commission consent order (regulation animating markets again!) prohibiting any company with sales of more than $100 million from acquiring one with sales exceeding $10 million.

If an industry competes vigorously in domestic markets, it can innovate and keep prices low, despite shelter from low-wage foreign competition. In fact, the shelter is sometimes conducive to modernization. Students of modern managed capitalism should hardly be surprised that market stability and new investment go hand in hand.

New Rules of the Road

We are already well down the road toward a managed-trade regime. It would be far better to acknowledge that reality, and seek a set of reasonable rules, than to pretend that Ricardian trade is the norm and allow mercantilist states to overwhelm U.S. industry and ratchet down wages, in the name of free trade. Managed trade, on the model of the Multi-Fiber Arrangement, offers an alternative regime, one that is more consistent with economic planning and distributive equity. Most economists, however, are loath to weigh the practical costs and benefits of a managed trade regime, for they already "know" that the best possible trade regime is the Ricardian one.

Nonetheless, we can glean the outline of such a regime, for many of its elements already exist. Under managed trade, imports do not cease, but their market share and growth rate are explicitly limited and politically bargained. The United States, notwithstanding its protestations of free trade, has negotiated such limitations in steel, autos, textiles, televisions, and of course agriculture. The EEC has done the same for those products plus a wide range of consumer goods.

The contrast between steel and textile cases suggests that economic models do not predict the relationship between protection and the dynamism of the protected industry. Industrial policy — planning— is a necessary concomitant to assure that protection doesn't become just an umbrella under which oligopolies can stagnate, as the steel industry did. Some protection may be necessary to incubate a restructuring, but it surely is not sufficient.

Besides import limitations linked to industrial restructuring, a managed-trade regime includes shared-production deals, often called domestic-content agreements. Content agreements for autos are widespread throughout the developed and developing world. All told, twenty-eight nations impose some form of content requirement on automakers. Since the 1950s, Australia has required automakers wishing to sell in the Australian market to locate plants there. Brazil and Mexico used stringent content requirements to produce jobs and compel automakers to transfer technology. Under the Mexican approach, auto manufacturers must produce in Mexico at least 70 percent of the value of cars sold to Mexican buyers. Alternatively, they may produce other auto components in Mexico for export and receive credit for their value. American automakers have chosen to locate a substantial portion of their worldwide engine production in Mexico, in order to fulfill Mexican content requirements.

The Japanese have negotiated numerous content requirements in the form of coproduction agreements. In the recent sale of 100 F-15 fighters to the Japanese military, the Japanese government negotiated the following deal: Only 14 of the planes will be made entirely in the United States; 8 will be delivered in kit form, to be assembled in Japan; 78 will be produced in Japan, under license from McDonnell-Douglas. According to one estimate, this deal is costing the Japanese $1.8 billion more than the price of buying the planes straight off the American production line, but the Japanese have calculated that the additional high-technology jobs and the gain to its infant aircraft industry are well worth it. The Japanese have exacted similar content requirements for sales of commercial aircraft. There is also a NATO coproduction agreement, which gives each NATO buyer of the F-16 domestic production of 40 percent of its value.

In theory, content agreements are an affront to the logic of the market. Yet they are certainly preferable to tariffs, quotas, and the other forms of defensive protectionism that are so popular in Ricardian America. Japan currently operates under a U.S. import quota of 1.86 million cars a year (in order to comply with the letter of GATT rules, this quota is technically voluntary). It effectively makes Japanese cars scarce goods, as any buyer soon discovers when he has the effrontery to seek a discount on a Japanese import. Unlike an import quota, the content approach would keep the competitive pressure on the entire auto industry, because it would place no quantitative limit on the number of Toyotas and Datsuns Americans may buy. It would only require that a portion of their total value be produced in the United States.

Interestingly, when stiff tariffs were levied against Japanese heavy motorcycles, one Japanese producer was quite unperturbed. The Kawasaki company was immune to the big tariff increases; it produces motorcycles for the American market at its plant in Nebraska. Most likely, content legislation would produce just the sort of retaliation we need. Foreign manufacturers producing for the American market would locate more of their production here. This is precisely what occurred in Europe, after the EEC adopted import limitations to protect its domestic market in consumer electronics. Mitsubishi, Matsushita, Sanyo, and Hitachi all retaliated — by announcing plans to build plants in Europe.

Moreover, content agreements may produce a positive-sum gain by accelerating technology diffusion — another dynamic effect unrecognized by the Ricardian model of trade. If Japanese mercantilism runs true to form, Japan will take the American aircraft technology acquired via its coproduction arrangement — and ingeniously refine it. The world will gain advances in aircraft technology that would not have been possible in the absence of the content requirement.

Yet another element of a managed-trade system is what's sometimes called counter-trade. The buyer of an imported product will require the supplier to market a like share of goods from the customer's country. General Electric, for example, won a contract to supply jet engines for the Swedish air force — but only on condition that GE market Swedish industrial goods. This kind of counter-trade is called an offset agreement. The Swedes, in this case, are not content to cast their bread upon the waters and trust that the fillip to global demand represented by their purchase will eventually cause someone else to buy some Swedish product. They took a more direct step to assure that the deal would produce tangible benefits for Sweden.

A common element in all of these devices is the principle that domestic purchasing power ought to produce domestic employment, and that the details are subject to explicit bargaining. Unlike pure protectionism based on prohibitive tariffs and tight import quotas, managed trade is quite consistent with increased trade. No doubt, this system is rather messier than the ideal of pure free trade. But free trade does not exist except as an ideal. In fairness, managed trade should be weighed against unmanaged, competitive mercantilism, for that is the practical alternative. Managed trade can be fully consistent with more trade.

Proponents of managed trade are often accused of fomenting "beggar-my-neighbor" protectionism. The specter of retaliatory trade barriers is evoked, epitomized by the 1930 Smoot-Hawley tariff. But what we have today is in many respects worse than beggar-my-neighbor protection: It is what the British economist and Labour M. P. Stuart Holland calls beggar-my-neighbor competitive deflation. Each country seeks to depress domestic consumption, trim its wage costs, and revive its economy through exports. But by definition, this is a zero-sum game — one in which one player's gains are another's losses. One country's exports are another's imports. If all the world's nations are depressing their domestic consumption, then global markets must be shrinking. Japan may have kept its unemployment low by achieving a $100-billion trade surplus in manufactured goods, but there is room for only one Japan. Japan's imitators are trying to repeat her success by lowering their labor costs. Industrial countries are trying to duplicate the Third World's comparative advantage in cheap labor by introducing "enterprise zones" and other measures to reduce their own wages. It is a strategy that might be termed, "beggar-my-*self*" protectionism. Reduced wages are nothing but reduced purchasing power — and ultimately reduced well-being.

A more stable system of trade relationships, far from beggaring neighbors, can be in the mutual interest of producing countries generally. Universal excess capacity, after a time, benefits no country. Korea rapidly developed an export industry in color TV tubes. When Korea's rapid penetration of the American domestic market reached intolerable levels, we slammed shut an open door. Overnight, Korean TV production shrank to 20 percent of capacity. Predictable, albeit more gradual, growth in sales would have been preferable for both buyer and seller.

Third-World Development

It is tempting to conclude that *any* restriction on the growth of Third-World exports to consumers in the industrial West unjustly limits

Third-World development. There are two fair responses to that charge: First, a sustained recovery of the advanced countries is very much in the interest of the Third World. Because of slow growth, high unemployment, and depressed purchasing power in the United States and Europe, commodity prices are now at their lowest real level since World War II. Competitive deflation has also led to very high real interest rates, worldwide. The combination of low commodity prices, tight money, and depressed demand is devastating to Third-World economic prospects. Some limitation on low-wage exports to the industrial North, as part of a program for worldwide recovery, is surely more in the interest of the Third World than the present course. If the industrial nations can re-emerge from the cycle of competitive deflation, there will be more markets to consume Third-World goods.

Moreover, it is also reasonable to insist that Third-World countries producing for export to industrial markets begin paying wages more commensurate with those in the industrial world. Once that adjustment is made, more purchasing power will be left in the Third World to consume products made in the Third World; competitive advantage will again reflect genuine advantages of specialization and not just operate as a global competition to lower wages. At present, demand deficiencies in the low-wage Third World are being made up by the purchasing power of the industrialized countries. This cannot continue indefinitely.

In devising strategies to reconcile growth with equity, it is crucial to keep in mind the new reality of world trade: mass-production technologies have grown so productive and so portable that one of the world's major trade areas all by itself could easily meet major consumption demands of the entire world, given the present distribution of purchasing power. If the United States permitted totally free entree to all goods, the Far East could easily supply all our textiles and apparel, all our cars and trucks, and all but the most sophisticated consumer electronics products. Or the United States could happily supply most of the world's cars, televisions, and consumer appliances, as we did in the short happy decade after World War II. Or Europe could supply all the world's steel, its computers, its autos, and clothing. As long as this fundamental overcapacity remains, we can expect that each of the industrial nations of the world will bargain fiercely for its share of domestic production, based roughly on relative shares of purchasing power.

Growth can solve much of this problem, for the material needs of the world are nearly infinite. To a Keynesian, there is no such thing as an excess of productive capacity, there is only a shortage of effective demand. But growth fueled by a competition to lower real wages in the advanced countries will only stifle itself. That path, as Wassily Leontief once observed, leads to a fool's paradise with plenty of products on the shelves and insufficient wages to buy them.

Admittedly, any departure from the ideal of free trade is administratively messy and vulnerable to political abuse. One can look back through industrial history and find illustrations that cut both ways. For decades, the British "Corn Laws" levied increasingly onerous tariffs on importation of grain, solely to protect the landlord class. By the time of the Napoleonic Wars, a bushel of wheat was selling for nearly twice a workman's weekly wage. (In America today, a bushel of wheat costs about 2 percent of the average weekly wage.) Not until the 1830s were the Corn Laws repealed and cheap grain imports permitted into Britain. But in the same nineteenth century, high tariffs were crucial to the development of fledgling American industry. And in our own century, one can point to examples of "protectionism" that enhanced commerce and protectionism that plainly retarded it. Industrial history is filled with efforts by industry to stabilize markets in order to make capital investment rational. The ideal of free trade never existed in practice, except when one nation like nineteenth-century Britain or post–World War II America enforced a "free-trade" regime that was really a system for restricting competition from other potential industrial rivals and promoting trade on terms favorable to the mother country. A worldwide free-trade system along textbook lines would be far too unsettling to be tolerated even if it could be approached.

The View from Brussels

For Western Europe, the stakes of managed trade are higher than for the United States or Japan. Thus far, the Japanese have emerged as the big winners of the present world regime, in which they play by mercantilist rules and the United States still tries to champion free trade. The United States probably comes out second; we have a huge domestic market, we have genuine comparative advantages in many agricultural and mineral products, and although our dominance is eroding, we still have a healthy surplus in capital goods trade. Of the three major industrial producers, Europe is the most vulnerable.

Though it has made major strides toward establishing a true common market, the European Economic Community (EEC) remains ten distinct nations, with separate currencies, frontier restrictions, and legitimate regulations (such as health requirements) that can easily degenerate into cannibalistic protectionism. Western Europe also has a social contract based on strong trade unions, high real wages, and an egalitarian (and expensive) welfare state. Today, American real wage costs are substantially below those of most European countries. If comparative advantage is based on portable technology and cheap labor, Europe loses.

Although Ricardian economists are loath to acknowledge it, the golden age of European economic recovery and regional economic integration was an era of substantial de facto protection. In the 1950s and 1960s, American-made goods did not compete in European markets, because the dollar was heavily overvalued. Japan and the other newly industrialized countries were not yet players. As Michael Noelke and Robert Taylor observed in a study of European protectionism, "Europe's era of rapid growth and full employment combined the advantages of free (regional) trade and the scale economies and specialization this allowed with a near-total de facto protection vis-à-vis the larger world environment."

In the 1950s and 1960s, both Europe and North America could build full-employment, high-wage economies, in splendid isolation. But, as Noelke and Taylor observe,

> The effective entry of non-Atlantic producers across virtually the whole range of manufacturing (and some exportable services like contracting and shipping) has revealed Europe for what it is: a high-cost area of production. . . . The delicate balance between production, investment, consumption, and employment which characterized Europe in its period of de facto protection and hence isolation from international market forces is unlikely to be re-established on a world level, least of all by "natural" forces of adjustment.

By 1970, Europe's period of splendid isolation had eroded, from multiple causes. Not only did Japan and the other new industrial exporters make the same inroads in European markets as they did in the United States, but as the overvalued dollar declined, U.S. products made substantial inroads as well. In addition, the growing vulnerability of European markets to import penetration also had a peculiarly European dimension. As Europe progressively dismantled its internal trade barriers, the Common Market came under growing pressure from the free-trade ideologues, notably the Americans, to lower their external barriers as well.

As external tariffs around the EEC have come down, defensive protection within the EEC has increased; because Europe remains a community made up of sovereign states, it is very easy for the EEC member nations to slip into extralegal, defensive forms of protection directed against each other. Belgium, for example, requires margarine to be marketed in cubes, rather than bars, which neatly excludes German shipments. Germany has an esoteric series of health laws, which keep out French beer. French telephones have specifications that can be met only by French producers. And so on, ad infinitum. "When you have mixed economies, as we do," says Pierre Defraigne, the chief of staff to the EEC directorate in charge of industrial policy, "there are just too many tricks at the government's disposal."

Today, many European integrationists, conservatives, and liberals, as well as social democrats, believe that the premature opening of EEC markets to extra-European imports — before European integration was completed — constituted a very bad bargain. Free trade with non-European nations has undermined liberalization of trade within Europe itself. It is widely argued in Brussels that the only way to get Europe back on a path of internal liberalization is to grant the EEC as a whole a greater degree of "Euro-protection."

According to Defraigne,

> We got caught up in the spirit of the Tokyo Round. Our big mistake was to lower our common external tariff before we had achieved greater political integration. When you do that, you force the weaker member states to resort to other instruments to protect their own economies. They resist further unification of the EEC's internal market. They try to protect against external penetration, but they end up protecting against their EEC partners. For us, Euro-protection is much more efficient than country-by-country protection. We can trade off Communitywide protection for the dismantling of country restrictions.

In the first year of the Mitterrand government, the French were very much enamored of a strategy they liked to call "reconquest of the domestic market." Planners at the Commissariat du Plan pointed to growing import shares of the French domestic market for basic consumer products; they suggested Japanese-style targeting of key industries, combined with some shelter from imports. But there was no way for this strategy to succeed within the framework of the Treaty of Rome. French targeting of a purely French consumer electronics industry infringed on other European producers. Given the free-trade rules of the Common Market, one-country industrial strategies are not feasible, except at the expense of the whole EEC system. Mitterrand quickly amended the strategy: reconquest of the domestic market was elevated to a pan-European strategy. European manufactures can serve European customers in all of the advanced products — but not if their market has been taken over first by Japanese and American multinationals.

In the past, the EEC has had some success in negotiating Communitywide restructurings of particular key industries, such as shipbuilding, textiles, and steel. But even more than in the United States (which is a single country), industrial policies for European industries require relief from imports. A good example is the so-called Davignon plan for restructuring of the steel industry, which resembles a Japanese-style recession cartel. The plan was devised in 1977 by the EEC Commissioner in charge of industrial policy, Etienne Davignon.

Under the plan, a floor price was established for steel, and each member country of the EEC receives an annual production quota. "Self-limitation" agreements have been negotiated with 15 non-EEC steel producers, to restrict imports. Within the EEC, capacity reduction and reinvestment in more modern steelmaking technology were painstakingly negotiated, so that no one country bore disproportionate burdens. Between 1975 and 1980, the EEC steel industry closed 42 steelmaking plants, and laid off 200,000 workers — one fourth of its work force. The Davignon system has not been without strife; it has caused labor hardship; it has repeatedly had to fend off attempts by one member country to protect its national steel industry, because of the political outcry that results when more capacity is shut down. And the EEC still projects 25 percent excess capacity in basic steel by 1985. But obviously, if Japanese steel had been permitted to take up the slack, the whole exercise would have been for nought.

Unlike American policymakers, who are equivocal on the issue of whether domestic steel production is indispensable for the United

States, the Europeans intend to do whatever is necessary to retain their steel industry. "Europe cannot give up steel production," states an official EEC steel policy document unapologetically, "since to do this would be to do away with one of the essential links in the production chain for a whole host of products, creating extra dependence at the cost of half a million jobs."

If America, out of a miscast loyalty to Ricardian trade, opposes Europe's efforts to devise a managed-trade regime, we will be helping to wreck the Common Market, whose success we are so wont to celebrate. It is not surprising that Europeans have trouble understanding American views on trade. Our stance seems contradictory, if not plainly hypocritical. And it is.

Ideology as Utopia

In America today, there is a near-total absence of professional economists and diplomats willing to challenge Ricardian assumptions. To be an economist is to be a free-trader, just as all astronomers were once Ptolomaic. The small fraternity of disinterested dissidents includes a handful of planners, political scientists, and students of comparative economic institutions. There is no research institution, respectable or otherwise, studying managed trade as an alternative paradigm.

Among planning advocates, it is fashionable to assert that industrial policy need not violate Ricardian norms; planning merely accelerates "adjustment" to new industries where we retain a natural comparative advantage. These, presumably, are ultrasophisticated, "flexible production" capital goods, which only white Americans have the sophistication to fabricate. Even more miraculously, despite the boundless productivity of their manufacture, these new sunrise industries will somehow provide enough work for the Americans being displaced from hand-me-down traditional industries now passed along to the Third World. There is also a conservative school of planning, which holds that the United States should become as fiercely mercantilist as the Japanese. According to this view, we should target domestic industries — but also jettison trade unions, high wages, and expensive social programs, so that American producers can compete openly on the basis of price.

The hegemony of the free-trade ideal is both professional and generational. Anyone socialized as an economist or a trade official during the American imperium saw its very success as the practical vindication of Ricardian theory. Diplomatically, free trade defined as access to the big U.S. market came to be a very handy carrot. Colonial access to the market of the mother country has long been an attraction of imperial trading systems, whether the British, the Roman, the greater Japanese co-prosperity sphere, or the American. After World War II, access to the U.S. market was a key benefit of joining Our Gang. America no longer makes the world's economic rules, but we find it very hard to break old habits. The U.S. market is still viewed as a bottomless reservoir, access to which can be traded for other diplomatic objectives.

There are also very powerful interest groups in America that reinforce the free-trade ideal. They include banks, which finance trade, and multinational corporations, which dislike any restrictions on their freedom to locate. Both, nonetheless, have figured out how to coexist with all manner of content, counter-trade, and offset requirements. But they continue to be ideological mainstays of the free-trade regime. There is also a huge "Japan lobby," made up of very well paid, former high trade officials. Nearly every former U.S. special trade representative or deputy representative is now a lawyer or trade consultant with Japanese clients. In effect, these ex-officials are paid to invoke Ricardian ideals in defense of open access for mercantilist Japan. Nobody seems to mind the contradiction.

Free trade is not an absolute value, like free speech. It is a means, not an end. The end is economic well-being, broadly distributed. It will take a long time, I suspect, before the ideal is revised in line with our real interests as a society. After World War II, Western Europe and North America evolved a social contract unique in the history of industrial capitalism. Unionism was encouraged; workers got a fair share in the fruits of production and a measure of job security. It enabled the West to defy Karl Marx's prediction that under capitalism workers had to become progressively worse off.

The world of free trade today looks rather more Marxian. Global capital has intimate access to a worldwide reserve army of underemployed and unorganized workers. Overcapacity and underconsumption are again serious problems. We are advised that in order to defend our standard of living, we must first lower it; that, to remain competitive, the West must jettison the very social baggage that assured us a comfortable passage. That conclusion, surely, defies common sense. From the viewpoint of the Ricardian entrepreneur, wages are an unfortunate cost of production. From the perspective of society, they are the stuff of stability. From the perspective of macroeconomics, they are the stuff of purchasing power.

The transformation of a primitive production machine into something approximating social citizenship is an immense achievement, not to be sacrificed lightly on the altar of an abstraction. Given a choice between idealized free trade and high, broadly distributed living standards, free trade is the more expendable.

If we are to enjoy continuous near-full employment, without changing the institutions and habits of industrial bargaining, we shall suffer from inflation. It is neither the fault of the trade unions, fulfilling their proper function of demanding a fair share in rising profits, nor of businessmen trying to preserve profits by raising prices when costs go up. It is the fault of an economic system inappropriate to the development of the economy. This seems to be dawning at last on official opinion.

— Joan Robinson

4

LABOR

KEYNES OBSERVED, in the famous last sentence of his *General Theory,* "But soon or late, it is ideas, not vested interests, which are dangerous for good or evil." Ideas matter. As Keynes's colleague Joan Robinson suggests, institutions also matter. The kind of industrial-relations culture in a given nation makes an enormous difference in that nation's ability to broker positive-sum gains in productivity, employment, growth, and distribution. In this chapter, I will suggest that societies with strong unions and highly refined social bargaining machinery do a much better job of maintaining full employment, promoting distributive justice, reconciling technological progress with social needs, and moderating inflation. This conclusion flies in the face of classical economic theory and much conventional wisdom about the role of unions.

Economists habitually ignore institutions. Their professional training instructs them to pierce the institutional veil and look beyond institutions to rational, "optimizing" individuals. Social institutions are messy; they resist rigorous quantitative modeling. Most economists leave the study of institutions to lesser disciplines, like sociology. However, when individuals come together to form certain institutions such as trade unions, economists suddenly take notice. Institutions matter after all, and their effect is presumed to be negative. Despite their obvious interest in full employment, unions are said to be the enemy of full employment. According to classical economics, this occurs because unions conspire to push wage levels beyond the point where industry can afford to employ everybody who seeks a job.

When unemployment rates were high and profits low during the Great Depression, orthodox economists therefore counseled wage reduction. Once wages fell to their natural "market-clearing" level, profit margins would be restored, industry would resume hiring workers, and the economy would return to equilibrium. Trade unions were wickedly keeping the market from enforcing necessary wage cuts; unions thus were pricing workers out of jobs and keeping unemployment high. It fell to Keynes to point out that wage reduction in a climate of slack demand only deepens depression. In fact, the Western nations climbed out of depression not by depressing wages, but by stimulating demand. In Germany, the Nazi regime accomplished this via public works and rearmament. In Britain, a devaluation and controls on imports began a recovery by the mid-1930s. In Sweden, the government engineered a recovery through domestic public works, budget deficits, and exports to Germany. In the United States, the Depression persisted until World War II revived purchase orders. In all cases, the share of profits rose with recovery — not because wages dropped, but because output increased.

Today, profits are again being squeezed and real wages have outrun productivity gains. And there are two new elements. Unlike in the 1930s, when prices were falling, we now have inflation as well as slow growth; and unions are held responsible for driving inflation, too. In addition, the rising specter of worldwide competition is said to make wage discipline all the more urgent. In this context, unions are blamed for pricing the United States (or Britain, or Germany — fill in the name) out of world markets. According to conventional economics, there is a common remedy for unemployment, inflation, profit squeeze, and sagging productivity: lower wages. Yet a competitive race to reduce wages must add up to a worldwide drop in purchasing power. It is as if the Keynesian revolution and the lessons of the Great Depression never happened.

EQUALITY, EFFICIENCY, AND UNIONS

Trade unionism is another of those subjects, like trade, where laissez-faire economists have little disagreement with the mainstream bastard Keynesian school. To be an economist in America is to dislike unions. Here is Milton Friedman on the subject of trade unionism:

> If unions raise wage rates in a particular occupation or industry, they necessarily make the amount of employment available in that occupation or industry less than it otherwise would be — just as any higher price cuts down the amount purchased. The effect is an increased number of persons seeking other jobs, which forces down wages in other occupations. Since unions have generally been strongest among groups that would have been high-paid anyway, their effect has been to make high-paid workers higher paid at the expense of lower-paid workers. Unions have therefore not only harmed the public at large and workers as a whole by distorting the use of labor; they have also made the incomes of the working class more unequal by reducing the opportunities available to the most disadvantaged workers.

In fact, unions have not been strongest among groups who would have been high paid anyway, but most American economists would agree with Friedman's other conclusions. In free-market economics, trade unionism is an almost unmitigated evil. Unions use their power to raise the wages of their members beyond what their work is "worth" to the free market. By definition, this is said to distort the allocation of resources. In an economy like ours, where the unionized sector of the work force is relatively small, organized workers further stand accused of taking their wage gains at the expense of the unorganized, who are often poorer to begin with. Higher wages for the unionized, it is assumed, mean lower wages for everyone else.

By raising labor costs, union wages supposedly increase unemployment, for industry can afford to hire fewer workers. By demanding uniform rates for wages and using seniority as the standard for promotion or layoff, unions break the link between merit and reward. Moreover, in their effort to protect wage gains and worker influence, unions often rely on defensive strategies that include protectionism, restrictive work rules, and opposition to labor-saving technology. In their defense of excessive wages, unions also become coconspirators in oligopoly. By pressing for wage increases that outrun true increases in productive output, labor unions make domestic industry uncompetitive and squeeze profits that are needed to be invested in productive capital. By leaving industry no choice but to pass along increased labor costs as increased prices, unions are also prime contributors to inflation.

Thus runs the economist's bill of particulars against trade unionism. The misguided drive for equality via higher wages incurs dreadful efficiency costs. If workers understood their long-term self-interest, they would throw out the union and defer to the superior wisdom of the Market (in this case played by management). It is a familiar tale: again, the egalitarian impulse harms economic efficiency.

The trouble with this view is that it generalizes (and caricatures) one particular model of trade unionism. It is a model sadly familiar to American and British readers. The UAW looks like a bunch of ingrates when Detroit is losing markets and it tries to increase wages that are already nearly double the average industrial wage. PATCO (Professional Air Traffic Controllers Organization) looks plain silly and hands union-busters an easy victory when it tries to depict a $35,000-a-year proletariat. With the deregulation of interstate commerce and new competition from nonunion companies, Greyhound drivers and TWA pilots lose their bargaining power to exist as high-wage islands. When unions represent only a fraction of wage earners, they contribute to economic dualism — an economy in which some workers cling to high-wage jobs while others fall into an abyss of minimum-wage service jobs, or no jobs. Unions cease to be the representative of the underprivileged, or of social justice generally. They become just another special-interest group resisting constructive change and contributing to a zero-sum stalemate.

But there are many versions of trade unionism. Contrary to the conventional view, unionism sometimes can lead to a more efficient and productive work place. A number of studies have shown that unionism can improve productivity in several respects. By giving workers a formalized voice and removing some of the arbitrariness of working life, unions contribute to employee morale. The union influence compels management to learn from what workers know about their jobs — *if* unionism takes the trouble to focus on work organization and work quality rather than just wages and fringe benefits. Statistically, unionized workers are often more highly motivated and more self-directed than nonunion workers in the same trade, which saves management money by removing the need for layers of supervisors. Studies of the construction industry have shown that the higher productivity of union workers more than makes up for their higher wage costs. Moreover, the premium wage and the job security associated with unionism promotes a more stable work force. Workers enjoying a slight wage premium don't quit so often; this creates a more experienced and more competent work force and reduces management's retraining costs. In short, when unions are not beleaguered and defensive, organized industrial relations can introduce greater industrial harmony — which improves efficiency — as well as more industrial democracy — which enhances equity.

This positive function of unionism, of course, becomes more difficult when unions are fighting for their very lives. The more fragmented, isolated, and defensive unions are, the less they can show their constructive side. In contrast, broad union representation also makes possible social bargaining more explicit and systematic, and thereby improves its outcomes. The strategy of trade unions in Northern Europe demonstrates how full employment coupled with wage moderation and pressures for egalitarianism can improve efficiency and equality at the same time. To execute constructive social bargains, however, labor first needs a degree of institutional power and cohesion far greater than it currently enjoys in America. Paradoxically, positive-sum social bargaining first requires strong, cohesive unions. A splintered labor movement is the worst of all worlds. Professor Friedman should either support banning unions, or he should encourage more workers to join.

Unions and Full Employment

As I suggested early in this book, full employment is the centerpiece of positive-sum equity/efficiency bargains. A high-employment economy promotes high real wages and rapid productivity growth. In a high-wage economy, human workers are too expensive to waste on trivial tasks, so industry is encouraged to substitute capital for labor. Under a laissez-faire regime, that substitution process leads to episodes of high unemployment as too few jobs are created at decent wages to take up the human slack, and total purchasing power falls. But a social commitment to full employment assures that as capital replaces labor in one sector, workers can be shifted to other useful tasks.

A full-employment economy thus enhances labor's flexibility by separating *employment* security from the security of holding a particular job. It makes workers less insecure about new technologies and unions less fearful of productivity gains. Almost by definition, a full-employment economy must be more efficient than a high-unemployment economy, for an idle worker contributes nothing to GNP but goes right on consuming goods, services, and tax dollars.

The obstacles to a full-employment society are both political and technical. Politically, business groups are at best ambivalent about full employment. Admittedly, full employment is associated with high growth, which is good for business. But it is also associated with tight labor markets, increased labor bargaining power, higher wage costs, and the reinforcement of the institutional power of trade unions. A whiff of unemployment does wonders for "wage discipline." Moreover, the means to maintain real full employment require a degree of state influence over the private economy that makes most owners of capital uncomfortable, especially in laissez-faire America.

Despite an apparent interest in stability and in high rates of growth, business on balance usually opts for policies that tolerate some joblessness. After World War II, businessmen backed away from their flirtation with full employment as soon as market forces produced a tolerable consumer boom. Thus in America and Britain, where business is largely unreceptive toward a full employment bargain and labor is relatively weak, organized labor has never quite been able to negotiate such a social bargain. Instead, it settles for a second best — vigorously representing the material interests of those workers who belong to unions.

The *technical* obstacle to a stable, high-employment economy is that the realization of full employment through demand management is inflationary, other things being equal. When tight labor markets lead to wage increases that outrun productivity gains, business passes its costs along through price increases. In an open economy subject to foreign competition, unjustified price hikes mean the loss of markets. If business chooses to absorb the higher costs, then there is a squeeze on profits, and eventually a reduction in productive investment. Thus, when full employment produces excessive wage costs, it can indeed produce inflation and harm economic growth.

But other things are seldom equal. Surprisingly enough, strong trade unions can be the key social instrument through which positive-sum bargains can be negotiated. Contrary to Professor Friedman, unions can serve to minimize inflation in a full-employment society. Unions can accomplish this by choosing to subordinate short-run wage demands to other labor goals: full employment, egalitarian wage distributions, retraining opportunities, welfare objectives, workplace enrichment, and greater labor influence over industry. A second paradox is that this bargaining outcome seems to depend on a powerful, cohesive labor movement. It is not possible to broker where unions are weak and fragmented.

POSITIVE-SUM UNIONISM

When unions represent a substantial majority of wage earners, industrial relations are necessarily transformed. It is no longer possible for union members to make gains at the expense of nonunion workers, for most people belong to unions. Nor is it so simple to increase labor's total share of national income at the expense of income that goes to capital, for even socialists recognize the need for capital investment. When trade unionists have substantial influence over public policy, their definition of self-interest broadens. They become a key constituency for positive-sum gains. In countries with very strong union movements, politics are also transformed; for the labor movement provides a well-mobilized constituency for social democratic or labor parties. Trade unionists get a chance to govern; practical approaches that reconcile equity with efficiency can be tested, proven successful, or refined. There is at least the possibility of close collaboration between organized wage earners and the State.

For the sake of simplicity, we can divide Western trade unionism into three broad types: Northern European, Southern European, and Anglo-Saxon. In Britain and her one-time colonies, unionism tends to be fragmented, often militant, but ideologically inchoate or divided. British and American unions in particular are very decentralized administratively; the nationwide federations, the American AFL-CIO and the British Trades Union Congress (TUC), have little influence over their constituent unions. This is not simply the fault of

America's size or its federal system, for Britain's unions are far more of a patchwork mess than ours.

Despite national legislation permitting a union-shop or closed-shop arrangement in which workers in a unionized bargaining unit must join the union, British and American unions represent only a minority of workers. Bargaining tends to be very pragmatic and limited to narrow work-place issues.

Southern European unionism (Italian and French) tends to be highly ideological, yet relatively weak. Collective bargaining is not well institutionalized, and cooperation between the labor movement and the state is poor. In Italy and France, the strongest unions are affiliated with the Communist Party. Neither Italy nor France permits a closed shop, so that union members and nonunion members often work side by side on the shop floor. In France the tradition of well-ritualized collective bargaining is recent and poorly established. Strikes tend to be sporadic and intense. Moreover, there is little opportunity for labor to use the machinery of the state, for unions in France and Italy are usually at odds with the elected government. With the exception of two brief interludes, the Right held power in France between 1947 and 1981. Similarly in Italy, which has been dominated by conservative Christian Democratic governments since World War II, there was no effective policy collaboration at the national level between the radical labor movement and the conservative state. Most of the welfare-state gains in Italy and France came via state subsidy and income-transfer programs rather than labor-market innovations.

For our purposes, Northern European unionism presents the most interesting model. The countries include Germany, Austria, Holland, Belgium, Norway, Sweden, and Denmark. There are of course notable differences, but in general they have these elements in common:

• A union movement with a more or less social democratic outlook closely allied to a Labor or Social Democratic party.

• A small number of national unions, with a high degree of centralization and a very inclusive membership.

• A union strategy that emphasizes classwide gains, especially increasing wages of the lowest-paid workers and assuring full employment.

• A willingness to subordinate short-run wage gains to longer-term political and class objectives; and a very strong commitment to egalitarianism as an end in itself.

These labor movements exist in political cultures that are often called corporatist. The term refers not to the influence of corporations but to a form of social bargaining in which large interest groups are very well organized, represented by fairly centralized associations, and accorded quasi-official status. Thus, most of Northern Europe has highly developed labor federations, employers' federations, farmers' associations, religious bodies, and other groups broadly accepted as representatives of their members' interests, with a mandate and a capacity to bargain effectively with each other at the national level.

Organized Labor and Corporatism ·

Corporatism has many faces. In the 1930s, Fascist Italy offered a model of totalitarian corporatism. Roosevelt's brief experiment with tripartite industry committees through the NRA (National Recovery Administration) attempted to introduce democratic corporatist institutions to the United States. Japan now offers a more or less corporatist model but with weak labor representation. In the democratic corporatism typical of Northern Europe, unions play a decisive role.

Democratic corporatism operates not as a substitute for parliamentary democracy but as a complement to it. By almost any standard, the nations of Northern Europe are among the world's most democratic. Voting participation is high; the press is free; the political culture is vigorous and by American standards uncorrupted; democratic participation has been expanded to economic institutions to a greater extent than in other political democracies; civil liberties are unparalleled. The centralized nature of interest-group representation does not seem to take a toll on political liberty. Although a high degree of centralism facilitates bargaining, the nations of Northern Europe are fairly skilled at leaving the details of bargains to local affiliates; their unions are highly democratic internally. So the undemocratic aspects of centralized bargaining are substantially leavened by accountability and participation.

In general, this social model seems to work best in countries that are relatively small, with parliamentary and unitary systems of government. A small, unitary nation is more likely to engage in successful social bargaining for a variety of reasons; most obviously, a small nation is more manageable; decision makers tend to know each other.

And in a unitary and parliamentary system of government, bargains can be negotiated and carried out with a minimum of extraneous politicking. More subtly, a small nation is liable to be more vulnerable to the international economic system and doesn't have the luxury of domestic fractiousness. The vulnerability of Switzerland, though a nation that is highly federated both ethnically and constitutionally, helps explain why that nation has many of the characteristics of corporatist social bargaining. But the correlation between small size and corporatist characteristics is far from perfect. History and politics also play a key role. Norway and Sweden have maintained successful social bargaining. But in Denmark, with just 5 million inhabitants, a compact geography, a uniform culture, and a unitary government, corporatist bargaining has broken down almost totally. West Germany, with 62 million people and a federalist constitution, is fairly successful at corporatist-style bargaining. So is Japan, with a population of 119 million.*

In recent years, a number of academic studies have quantified the relative success of different economies in the years before and after 1973. All have concluded that the "labor-corporatist" or "neocorporatist" nations have been among the most successful at reconciling high rates of employment, productivity growth, and social equality with low rates of inflation. This is all the more surprising from the laissez-faire view, since these are the very nations with big public sectors and strong unions. The success of democratic corporatist economies provides a key illustration of equality and efficiency working in tandem and of the importance of social institutions in bringing that result about. It refutes the presumption that the gains of "organized labor" must be losses for the larger society. These positive-sum gains reflect the value of strong and responsible unions as brokering and representational institutions, which look beyond the short-term self-interest of their members. In a society where organized and responsible labor unions are powerful, "efficiency" comes to be defined as something social and collective as well as individual and economic.

---

*Japan's political structure differs from Northern European corporatism in many respects — Japan's unions are weaker; its private welfare state (which ties benefits to employment) is far more important. But the Japanese experience does suggest that corporatist social bargaining can function in a fairly large country.

Social Efficiency

In 1976, the sociologist Harold Wilensky predicted that the corporatist democracies would be relatively more successful than laissez-
faire democracies at coping with the worldwide slump of the seventies, both economically and politically. Looking at the widespread
phenomenon of voter backlash against high taxes in the face of slower
growth, Wilensky noticed that high overall tax levels did not correlate
very well with where backlashes occurred. Tax revolt broke out in
Denmark, but not in Sweden; in low-tax America but not in high-
tax West Germany. Again, democratic corporatism seemed to make
the difference: Fairly centralized institutions of government coupled
with well-organized interest groups, especially unions, facilitated
more effective social bargaining, with positive results for equality,
efficiency, political responsiveness, and voter satisfaction. Several statistical studies conducted in the early 1980s confirm this
insight.

The Yale political scientist David Cameron (in 1982) tabulated
a variety of indicators of economic performance, and on almost every
count, the labor-corporatist nations enjoyed a superior performance.
Between 1965 and 1981 for example, the average industrial nation
experienced an increase in unemployment rates of fully 3 percent of
the labor force, but the rise was below one percent in Sweden, Austria,
and Norway (also in Switzerland and Japan). Germany, Austria,
Belgium, Holland, Switzerland, and Japan had the most modest increase in inflation rates. Taking unemployment and inflation together
and comparing them across countries, Cameron found that contrary
to the Phillips curve hypothesis (which associates full employment
with inflation), *low* inflation and *low* unemployment often went together. But this achievement required a corporatist political culture.

Statistically, Cameron found, "Full employment is not associated
with price acceleration, but instead with price moderation..." A
follow-up study by Jeffrey Sachs, a Harvard economist, agreed that
the corporatist countries indeed accomplished superior inflation-employment outcomes.

Following this general approach, it is possible to rank nations
according to the famous "misery index" (the unemployment rate
plus the rate of inflation). The seven nations with misery rates of
below 9 percent include five that can be considered "labor-corpo-

ratist" — Austria, West Germany, Sweden, Norway, and Holland. Of the other two, Switzerland is something of a special case, and Japan has substantial elements of corporatist social bargaining. The worst mix of high inflation and high unemployment is found in Britain and the United States. There, high unemployment did not succeed in bringing down inflation until it reached levels above 10 percent; while in Northern Europe, near-full employment was maintained and never led to unacceptably high inflation.

The several studies also reported that corporatist countries enjoyed more labor peace, despite strong unions. Sweden, Holland, Austria, Norway, and Germany had the fewest working days lost to strikes, although they rank near the top in terms of union membership and influence. Finally, an influential labor or social democratic party seems to be a key ingredient in a successful corporatist bargain. Cameron ranked countries according to the percentage of cabinet portfolios held by democratic left parties between 1965 and 1981. And again, the countries with the best employment/inflation tradeoffs correlated closely with governing social democratic parties. The ability to participate in government gave labor unions an alternative to inflationary wage demands. A subsequent study, by political scientists Peter Lange and Geoffrey Garrett, concluded that both a cohesive labor movement and a strong, effective social democratic party were necessary to make the corporatist model perform well. The absence of either a cohesive union movement or an effective left party only magnifies social strife.

For example, in Britain and Denmark, left parties sometimes govern but have failed to bring about political consensus or constructive social bargaining; economic performance is well below average. This is not surprising, for both nations have political cultures in which the labor movement is fragmented and organized along craft lines, and the left party (though it often holds office) is almost equally fragmented. In Britain's one major experiment with an explicit "social contract," the Callaghan Labour Government of 1975–78, Labour's margin in the House of Commons was so thin that the rival Liberal Party held an effective veto. In Britain, a badly splintered Labour Party now competes with two other left parties. In Denmark, the Social Democratic Party is the largest single party, but it has always had to govern in coalition with antisocialist parties. The trade-union federation and the Danish Social Democratic Party have never been sufficiently strong to broker a Swedish- or German-style social contract based on wage restraint and full employment. Instead, liberal Denmark has suffered high unemployment and paid very costly compensatory benefits through its welfare sector.

In sum, the labor-corporatism model seems to offer a social bargain in which a well-organized and powerful labor movement exchanges overt class conflict and militant bargaining over wages for a high-employment society with a generous social wage, a state policy commitment to greater equality, and substantial institutionalized influence for organized workers. Thus, democratic corporatism creates social institutions that facilitate positive-sum gains. For an egalitarian, the particular value of corporatism with strong *labor* influence is that the positive-sum outcomes enhance social justice. Labor's willingness to trade its substantial influence for broader egalitarian goals such as work-place democracy or generous retraining and retirement benefits leads to other gains that are good social policy in their own right.

Democratic corporatism with substantial labor influence provides an important counterpoint to the idea that a society dominated by interest groups must lead to a stalemate. In his recent influential book *The Rise and Decline of Nations*, Mancur Olson observed that collective action by organized interest groups usually comes at the expense of the well-being of the larger whole, because a society of hyperactive interest groups adds up to a stand-off. But the exception to this rule was what Olson called an "encompassing" organization — one so large that it must worry about the health of the larger collectivity. Olson wrote, "The members of the highly encompassing organizations own so much of the society that they have an important incentive to be actively concerned about how productive it is." That is not a bad description of Northern Europe's trade unions.

SOCIAL BARGAINS

Sweden, Austria, Norway, and West Germany offer instructive variations on the theme of labor-corporatism. I shall dwell on Sweden in greatest detail, because in Sweden the model is most refined and ideologically explicit.

The Swedish Model

Sweden undoubtedly provides the purest illustration of successful labor-corporatism. Sweden has by far the highest union membership and the most dominant Social Democratic Party in the West. In Sweden, about 90 percent of blue-collar and 70 percent of white-collar workers belong to unions. The two major union federations, the industrial LO and the white-collar TCO, account for the vast bulk of union membership. The ties between the labor movement and the Social Democratic Party are long-standing and intimate. Most of the groups that came together in 1889 to found the Social Democratic Party were unions. Since 1906 Sweden has also had a fairly centralized national employers' confederation, the SAF, which was itself organized in response to the rise of unionism.

In the early part of this century, Sweden experienced a very high degree of social discord. Industrial disputes were frequent and acrimonious. The labor movement was powerful, but it had not yet been accorded a constructive role in the economic and political system. In 1909 a bitter general strike was crushed. Labor's electoral influence, however, expanded very rapidly. By 1917, the Social Democrats were already the largest parliamentary party, and in 1932 they received enough votes to form a majority government in coalition with the Farmers' Party.

During the 1930s, Sweden's social discord gave way to a new social contract. Politically, the coalition of industrial workers and fairly conservative farmers served to tone down the more extreme socialist impulses. In the coalition bargain of 1932, the socialists agreed to subsidize agriculture, and the farmers agreed to support a major expansion of the welfare state.

There was no socialization of industry. Instead, the government opted for a strong Keynesian strategy of demand stimulation, which spared Sweden much of the impact of world depression. By 1936, Swedish unemployment had already dropped to pre-Depression levels. With the Social Democratic Party heading the government, organized labor's constructive influence grew. Industry was forced to become more accommodating to the trade unions.

In 1938, the LO and the SAF met at the seaside town of Saltsjö-baden near Stockholm and concluded an industrial concordat. Under the Saltsjöbaden agreement, which is a key event of modern Swedish history, both parties recognized each other as equals. They established a framework for collective bargaining, increased labor's influence within enterprises, prohibited strikes during the life of contracts, and centralized control over most wage negotiation. Saltsjöbaden ushered in forty years of industrial peace. Soon, Swedish strikes and lockout rates were among the world's lowest. Saltsjöbaden was doubly impressive because it was not imposed on the labor market by the state. Swedish labor and management have continued to prefer to make their bargains without state interference.

Sweden, as a noncombatant, suffered no industrial damage during World War II; instead, the Swedes substantially expanded their export markets and came out of the war years enjoying a booming economy. The Social Democratic Party consolidated its strength. It no longer needed the Farmers' Party as a coalition partner, and its program became more venturesome.

By the late 1940s, the conventional Keynesian approach of macroeconomic demand stimulation was producing unacceptable inflation. After a brief and unpopular episode of wage controls, the LO devised an ingenious alternative. In 1951, two LO economists, Gösta Rehn and Rudolf Meidner, were grappling with the problem of how to maintain full employment without inflation, while at the same time promoting social objectives. In the 1950s, most other Western nations were shifting away from a Keynesian welfare strategy and relying more on market economics. Conservative governments were in power in every large Western nation. In Sweden, however, the Rehn-Meidner model pressed the Keynesian strategy outward. The economists devised a twin strategy, which combined an "active labor-market policy" with a "solidarity-wage policy."

The active labor-market policy would be a microeconomic substitute for excessive demand stimulation. Instead of expanding aggregate demand to the point where the whole economy overheated, the government would intervene selectively to soak up unemployment. This approach eventually evolved into a remarkable system of labor-market boards. A national board, the AMS, is mandated to coordinate job training, relocation, placement, and job creation. Local tripartite boards, made up of representatives of business, labor, and local government, can design local programs to spend AMS funds.

The fact that Sweden uses a labor-market mechanism — rather than capital subsidies — to plan economic transitions had led some observers to conclude that Sweden doesn't go in very much for economic planning. But in reality, the labor-board system is indeed a planning mechanism and a very efficient one, at that.

When the world economy is in recession, labor-market board measures can take up the slack and keep Sweden close to full employment. During the 1970s, the board used temporary public service jobs, stockpiling of goods, early retirement, investment subsidies, and retraining sabbaticals. Allan Larsson, the director of the national AMS, described one typical case. In the town of Arvika, the principal employer is Thermia-Verken, a maker of hot-water heaters and furnaces. In a recent construction slump, products were piling up, and management began considering a layoff. Instead, the AMS approved the company for temporary training-grant aid; the union local working with the local AMS board and the company devised a training sabbatical program. Instead of suffering a layoff, 76 workers got a paid training sabbatical to improve their skills.

When local unemployment is more severe, the board can pay relocation expenses, or use wage subsidies to help attract new industry. In the early 1980s while unemployment in the West increased to the 10–11 percent range, Sweden's labor-market system kept total unemployment below 3 percent most of the time. Unemployment briefly peaked at 4.4 percent — a rate that most countries would consider full employment. The labor-market boards spend as much as 3 percent of Sweden's GNP, and most Swedes consider the outlay well worth it. (By contrast, in the United States retraining and job-creation measures together account for about one quarter of one percent of GNP.) The system keeps Sweden near full employment with all the secondary benefits that brings, without triggering unacceptable levels of inflation.

Not only is the active labor-market beneficial during periods of economic slump. It also acts as an anti-inflation tool during periods of boom. Booms produce labor shortages. In a laissez-faire system, full employment is inflationary because it creates labor bottlenecks. Skilled workers in short supply are able to demand excessive wage increases. The active labor-market policy, however, allows Swedish planners to anticipate bottlenecks and train workers for skills where shortages are forecast. Thus, when labor shortages arise, the result is new job opportunities and wage restraint rather than windfall wage gains for existing workers. That outcome would be impossible without centralized wage bargaining and active labor-market policy. The national commitment to retraining also creates a labor-market climate much friendlier to technological advance, for workers are confident that new technology equals new job opportunity, not unemployment.

Sweden's ability to maintain full employment without unacceptable inflation generated spectacular productivity gains during the 1950s and 1960s. During that 20-year period, Sweden's annual rate of productivity growth was exactly double the American rate. Even more strikingly, Sweden maintained full employment despite the world's highest rate of labor force participation. According to the Organization for Economic Cooperation and Development, 81 percent of Swedes between ages 15 and 64 are in the labor force. The comparable figure for the United States is 72.4 percent. If America had Sweden's participation rate, our unemployment rate would exceed 18 percent.

The second pillar of the Rehn model is the so-called solidaristic or solidarity-wage policy. The idea is that collective bargaining should aim toward a more nearly equal wage structure — equal pay for workers doing the same kind of work in different firms but also a narrowing of wage differentials between low-skill and high-skill workers, between blue-collar and white-collar workers, and between men and women.

Obviously, this approach produces equality gains, but Rehn also shrewdly noted the efficiency gains: If all employers in an industry must pay essentially the same labor costs, then the more efficient companies reap a competitive advantage. By taking wages out of competition the system allows more productive companies to keep profits that otherwise would be bargained away in wage increases. By the same token, inefficient producers are no longer able to compete by making their workers bear the costs of their inefficiency through lower wages. The more efficient firms will pay wage increases out of productivity gains, rather than with inflationary price increases to consumers. A degree of wage *inflexibility,* paradoxically, produces an efficiency gain. Relatively unproductive and poorly managed firms are forced to become more efficient, or lose market share and perhaps go out of business. Inflationary wage pressures are moderated. Labor thus simultaneously serves the national goal of a more productive economy and its own parochial goal of an egalitarian wage structure.

A second efficiency gain is that workers are much more easily transferred among industries. In the United States, if an autoworker earning $12 an hour is replaced by a machine and is offered a new job in electronics, he suddenly faces a wage cut of 50 percent, for in America electronics is a low-wage, nonunion sector. No such problem exists in Sweden, because wages in different industries are so comparable, and virtually all sectors are unionized.

In Sweden's important export sectors, this has had some negative effects, but also important positive ones. For example, in industries like textiles, where prevailing world wages are very low, this tends to overprice Swedish labor. It means that Sweden loses export markets, or is limited to specialty products — it also forces Sweden to substitute capital for labor and compete on the basis of more efficient production technology. Even more important, in high-skill industries, like metalworking, Sweden's solidarity-wage policy produces major export advantages, for it tends to keep wages of highly skilled workers below what they otherwise would be, and keeps them moderate relative to Sweden's competitors. As Willy Bergstrom of the Swedish Center for Working Life quips, "Solidarity wage policy has given us the world's most expensive textile workers, and relatively cheap autoworkers."

This model cannot be understood as just a technical fix. Although it "works" technically, its more notable aspect is political. It is significant that the idea for this strategy came from trade unionists; that fact both reflects and reinforces labor's remarkable influence in the Swedish political economy. The model underscores organized labor's stake in the economic viability of the larger system. It offers some very tangible benefits — full employment, mobility, opportunity — in exchange for the sacrifice of forgoing possibly inflationary wage gains.

Second, the model accomplishes an important ideological purpose. It serves to reinforce labor's (and Sweden's) commitment to an egalitarian society, based on labor solidarity. In very few countries would more highly skilled workers forgo wage gains because of the knowledge that wage restraint and wage equity benefit the bargaining strength of the labor movement and the productivity of the society in the long run. The success of the solidaristic-wage policy cements labor's political and — if we may be forgiven the term — its *class* solidarity. As we shall see, worldwide depression has pushed the solidarity model almost to its breaking point, for Sweden is an open economy, vulnerable to global trends.

The contrast with the American labor movement is instructive — and depressing. In America, successful unions such as the UAW and the Steelworkers are being asked to give up wages as a sacrifice to a competitive American economy, just as some Swedish workers do. But unlike the Swedes, the American wage earners will get nothing in return — not job security, not worker influence, not full employment. Unionized workers are vulnerable in America because so many workers are not unionized. The United States possesses neither the institutions of constructive social bargaining nor a labor movement with broad influence and legitimacy. Thus, even if the UAW wished to trade wages for job security and meaningful retraining opportunities, or for wage gains in other industries, or for more institutional influence for the labor movement generally, there is no machinery to broker such a deal.

For example, the Swedish labor market system has a feature that allows all workers in a plant to share the pain of an economic downturn and minimizes the hardship to any one worker. The device is known as short time. If orders fall off and there is less work to be done, the union local can agree to take the reduction in the form of a shorter work week for everybody, rather than layoffs for the most junior workers. In addition, the labor-market board can ease the burden by allocating funds for brief retraining sabbaticals, to soak up the temporary excess work force. This system, however, must be understood as the product of a deep commitment to labor solidarity, which in Scandinavia is more than just a slogan. In America, where there is less of that tradition, the usual practice is for junior workers to suffer the entire burden of layoffs. It is very rare for senior workers to agree to share a reduction in hours to spare their coworkers loss of employment. In fact, in the auto industry the company often requires senior workers to put in overtime even while some members are still on layoff. The union doesn't resist too strenuously, because overtime is a good deal for those senior workers who want to make extra money.

*   *   *

Since the early fifties, the Swedish labor movement has been the principal source of other social innovations. In Chapter 2, we considered Sweden's unique system of socialized savings. This was intended as a remedy to the problem of declining private capital formation in a highly egalitarian society. It was also an idea that originated with the labor movement. Its purpose was frankly ideological as well as technical. Understandably, socialized savings was bitterly resisted by Sweden's business groups, because it represented one more step away from a laissez-faire economy.

The latest embellishment in this series of labor-designed policy innovations is the so-called Meidner Plan. The plan, enacted in late 1983, diverts 20 percent of major company profits annually to a series of "wage-earner funds." The funds will be partially controlled by Sweden's unions. The funds will use their growing capital to buy corporate stock; and by the year 2000, they will own a substantial portion of Swedish industry. Labor's direct wage gains will be restrained because a portion of their compensation will take the form of stock ownership through the funds. But unlike a conventional profit-sharing plan, ownership will remain collective.

The plan is intended simultaneously to increase Sweden's overall rate of capital investment and to restrain labor costs — the same macroeconomic goals projected by Reagan and Thatcher — *but in a manner that broadens the distribution of wealth and economic power.* No firms will be "nationalized." Competing firms will continue to be subject to the discipline of the market. Investors will still seek the highest source of return. If the plan succeeds, it will accomplish an entirely novel form of market socialism.

The Meidner Plan was inspired by the need to solve several seemingly distinct problems: Sweden's relatively low rate of capital formation; Sweden's concentrated ownership of productive wealth; and the tendency for cycles of high profits to undermine the system of wage solidarity and wage restraint. Centralized wage bargaining, Swedish style, gives rise to a problem that doesn't even exist as a concept in laissez-faire America: "Wage drift." The term refers to the tendency of the more highly skilled Swedish workers to negotiate local wage settlements that exceed agreed-upon central guidelines. Since the solidarity-wage policy compresses the distribution of wages by raising the lowest paid workers disproportionately, higher paid workers (who usually have more bargaining power) often seek to maintain their relative status by negotiating extra wage or fringe benefits locally. Employers in profitable industries are willing to give their workers raises that exceed national norms. Thus, it is not unusual for the LO and the SAF to agree that wage increases will average, say, 4 percent — but when the dust settles the overall cost will be 6 or 7 percent. During the 1950s and 1960s wage drift accounted for almost half of Sweden's total increase in wages.

Wage pressures are particularly acute in phases of the business cycle when business is enjoying above-average profits. The unions then respond with demands for proportional wage increases that often outrun productivity gains and set in motion an inflationary wage push, and occasionally wildcat strikes. The wage-earner funds will help deflate that psychology by soaking up a share of profits and by assuring that they will be reinvested, rather than leaving them vulnerable to inflationary wage bargaining.

The Swedish model — social brokering with substantial labor influence — also permits other forms of compensation that serve to moderate wage inflation. In the 1970s, when most union leaders agreed that Sweden's wage costs were making the Swedish economy uncompetitive internationally, the unions turned to a series of non-wage demands. The 1971 Congress of the LO called for a comprehensive program of work-place democratization. The Social Democratic Prime Minister, Olof Palme, proclaimed the seventies the decade of economic democracy. Laws were passed expanding worker representation on company boards, expanding the authority of shop stewards, and increasing pre-notification requirements in cases of layoff; and a far-reaching Work Environment Act created a system of worker-enforcement of health and safety laws, which made health and safety compliance more cost-effective as well as more worker-oriented. All of these industrial-democracy laws grew out of union initiatives. Another model law, permitting phased retirement after age 60, was the result of a proposal by the metalworkers union.

In a system of centralized corporatist bargaining like Sweden's, tax policy and wage policy are also closely coordinated. A tax reform in 1982 reduced the top marginal income tax rate on most Swedes to a maximum of 60 percent. There was no net revenue cost to the government, since certain loopholes were closed and other charges were increased. In this tax reform, the higher-paid manual workers gained disproportionately, since they had been in income tax brackets with higher marginal rates. In the wage bargaining, wage increases for highly paid workers were restrained, because they had gained a tax benefit not shared by other workers.

Once again, the contrast with recent American history is instructive. In the Reagan tax program, there was no attempt to bargain over the distributive aspects of the tax cut, or to use it as a tradeoff to attain wage restraint. On the contrary, the tax cut was skewed to the very wealthy, because that conformed to the administration's view of how to increase capital investment. When all the tax changes are added up, workers earning less than about $30,000 lost. Those unions with sufficient power could bargain for wage increases, but weaker unions and the unorganized lost doubly. Several hundred billion dollars' worth of tax cut might have been traded for wage restraint, but such a social bargain was impossible, both ideologically and institutionally.

Some liberal American economists have been promoting an idea they call TIP, which stands for *Tax-based Incomes Policy*. The idea is that even though Swedish-style centralized wage bargaining is not possible in the United States, it is possible to create tax incentives (what else?) for wage restraint. Under TIP, workers in firms that agreed to keep contractual wage increases within certain national guidelines would enjoy a tax credit. Thus collective bargaining would remain decentralized, but the government would nonetheless induce compliance with a wage standard. As inflation has given way to unemployment and most unions are negotiating about wage cuts rather than wage hikes, TIP is off the front burner. But it is instructive to reflect on the political history of the idea.

In the late seventies, when inflation was raging, advocates of TIP wondered why the plan received such a lukewarm reception from the unions. The reason should be all too obvious to students of comparative politics. Unions in Northern Europe go along with incomes policies because they get something in return. In the case of Sweden, unions get a national commitment to full employment, egalitarian wage policies, substantial industrial democracy, a generous system of social income, and a good deal of institutional legitimacy. In America, TIP would be a one-way deal.

Given the power of Sweden's trade unions, their degree of wage restraint since 1980 has been astonishing. Unions have agreed to real wage cuts that will equal about 6 percent over a three-year period, depending on the rate of inflation. Even more remarkably, Sweden accomplished this in the context of near-full employment. American labor costs have also been coming down, but in the United States wages have been *driven* down by 10 percent unemployment. Even Keynesian economists in the United States now believe that unemployment rates below 6 percent must trigger inflation. Full employment has been redefined as 6 million people involuntarily out of work. In Sweden, the pain of deflation has been distributed equitably. In America, it has fallen on low-wage workers and on the unemployed. Macroeconomically, the decline in labor costs in Sweden and America since the mid-1970s have been roughly comparable, but socially, the difference is extreme. There is no doubt about which approach is the more equitable. And it would be hard to argue that America's technique for moderating wage costs — 10 percent unemployment — was the more efficient.

Sweden has been able to lower its wage costs without depending on high unemployment to discipline its work force because it has in place institutions of social bargaining — not devices whose virtues are technical, like TIP, but institutions that reflect a powerful labor movement as the instrument of a viable social contract. Another good illustration of the power of this kind of social bargaining is Sweden's recent devaluation. Upon taking office in the fall of 1981, after six years in opposition, the Social Democratic government immediately devalued the Swedish krona by 16 percent. This was intended to make Swedish exports more competitive in world markets and to depress consumption of imports. Usually, such devaluations fail. They raise the cost of imports; unions demand compensatory wage increases; the rate of inflation rises; and the country ends up about where it began, but with a debased currency.

This devaluation, however, is working. The unions, with their stake in the larger economic strategy, have held down their demands. Thanks to the devaluation and the wage restraint, Sweden's wage costs relative to her trading partners are at their lowest level in twenty years. Exports are up smartly; and the stock market is booming. As profits rise, the government hopes that the unions will settle for the gains of the new Meidner profit-sharing plan, rather than press direct wage demands. There is a high likelihood that this will happen, for the unions designed the plan.

Austria

Austria offers an even more explicit system of social bargaining than Sweden, though the power of the labor movement is less pervasive. To an even greater extent than Sweden, Austria relies on a system of national economic planning and government allocation of capital. Most of Austria's basic heavy industries are nationalized, and the state allocates an estimated 40 percent of investment capital in the economy. Along with Norway and West Germany, Austria also is the outstanding economic success of the post-OPEC period. Inflation peaked in 1981 at 6.8 percent, at a time when other countries were suffering double-digit rates. Unemployment has remained below 4 percent. In 1982, when the European rate averaged 10 percent, Austria's was 3.7 percent. In fact, throughout the early 1980s, Austria was the one European nation where foreign workers still outnumbered total domestic job seekers. Austria is also one of the few countries where real wage gains continued in the years after the oil shock. In 1983, wages were about 58 percent above their 1976 level, while prices had increased only 38 percent. Despite a very strong labor movement, Austria has Europe's lowest level of strike activity.

In Austria, as in Sweden, there is a strong government commitment to Keynesian demand management to maintain full employment, coupled with centralized wage bargaining and wage moderation, to hold down inflation. This mix of demand management at a macro-economic level, planning at a microeconomic level, and bargained wage stabilization is sometimes called Austro-Keynesianism. With its low inflation rate, Austria also manages to retain a "hard" currency, with the strong Austrian schilling tied closely to the deutsche mark.

Austria does not quite share Sweden's commitment to equalization of primary wages, preferring instead to rely on social spending to equalize effective purchasing power. Nor is there the same reliance on an "active labor market policy," since unemployment has remained quite low without heroic job-creation measures. Between

1970 and 1980, Austria had the highest growth rate per capita of all 22 OECD nations, including Japan.

The institutions of Austrian corporatism date back to the nineteenth century and are probably the most firmly established in the world. Both a Chamber of Commerce (dating to 1850) and a Chamber of Labor (1920) are established by legislation. Workers are represented through the Chamber of Labor, in which membership is compulsory, through their unions, in which membership is voluntary, and through works councils at the factory or office level. Since World War II, all sixteen Austrian unions have been part of the Austrian Trade Union Federation, the Oesterreicher Gewerkschaftsbund (OeGB), which gives Austrian unionism an unparalleled degree of cohesion. According to a comprehensive study of European unionism by labor economists Robert Flanagan, David Soskice, and Lloyd Ulman, Austria suffers "none of the fragmentation of the labor movement along political, confessional, or occupational lines" that plagues other union movements. Moreover, they report,

> The centralization of authority in the OeGB probably exceeds that of any other democratic trade union movement and vests the federation with considerable influence over the activities of the affiliated unions. In particular, the OeGB controls the finances of the sixteen unions and appoints and employs the secretary of each.

Austria's wage policy is based on a shared premise that wage gains should parallel real gains in labor productivity. As a small, open economy, Austria is very sensitive to the need to remain competitive internationally. Thus, wage restraint, price restraint, international competitiveness, and balanced growth are equal goals for national policy.

The present regime of social bargaining dates to the post–World War II reconstruction period. *Ad hoc* arrangements of the late 1940s gave way to a more formal system in the 1950s. A Joint Wage and Price Commission, or "Parity Commission," established in 1956, has subcommittees on wages and on prices. The wage subcommittee reviews the broad outline of proposed wage settlements prior to the beginning of formal bargaining, but leaves the details of settlement to labor and management. The subcommittee on prices requires companies in key industrial sectors to submit requests for price increases, which can be approved or disallowed. A new labor code, approved by the Austrian parliament in 1973, substantially expanded codetermination. The works council, elected by a firm's employees, now gets to appoint one third of the firm's board of directors.

Since social income looms larger in Austria than in Sweden, it provides a key rationale for wage restraint. Most students of Austrian corporatism have concluded that full employment is a more important goal to Austria's unions than wage gains. As a result, direct wage costs for Austrian industry are comparatively low. But Austrian employers pay higher-than-average payroll charges to finance social benefits. Social charges as of 1982 were about 16 percent of GNP, third highest in the world after the Netherlands and France. According to the OECD, Austria's system of income transfers is one of the most redistributive in the world. An average production worker has take-home pay after taxes equal to 77.4 percent of gross wages; but after social benefits are added in, the effective take-home income rises to 91.1 percent. Thus, while the public sector in Austria is substantially larger than in America, the effective tax burden on an average-wage worker is much lighter.

A final element worth noting is the dominance of two parties, the conservative Austrian Peoples Party and the Social Democrats. Both are very strongly committed to the Austrian system of democratic corporatism, and together they have over 90 percent of the vote in most parliamentary elections, Europe's highest two-party share. Since 1970, the Socialists have been the party of government; for more than a decade, the prime minister was the uncommonly gifted Bruno Kreisky.

West Germany

German unions are less powerful than those of Scandinavia or Austria; union membership today is about 40 percent of the work force. German law in many respects constrains the power of unions. Strikes are prohibited during the life of contracts; and the closed shop is illegal. Yet the German labor movement is nonetheless a well-established partner in an effective system of social bargaining.

The postwar success of the West German economy has been built on a broad social consensus that favors, above all, economic stability. This goal was codified in the 1967 Act to Promote Economic Stability and Growth, which specifies as national goals: stable prices, appropriate growth, high employment, and balanced trade.

Until 1981, Germany had the best record in the West of reconciling high employment, rapid growth, and low inflation. Throughout the 1950s and 1960s, Germany was at *over-full* employment. The slack was taken up first by immigrants from East Germany, then by foreign "guest workers." Between 1960 and 1973, the vacancy rate (jobs available) exceeded the unemployment rate in every year but one. Despite over-full employment, German inflation has been below 6 percent in seventeen of the past twenty years, and never above 8 percent. Germany also enjoys one of the lowest levels of strike or lockout activity in the West. German labor has settled for a bargain that includes full employment, substantial plant-level influence via codetermination, generous social legislation — and wage moderation. Since 1980, however, world recession has placed severe strains on this social bargain, as German unemployment has risen to a postwar high of over 9 percent.

Probably the dominant economic policy institution in West Germany is the unusually powerful central bank, the Deutsches Bundesbank. The central bank's main objective has been monetary stability (as opposed to monetarism), and it has succeeded admirably in keeping interest rates low and stable. Occasionally, when inflationary pressures have been excessive, the Bundesbank has gone against the wishes of the government and tightened money to the point of provoking recession. But the Bundesbank is far more consistent and competent than its American counterpart, the Federal Reserve. Germany's commercial banks, as noted, play a dominant role in industrial financing and planning.

Germany's labor movement is similar to that of other corporatist nations, in that it is highly centralized. Some four fifths of union members belong to unions affiliated with the national labor federation, the Deutscher Gewerkschaftsbund. As in the case of Austria, the relative centralization of the German labor movement is a legacy of postwar reconstruction; in 1949, the fragmented remnant of Germany's pre-Hitler free labor movement was merged into 16 national unions, organized mainly along industrial lines. Employers' associations are similarly centralized.

Formal incomes policy in Germany dates to the 1960s. A "Council of Economic Experts," created in 1963, was charged with making recommendations on how to maintain both full employment and price stability. The 1967 Act to Promote Economic Stability and

Growth requires government to undertake "concerted action" among the unions, employer associations, and government officials, including the Bundesbank to promote noninflationary full employment. That Act gave tripartite social bargaining a fresh impetus.

The coming of age of the Social Democratic Party (SPD), in the late 1960s, first as a junior coalition partner and after 1969 as the party of government, also served to reinforce corporatist bargaining. Under the SPD, Germany's famous system of codetermination (*Mitbestimmung*) was substantially expanded. Since the early 1950s, German workers have been represented through plant-level works councils; and workers in the coal and steel industry have been able to elect half of the corporate board. In 1976, workers in all other companies with over 2000 employees were granted the right to elect 50 percent of company supervisory boards. However, the chairman, representing management, is empowered to cast the decisive vote in case of a deadlock. The expansion of codetermination was resisted bitterly by many employers' groups, while labor has criticized it for not going far enough.

Despite the Social Democratic leadership of the government (between 1969 and 1982), the labor movement has been unable to achieve two other cherished goals. A German version of the Meidner profit-sharing plan has been on labor's agenda for better than a decade (Meidner himself credits the idea's German origin). But the German labor movement has been unable to persuade the SPD to make the proposal its own. Nor have the German unions succeeded in their other major objective, a substantial shortening of working time. Only in 1984 did the metalworkers union succeed in negotiating a slight reduction in the basic workweek, to 38.5 hours.

Despite German labor's wage restraint, German companies have found themselves in a profit squeeze. The relative strength of the German economy, coupled with the conservative monetary policy of the Bundesbank, has made the deutsche mark an increasingly expensive currency. Even though wage costs have not outrun productivity gains, Germany nonetheless has become a nation with high labor costs on international markets. Moreover, in a climate of slow growth, Germany is paradoxically harmed by her high productivity growth. As capital replaces labor, jobs are lost, and the slowdown in growth limits Germany's ability to place workers in new jobs.

Thus, in many respects, Germany can be seen as an example of incomplete labor-corporatism. The labor movement benefited for two decades from Germany's strong competitive success. The conservative government, which was in power until 1969, was generous with social benefits (a noblesse oblige tradition dating to Bismarck). Labor, for its part, was fairly docile. When Social Democrats led the government during the 1970s, they did so in coalition with the anti-socialist Free Democratic Party; and there was not nearly the close collaboration between the labor movement and the state that has operated in Sweden. In 1982, the Free Democrats shifted their allegiance to the conservative Christian Democrats, and at this writing Germany again has a conservative government. In the absence of more substantial labor influence and more venturesome strategies to maintain full employment via either demand stimulus or heroic labor-market policies, Germany's version of a social contract is today rather precarious.

Norway

The Norwegian system is very similar to the Swedish. If anything, the bargaining over wages and income shares is even more highly institutionalized than Sweden's. As in Sweden and Austria, a high dependence on foreign trade forces the Norwegian labor movement to make sure that wage settlements do not lead to a deterioration of Norway's international competitiveness. According to one study, labor-market bargaining in Norway has three explicit objectives: to maintain the country's share of international markets, to achieve and maintain full employment, and to redistribute income. In Norway, indexation formulas are used to give disproportionate wage increases to the lowest paid workers. Instead of using a percentage increase to offset inflation, a flat wage increase is set at so many ore per hour for each percent of increase in the consumer price index. Thus, every time there is a cost-of-living adjustment, the wage spread narrows. In America, where the lowest paid workers tend to be unorganized, cost-of-living formulas tend to widen disparities.

Like Sweden, Norway has highly centralized bargaining, with one union federation that represents all production workers, the LO, and one employers' federation, the NAF. As in Sweden, the Social Democratic Party held power for an extended period (1936–1965), although it has been somewhat weaker since then, alternating with nonsocialist coalition governments during the 1970s. The conservative government that assumed power in 1965, however, was very friendly to centralized wage negotiation. That government appointed a nonpartisan committee headed by an influential economist, Odd Aukrust, to create a sophisticated economic model that would predict the consequences for wages, prices, economic growth, and income distribution of different possible wage settlements. This model, which is widely accepted as technically valid, allows bargaining to be even more precise and explicit, as well as sensitive to the efficiency costs of different possible settlements.

Aukrust hypothesized that the Norwegian economy, with its heavy dependence on trade, must base wage settlements in the "open sector" of the economy on worldwide wages and prices. Labor could maintain its share of income in the open sector, but not raise the price of Norwegian products beyond worldwide levels. Moreover, wage settlements even in the "sheltered" sector had to be limited by what was reasonable for the competitive sector. Thus, international competition (about 40 percent of Norway's GNP is imports and exports) forces Norwegian unionism to exercise restraint. This "two-sector" model has a close counterpart in Swedish wage bargaining, and together they can be considered one "Scandinavian" model of labor negotiation.

In both Norway and Sweden, the worldwide economic slump of the late 1970s and early 1980s has put extreme pressure on this social model. In Norway, where North Sea oil reserves have become a major export, the result has been a substantial appreciation of the currency. Norwegian wage costs on world markets have risen substantially, not because of excessive wage settlements, but because oil sales have increased the value of the Norwegian krone against other currencies. In a sense, oil exports, which are very capital intensive, have substituted for manufacturing exports. In addition, the petroleum sector, with fewer than 50,000 workers, has become a principal source of wage drift. Because labor costs are such a small fraction of total costs in the petroleum industry, management has been willing to agree to settlements that are exorbitant compared to wage levels in other Norwegian industries.

The interludes of conservative government in Sweden (1976–82) and in Norway (1965–73, 1981–) have also added stress to the labor-corporatist model. Organized labor is of course a close ally of the Social Democrats. Conservative governments share neither the political interests nor the ideological outlook of the labor movement; trade unionists participate in socialist governments, but not in conservative ones. Thus, the conservative governments seldom engage in constructive bargaining with labor for common goals as effectively as do their Social Democratic rivals. There has been less inclination by conservative governments to liberalize social benefits or broaden labor's influence in the work place as a tradeoff for wage restraint. Wage drift has increased in both countries during the past decade, and labor's own solidarity has been stretched rather thin. Ted Hanisch, of the Norwegian Institute for Social Research, observes that an incomes policy, in conditions of economic stagnation, "*consumes* working class solidarity without reproducing it."

In Sweden, a major break with the system of centralized bargaining occurred in early 1983, when the important metalworkers union broke ranks and signed a contract far more generous than the prevailing LO standard. This, in turn, put pressure on the other LO unions to bargain harder next time. It remains to be seen whether the other policy levers available to the Social Democratic government — the distribution of taxes and social benefits, the new wage-earner funds — will be sufficient to keep wage restraint and labor solidarity from collapsing.

Despite these stresses, however, both Norway and Sweden have coped with stagflation far better than have the laissez-faire countries. Norwegian inflation has remained extremely low, while unemployment has stayed in the 2–4 percent range. Norway's growth rate has remained well above average. Domestic wage costs have been restrained, despite near-full employment. Though oil exports have made Norway a relatively high-cost nation, corporatist Norway has done far better than laissez-faire Britain has at keeping oil from turning from blessing to curse.

A Viable Bargain?

In Western Europe's labor circles and left academic literature, there is currently a good deal of debate about whether democratic corporatism is ultimately a sustainable bargain for labor. As the working class becomes more middle class, the solidarity necessary to maintain labor's bargaining influence begins to erode. As the logic of equality makes greater inroads on the logic of the market, capital either fights back or becomes less efficient or fights back *by* becoming less efficient. In periods of economic slump, the necessary social grease wears thin, the social bargaining grows testy; higher paid workers begin to conclude that egalitarianism no longer serves their interest. Corporatist leaders urging restraint for the common good begin losing the support of their members who above all want to sustain their own status. European neo-Marxists and labor intellectuals delight in pursuing the almost metaphysical issue of whether labor corporatism represents "class gain or class collaboration."

So far, labor corporatism has produced substantial class gain *by* class collaboration. It remains to be seen whether that model can adapt to the new global economy. It is possible that worldwide recession will progressively weaken the influence of corporatist labor movements, and market forces will reassert themselves. It is also possible — Sweden and Austria are bellwethers here — that labor will expand its influence and continue refining efficient democratic socialism.

The value of the labor-corporatist approach is that it offers a model of social bargaining that seems to outperform the laissez-faire alternative *in both equality and efficiency*. Both models have experienced strains in the post-1973 worldwide slump. But interestingly, the labor-corporatist nations outperformed the laissez-faire countries both before and after the slowdown; they did notably better at adapting to the period of slower growth.

The entire industrial world has slowed down since 1973, but it is doubly significant that the labor-corporatist nations outperformed most others, since they tend to be small, open economies, with above-average dependence on trade and on imported energy. As such, they are more vulnerable than most to external shocks, such as the quadrupling of oil prices, or the leaden influence of an American economy committed to high interest rates and deflation. Europe's small corporatist nations have had to contend with shrinking foreign markets, price competition from low-wage competitors, and imported high interest rates from America. This has put immense pressure on their ability to conclude domestic social bargains; yet they have still done substantially better than have laissez-faire Britain and America.

But the skeptics on the left must be taken seriously. In a period of slow growth and escalating competition for markets and jobs, there is a real question whether this model can endure. On one flank, the social lubricants of labor influence and public spending are threatened by the underlying dynamic of a Western economy that remains fundamentally capitalist. Profit-maximizing producers under global competitive pressure are constrained to lower costs; the social benefits that tempered the brutality of pure capitalism are seen as expendable frills. From the other side, labor's own solidarity — the indispensable ingredient in labor's ability to bargain — is worn thin as skilled workers and unskilled workers fight for their shares of a static economic pie. In a period of no job growth, multinational corporations have an easy time playing off national labor unions against one another.

Restored economic growth, therefore, is necessary not only for its own sake, but because it makes equitable social bargaining possible. The nations with strong labor movements, not surprisingly, have fought hard to maintain high employment. To the extent they have succeeded, they have preserved their ability to press equity claims and to make gains on other fronts. In countries like Britain and America, where unemployment is high and labor solidarity was much weaker to begin with, the labor movement is in open retreat.

But if growth is necessary, it is not sufficient. As the global economy shifts into a new era of labor displacement caused by increased world trade, capital mobility, and technological advance, an effective system of social brokering becomes all the more essential to reconcile efficiency and equality. With strong labor influence, the economic gains of trade and technology can become true social gains, broadly distributed. Without it, trade and technology "gains" can produce windfall returns for some, and persistent unemployment and falling wages for others.

THE NEW UNEMPLOYMENT

With the exception of a handful of countries, very high unemployment now plagues most of the industrial world. As I have suggested, when unemployment is high, an egalitarian welfare state disintegrates economically, fiscally, ideologically, and above all, politically. The cost of unemployment creates intolerable fiscal pressures, and the constituency for social justice falls apart. High unemployment produces social costs that are not distributed equitably. In both the United States and Europe, unemployment means particular suffering for younger people seeking to enter the labor force. In the United States, where the majority of workers are not organized, high unemployment revives the Marxian "reserve army" phenomenon, in which the large numbers of jobless lower the prevailing wages paid to all workers, particularly to low-skill workers, who are easily replaced.

In theory, the shift from a manufacturing economy to a service economy is a sign of progress. With a more automated and productive industrial sector, human labor is no longer needed to perform many arduous physical tasks. Just as the mechanization of agriculture freed human workers to perform more productive industrial tasks, the automation of industry should free workers to do more highly refined service jobs and to enjoy leisure time. Unfortunately, the workings of the market do not necessarily produce that happy outcome. For a variety of historical reasons, industrial work has been associated with relatively high wages. Henry Ford, in a sense, was the first Keynesian. He paid his assembly workers high wages so they could afford to buy his cars. When people came off the farms to take factory jobs, most of them improved their economic condition. But the shift to a postindustrial economy, in a historical period of slow growth, declining unionism, increased world competition, and demographic transition, means — for many workers — declining living standards rather than increased opportunity. Without an explicit effort to maintain decent wages and a full-employment context, this productivity paradox is likely to intensify.

Prolonged high unemployment pushes to stage center several issues of distribution: distribution of work opportunity, of income, and of leisure. There are really two distinct aspects to the job scarcity of the 1980s. The first is the interaction of trade and technology on the *total* supply of jobs in a laissez-faire economy. In the OECD countries, there is now a shortage of some 35 million jobs, and because industrial productivity and Third-World competition are increasing so rapidly, it is likely that unemployment will remain unacceptably high even given the modest economic recovery projected for the mid-1980s.

A second, more subtle problem, is the growing shortage of *good jobs.* This is a particular problem in nations like the United States and Britain, where unions are currently on the defensive and there is no public-policy commitment to wage equalization as a valid goal for its own sake. It is far less of a problem in the labor-corporatist nations, where an egalitarian pay structure is part of the social contract.

Dualism and the Declining Middle

There is substantial evidence that job opportunities and pay scales in America are polarizing. As the economy shifts away from its traditional manufacturing base into services and high-technology industries, the share of jobs that pay for a middle-class standard of living is shrinking. An industrial economy employs large numbers of relatively well-paid production workers. A service economy employs doctors, engineers, accountants, and executives at one extreme, but legions of salesclerks, typists, waiters, cashiers, and secretaries at the other. Without efforts to socially alter the structure of wages, a postindustrial labor market suffers from what might be called a "declining middle."

During the three decades after World War II, America not only generated lots of jobs; it generated plenty of good jobs. Between 1958 and 1968, for example, manufacturing added 4 million workers; state and local government added another 3.5 million. A working-class family's child with no education beyond a high school diploma could nonetheless choose among a number of relatively well-paid jobs, with a wage sufficient to buy a house and support a family, usually on one income.

These are precisely the jobs that are disappearing today. Manufacturing, which on average pays nearly three times the minimum wage, added only one million jobs between 1968 and 1978 and has lost nearly three million jobs between 1980 and 1982. Construction and production work, taken together, accounted for one job in four in 1950; they account for just one job in eight in 1984. State and local government, a key source of good service jobs, peaked in 1981 and has reduced its labor force since then by several hundred thousand workers.

The erosion of the middle of the labor market is easy to misinterpret because its roots are multiple. Demographic change is one important factor. In the past fifteen years an unprecedented number of women and young adults born during the baby boom entered the work force. During the 1970s, the American economy produced twenty million new jobs, two thirds of them in services; but twenty-three million new workers entered the labor force. This resulted in a mismatch between labor supply and labor demand, which depressed wages, especially at the lower end, where workers had less bargaining power.

The decline of well-paid production jobs also reflects the growth of capital mobility and world trade. Since the 1970s, global corporations have had an easier time shifting high-wage production jobs to lower-wage countries, or demanding that high-wage domestic workers moderate their wages. In addition, technology has influenced the polarization of available jobs. Fewer American workers would have been needed to make steel in 1980 than in 1960, even without the added pressures of foreign competition and world recession, because new technology made many of their jobs redundant. Finally, the high rate of unemployment caused in part by these other trends becomes an independent factor polarizing jobs and income. High unemployment disproportionately erodes the bargaining power of the poorest paid, while professional and unionized workers are able to defend their status more effectively.

It is a mistake, however, to blame job polarization on technology. The source of the conflict between efficiency (technological advance) and equality (loss of high-wage jobs) is fundamentally not economic, but social. Ultimately, the structure of labor income in America is polarizing not because of technology, but because of the ways in which technological impacts are distributed and the absence of brokering institutions to distribute gains equitably. When a more efficient machine replaces a production worker, both the firm and consumers as a group benefit. The loss falls mainly on the worker who is displaced. In a climate of full employment, that worker can be reemployed at a more productive job. But with unemployment high, the sum of individual losses adds up to a social loss. High-wage workers as a group suffer a fall in living standards, and the economy as a whole suffers a loss of purchasing power. Thus, the absence of a social mechanism to redistribute the economic gains of technology operates as a drag on the entire economy.

As it happens, production work in America is becoming heavily automated at a moment when the two most powerful agents of equal wage distribution — the trade union movement and the state — are in disfavor and relative decline. The correlation between high wages and highly skilled work or "high value-added per worker" is imperfect at best. There is nothing intrinsic about assembling cars, mining coal, or pouring molten steel that dictates high wages. These are all heavy, dirty, and semiskilled jobs. In America, these jobs pay well mainly because they exist in sectors with strong unions. But many other production jobs pay far less, not because the work is easier or at a lower skill level, but because unions are absent.

Just as high wages are not a necessary characteristic of factory work, low wages are not an inevitable hallmark of a service economy. But because American unions have organized few fast-food workers, typists, bank clerks, or even computer assemblers, most of the new service and electronics jobs that are replacing factory work pay far lower wages. Polarization of professional service salaries reflects social as well as economic factors. Library and schoolteaching jobs have been historically underpaid relative to their educational requirements, because they are traditionally "female" jobs. By the same token, there is no sound economic reason why a doctor's average income must be about six times that of a nurse. In countries with strong labor movements committed to egalitarian outcomes, such wage spreads are much narrower, and there seems to be no efficiency cost.

Statistically, there is persuasive evidence of the polarization of wage and salary income. A 1980 study by two economists in the U.S. Bureau of Labor Statistics found that, between 1958 and 1977, earnings of male workers at the 20th percentile of income (the bottom fifth) increased by 130.6 percent (with no adjustment for inflation), while the earnings of men at the 80th percentile (the top fifth) increased by 206.7 percent. Statisticians at the Labor Department also found that salaries in the twenty fastest growing occupations were fully $5000 a year lower than in the twenty occupations in steepest decline. Another telling indication of labor-market polarization is that the minimum wage, which was once as high as 52 percent of the average wage, is now only 37 percent; that means that low-wage workers are falling progressively further behind.

Brave New Work

The Labor Department ranked 1980 job openings by category and availability. The top fifteen categories, with one exception, are jobs that middle-class parents hope their children will avoid.

Of the top fifteen, only one, the grab-bag category "Managers and Administrators (not elsewhere classified)," suggests a well-paid line of work. The first profession to appear on the Labor Department's roster is job number thirty-six, Accountants, with 140,108 openings. Far, far down on the list come Computer Programmers (30,953), and Electrical Engineers (23,089). All told, the Labor Department projects that the American economy will generate some 19 million new jobs during the 1980s, of which only about 3.5 million will be professional and technical. Low-wage service and clerical work will account for almost 7 million of the new jobs.

Given the high rate of unemployment, it might be tempting to conclude that lots of low-wage "entry-level" service jobs are just

Job	Openings, 1980
Retail Salesclerk	757,750
Managers and Administrators (not elsewhere classified)	711,793
Cashiers	617,973
Secretaries	599,216
Waiters and Waitresses	465,628
Cooks	437,341
Stockhandlers	358,393
Janitors	333,309
Bookkeepers	304,789
Miscellaneous Clerical Workers	299,940
Nursing Aides and Orderlies	284,332
Child-Care Workers (private household)	277,525
Building Interior Cleaners	259,528
Typists	250,276
Truck Drivers	244,377

Source: "Occupational Projections and Training Data," 1982 edition (Washington: U.S. Department of Labor).

what the economy needs. Unfortunately, although these jobs do provide entry into the work force, they offer very few opportunities for advancement. The fast-food industry, for example, which now employs more workers than the steel industry, has jobs for a small number of managers and executives, but employs several hundred thousand cashiers and kitchen help who make about $3.50 an hour. That wage translates into an annual income well below the poverty line for a small family. With some variation, keypunchers, chambermaids, and retail salesclerks confront the same short career ladder.

Technological advances are not translating into gains for blue-collar workers. In industry after industry, the technology becomes more advanced, but the work becomes more routinized and lower paid. There are exceptions — industry still needs a small number of skilled technicians — but particularly in high-technology industry, production lines are more highly automated, and technical functions like quality control and maintenance are themselves increasingly done by machine. Despite the enormous growth of electronics, the projected demand for new electronics technicians is only about 15,000 a year.

In high-technology production work, assembly workers are semi-skilled, easily replaced, almost 100 percent nonunionized, and low paid. The typical wage of a worker employed to load circuit boards or to transfer silicon wafers between chemical baths is about $5 an hour. High-technology industry, far from being the savior of America's employment needs, is the epitome of a dual economy. Because of their scant bargaining power and the competition from low-wage countries in Asia, production workers in high technology have faced stagnating wages, while engineers and computer scientists have been in short supply and have enjoyed economic rewards. Polarization of wages in this growth field is widening. According to one study, production workers in microelectronics got wage increases that averaged only 7 percent between 1972 and 1978; their hourly pay rose to about $9000 a year. During the same period, the average salary of electronics engineers increased 33 percent, to $48,000. One has only to consult the want ads to appreciate that the openings are mainly for highly educated professionals.

Demographic pressures are likely to intensify the competition for scarce good jobs for at least a generation. In the mid-1980s, the baby-boom generation is finally tapering off; for the next two decades, relatively fewer new workers will be entering the labor force each year. But those already in the job market are only beginning to enter their prime earning period. In 1975, about 16.7 million were between thirty-five and forty-five years old. In 1995, almost 34 million people will fall into this age group. Twice as many people will be competing in 1995 for the limited supply of breadwinner jobs. And as women continue to demand equal opportunity, that pressure will only increase.

For some households, the rise of the two-income family has provided a defense against declining-wage income. The average wage lost about 16 percent of its purchasing power between 1974 and 1981, while average family incomes dropped by about 11 percent. But the averages conceal the trend toward polarization. In that respect, the two-income household is a mixed blessing. People tend to marry within their own socioeconomic class. Statistically, the wife of a male with a $50,000 annual income earns about $5000 more than the wife of a male earning $10,000. To the extent that two incomes are now necessary to sustain a middle-class standard of living, the one-income family is doubly punished. The vast majority of households in poverty are households headed by women. Given the low prevailing wages paid to women and the difficulty of supporting a family on one income in any case, family-income distribution is further polarized by the two-income household trend. A family with two professionals is that much further ahead; and a household headed by a sole woman wage earner is that much further behind.

The danger is that as good jobs remain scarce, the American economy will continue polarizing. Unionized workers and professionalized workers will cling to relatively high-paid jobs; others will have low-wage jobs, or no jobs. Since income from one's job is still the principal source of economic status and well-being, labor polarization will mean an increasingly unequal society.

Job Shortage and the Retraining Myth

The phenomenon of dual labor markets has been a controversial topic within the economics profession for better than a decade. In the early 1970s, several labor economists, most notably Peter Doeringer and Michael Piore, began analyzing the bifurcation of jobs.

The "primary" labor market, they found, is typically union-organized or professional, with relatively good wages, benefits, and job security. The "secondary" labor market, in contrast, is made up of jobs that are usually less rewarding and almost always lower paid. Its defining characteristic is instability: high turnover, and a disproportionate number of seasonal, part-time, and temporary jobs. Doeringer, Piore, and other analysts of the dual labor-market school also point out the preponderance of white males in "primary" jobs and argue that the dual system both reflects and reinforces race and sex discrimination. A large number of primary jobs, they note, do not have high formal entry requirements; skills are learned on the job. Sometimes, members of the secondary force — women — teach skills to members of the primary force. Through informal referral networks, white men are steered disproportionately into the better jobs, and women and blacks into lesser ones.

Economists of the rival "human-capital" school have responded to the dual-labor theorists by arguing that any labor-market schisms simply reflect differences of skill and education; the free market is just doing its job. If any residue of race and sex discrimination persists, it is of course to be deplored; but if some workers are only marginally literate, with little training and sloppy work habits, it is hardly surprising that they should land in marginal jobs. Indeed, it is fortunate that society provides jobs for such workers at all. According to human-capital theorists, the obvious way to upgrade jobs is to upgrade the quality of the work force. This approach has informed most of the federal job-training efforts, including the 1962 Manpower Development and Training Act, CETA, and more recently, the Reagan administration's Job Training Partnerships Act.

A favorite counter-example of the dual-labor school is World War II. All kinds of people who had never seen the inside of a factory quickly learned a variety of skills on the job. Even blacks and women (!) turned out to be competent to do skilled production work. The reason, of course, was that jobs were to be had. Job training, in the context of World War II–style mobilization for full production or a Swedish full-employment/active labor-market policy, serves to upgrade skills, increase opportunity, and make labor markets operate more efficiently. Job training, in the context of 10 percent unemployment, is mostly a cynical exercise in redistributing idleness.

In fairness, even with 10 percent unemployment, job-training programs aimed at areas of true labor shortage (skilled machinists) can be useful; and some special remedial training programs have managed to give the "hard-core unemployed" initial work experience. But the successful approaches have typically coupled job training with wage subsidies and job placement rather than relying on training alone. This is a central element of the Swedish approach. In Germany, workers in retraining are paid an income subsidy, which can equal 90 percent of the previous wage. In America, where the Reagan administration professes to support job retraining, wage subsidy has been largely removed from the program.

To be sure, upgrading the skills of the labor force, both in the schools and on the job, is a worthy goal. But with unemployment high, tending to the supply side of the labor market will not cause jobs to materialize. If the job market is polarizing because of high aggregate unemployment and shifting demands for workers, it is no solution to emphasize job training — unless we deliberately use retraining to soak up large numbers of workers, Swedish-style, and thereby reduce the pool of job seekers. But there is no such program in the United States. In fiscal year 1983, the United States spent about $30 billion on labor-market programs — the vastly greater portion, $24 billion, went for unemployment compensation.

Dualism in American labor markets is also reflected in the federal agency that administers the unemployment insurance and job-referral program, the U.S. Employment Service. The USES and its state affiliates date to the 1930s, when the new system performed a valuable service of matching workers to jobs as national unemployment rates slowly subsided. Since the 1930s, however, a large industry of private employment agencies and corporate personnel departments has taken over much of this function. USES generally gets the dregs of job listings. Increasingly, its function has become enforcer of a useless paper chase, in which people collecting unemployment insurance are made to go through the motions of looking for a job. Employers complain that when they give USES job listings, they are often sent applicants who are either underqualified for the job, or who are waiting for a better one and are interested mainly in an interviewer's signature to prove that they are dutifully pounding the pavement.

Interestingly, in Sweden, the law prohibits private employment organizations from charging a fee for the service; for-profit employment agencies do not exist. Swedish employers generally list their vacancies with the local labor-market boards. Consequently, the Swedish labor-market system is far more useful as a genuine referral and retraining organization. And there is far less segmentation of the process of job referral. In Western Europe, the percentage of hires in which national employment services have a role ranges from 25 percent to 60 percent. In the United States, the figure is 10 percent.

American conservatives draw the usual conclusion from the disarray of the U.S. Employment Service: one more government program doesn't work; what did you expect? It doesn't occur to them that success sometimes requires more public intervention, not less.

PRODUCTIVITY AND PROGRESS

Despite the welfare state, the overwhelming determinant of social status and economic well-being remains one's job. In America, the working-age population gets fully 85 percent of its income from wages and salaries. As the society becomes more productive, and less human labor is required to produce more physical output, distribution rather than production re-emerges as the key economic issue. Since jobs remain the principal source of income and status, jobs are central to the issue of distributive fairness. How are they defined? How wide are wage disparities? How are work and income allocated when market demand for workers is declining?

Wassily Leontief, the Nobel laureate in economics, argues that the loss of purchasing power from the decline in wages brought about by automation could doom the economy to a paradoxical state of rising productivity and rising destitution — an economy in which the shelves are loaded with goods, but there is not enough money in the hands of consumers to buy them. Ample supply, by itself, does not assure adequate demand. Technological unemployment in a climate of global competition and slow growth is just a variation on the Keynesian theme of insufficient purchasing power and the maldistribution of the private demand. As we saw in the discussion of foreign trade (Chapter 3), production is no longer the problem. Overcapacity is rampant. One country — Japan — could by itself supply half of the West's industrial needs if the West were to allow it.

Unlike the era when farm labor became higher-paid industrial labor, production workers dislocated into the service economy are not necessarily guaranteed a better economic life — not unless there are more creative social interventions to assure that the service jobs are good jobs. Leontief offers a parable of Adam and Eve, in which the new Paradise is a society where production is totally automated:

> Adam and Eve enjoyed, before they were expelled from Paradise, a high standard of living without working. After their expulsion they and their successors were condemned to eke out a miserable existence, working from dawn to dusk. The history of technological progress over the past 200 years is essentially the story of the human species working its way slowly and steadily back into Paradise. What would happen, however, if we suddenly found ourselves in it?
>
> With all goods and services provided without work, no one would be gainfully employed. Being unemployed means receiving no wages. As a result, until new income policies were formulated to fit changed technological conditions, *everyone would starve in Paradise* [itals added].

To prevent "starvation in Paradise," Leontief proposes an ever-shorter workweek as a means of redistributing available jobs and a greater reliance on government transfer payments to distribute non-wage income, create new jobs, and maintain consumer purchasing power. These remedies, of course, depend heavily on the sort of brokering institutions that are not well developed in the United States.

If we instead permit market forces to determine all of these outcomes, there is a likelihood of increasing dualism: polarized job opportunities, persistently high unemployment, pressure on workers generally to lower wages, resistance to occupational or technological change by working people located in occupations that happen to pay high wages. Unions come to be seen as islands of privilege rather than champions of the underprivileged. The irony is that an economic good — productivity — is turning into a social bad — unemployment and inequality. The market, left to its own devices, doesn't seem to point a way out. Luddism — smashing the machines — is surely the wrong response, for it is the machines that make the whole economy more productive and thus wealthier. The issue is how to reconcile an efficiency gain with an equity gain.

The American economics fraternity, led by the bastard Keynesians, insists that the only problem is to restore balance to macroeconomic policy. If deficits are reduced, interest rates moderated, currency misalignments fixed, and growth rekindled, then the market will eventually provide jobs at appropriate wage levels for everyone. There will be no need for messy social interventions. Competent macroeconomic policy indeed counts; but as we have seen, the evidence is that the nations with the best records of fine-tuning macroeconomic policy are also those with the most highly refined social institutions and the least fear of altering market-dictated outcomes in labor markets and social areas. By contrast, American policymakers have shunned labor-market interventions, distrusted unions, resisted income distribution — and made a unique mess of macroeconomic policy, too! As the experience with European labor-brokering suggests, good macroeconomics and decent social policy are complements, not alternatives.

In researching the effect of technology on the polarization of work, I was curious about whether the phenomenon applied equally to Western Europe. A Swedish trade union researcher was puzzled by the question. "How could occupational shifts widen income inequality?" she wondered. "We have a solidarity wage policy." A deliberate national policy of equalizing wages across occupations is one way of making transitions into new occupations less damaging to social equality. Such a policy doesn't spring full blown from the brows of policy technicians. It requires strong and broadly representative unions, both as constituents and as brokers. Unemployment is a problem in much of the industrial West, but dual labor markets are far less a problem in countries with effective labor movements, political commitments to egalitarian outcomes, and institutions competent to produce such outcomes.

In a period of rapid technological change and accelerating global competition, effective mediating institutions become all the more necessary. With more of the economy's goods being produced by fewer workers, we are clearly becoming a service society. But that phrase can mean many things. The kind of service society that results is ultimately a political choice. It can mean a society in which wealth is highly concentrated, and the owners of wealth create demand for lots of service employees — waiters, designers, hairdressers, psychoanalysts, salesclerks, plastic surgeons.

Or it can mean a service society in which wealth and income are broadly spread, working time is reduced as fewer workers are required in production, and the latent demand for human services is translated into economic demand. But that requires social interventions to equalize wages across industries, to progressively reduce working time, and to create more service jobs in the human services where private demand seldom equals social need: teaching school, caring for the elderly, aiding the handicapped, working in the arts.

One can glimpse the elements of this kind of social bargain from what we have seen in Northern Europe. It includes: wage moderation, especially in industries vulnerable to global competition; wage equalization among industries, so that sectoral shifts do not translate into wage losses for individuals and institutional losses for the union movement; industry acceptance of unions as constructive bargaining partners; progressive shortening of working time as a strategy of spreading available work; full employment, so that workers displaced by technical advances have someplace to go; a trade-union commitment to flexible work rules and job definitions; and the creation of new jobs through public spending. Full employment is a far better defense of workers' real interests than defensive work rules that obstruct technological gains.

As we have also seen, the American political economy is currently ill-suited to such a social bargain. It is a case of "If we had ham, we could have ham-and-eggs, if we had eggs." Clearly, each piece of this model depends on the others. Unions would dearly love to trade more shop-floor flexibility for a nonaggression pact with industry. But flexible work rules are self-defeating if the result is easier layoffs and union busting. Conversely, management acceptance of unions and labor solidarity doesn't work when certain unions demand wage gains that outrun productivity. Worker mobility requires full employment and wage equalization, or it just equals downward mobility. Increased productivity and shorter working time requires a complementary social commitment to maintain purchasing power and generate new job opportunities.

Short Time or Short Shrift

Consider the experience of the West Coast longshoremen. Harry Bridges, who was president of the International Longshoremen's and Warehousemen's Union (ILWU) from 1937 to 1977, was among the first labor leaders to bargain explicitly with management on the consequences of automation. For this he was hailed as a great labor statesman. As automation came to the West Coast docks, Bridges's main concern was to protect his existing members. In 1960, Bridges and the shippers negotiated the following agreement: The shipping companies would be free to automate, but ILWU members would not be laid off. The wages of longshoremen holding "A" cards would rise with productivity, while the number of longshoremen would gradually be reduced by attrition. Bridges liked to say, "At this rate, by the year 2000 there will be one longshoreman left on the West Coast. But he's going to be the best paid son of a bitch in the United States." As Bridges was quick to recognize, the deal was fine for ILWU members holding "A" cards, but not so good for the work force as a whole.

Shortening working time as industry becomes more productive is the right idea; but in the absence of a broader social commitment to find good jobs for new members of the labor force, automation buyoffs degenerate into extreme dualism — nice jobs for those who are grandfathered and diminishing jobs for newcomers. Harry Bridges, at least, made his separate peace with automation at a time when the larger economy was booming. It didn't matter that dockwork ceased to be a major source of new good jobs. Other work filled the social need for decent jobs. Technological unemployment as a broad social ill was staved off for a generation by very high growth and by the bargaining strength of other unions. Today, however, unemployment is high and unions in general are substantially weaker. We see the same symptoms of economic dualism in the concession bargaining being forced upon other unions.

Unionized airline pilots, autoworkers, machinists, and bus drivers are all under pressure to cut their wages. High unemployment and slow growth contribute to this bargaining climate; deregulation accelerates the trend. At this writing, the union representing Greyhound Bus drivers has just persuaded the company to accept a 7.4 percent wage *cut* rather than the 10 percent cut that was first demanded, and the union counts itself lucky. Greyhound drivers still earn nearly double the average wage. Pilots and autoworkers, in order to protect their privileged status, are abandoning broader solidarity goals, even at the enterprise level, and allowing management to hire new workers at much lower wages. This fosters yet another form of dualism, in which older workers have privileges at the expense of younger ones.

The relationship of deregulation to union busting is intriguing. Deregulation encourages new companies in industries that were previously sheltered by regulation of routes and rates. The new firms are typically nonunion companies, with much lower labor costs. Higher-cost established companies can't compete. They must lower their wage bill or go out of business. However, the origin of labor's deregulation predicament is not deregulation itself, but the fact that the workers in the new enterprises are unorganized. In much of Europe, this problem would not exist, for the workers in the new firm would also be union members and its wage costs would be comparable. Union shops could not use the lower wage costs of nonunion competitors as a rationale to undermine their own unions or their established wage structures. But American unions made the mistake of relying on cozy relationships with oligopolistic industries for their wage gains, rather than pursuing a strategy of broader labor solidarity. They kept piling up wage gains, while other workers remained unorganized. In an era of low growth and high unemployment, that failure returns to haunt unionism.

Japan, interestingly, is the other major industrial power with the same sort of dual labor market. The well-publicized Japanese workers in industrial giants who enjoy lifetime job guarantees represent only about one third of Japan's labor force. The "give" in the system is Japan's large and unpublicized secondary labor force, which suffers from lower wages and job insecurity. Even so, Japan's overall wage structure is more egalitarian than ours, and there is a greater commitment to job retraining when a worker is displaced.

What does it mean that Japan and the United States — the highest growth and lowest growth countries — both have dual labor markets, while Europe, which falls somewhere in between, has more highly developed social bargaining? Only that different social models for accommodating economic transition are possible. A nation can rely on imperfect market institutions to broker labor-market shifts, as America and Japan do; or a nation can devise imperfect social institutions to broker the changes and allocate the costs and benefits of transition somewhat more fairly. Either approach is compatible with relatively high or relatively low growth rates overall. The choice is political.

Spreading Work, Creating Jobs

The last time American society systematically attempted to reduce working time was in the 1930s, when social security legislation was passed. One objective was to protect the living standards of the nonrich elderly. But a key goal was to make it economically possible for older citizens to leave the work force, in order to open up jobs for younger workers. The New Deal also reduced the standard work week through wages-and-hours legislation. But there has been very little reduction of working time since then. On the contrary, the work week has stabilized at 40 hours, and the percentage of total population in the labor force has increased.

Rather than waste over $20 billion a year paying unemployment compensation, one could imagine a variety of devices to shorten working time and spread available work. Although millions of workers are involuntarily unemployed, millions more are working longer hours than they wish. The two obvious categories are people near retirement age and working parents. It should be possible to extend the social security retirement concept and have either the state or a prepaid supplemental retirement scheme partially compensate people who voluntarily drop to a 20-hour work week at age sixty. This would be good social policy — it would temper the sudden shift from full-time work to no work at all, which is typical of U.S. retirement. It would open new jobs to younger workers. Sweden has had such a program since 1973. Workers who drop to part time after age 60 collect a partial pension equal to 65 percent of the income lost by working reduced hours. When you add the paycheck to the partial pension, a "partial pensioner" takes home 85–90 percent of his or her previous full-time wage.

The French government has recently adopted an experimental similar program called "solidarity contracts." The Labor Ministry has a budget allotment that can be used to subsidize early retirement plans, which are negotiated enterprise by enterprise. If some workers choose to take early retirement or to drop to shorter working hours, the cost will be shared by the enterprise, the state pension system, and the Labor Ministry.

A second category of "overemployed" people is working parents. A family allowance might permit parents to drop to half-time work for nearly full-time pay, for a total of three years for each child up to, say, two children. This would also be good social policy. It would make it economically feasible for both parents to spend more time with young children. And it would be another means of reducing unemployment by spreading around available work.

Social Bargaining and American Labor

America is a long way from the Northern European societies in which trade unions enjoy broad legitimacy and, in turn, are engaged in positive-sum social brokering. Yet there are common needs that could bring us closer to that sort of unionism. I recently interviewed a trade unionist from one of the locals representing General Electric. GE is a company that would just as soon be rid of unions. It has embarked on a program of rapid automation, and it is shifting a good deal of human labor to its nonunion plants in the South. My union friend described the company's plans to weaken unionism, and then just as meticulously described how the union, in defense of the remaining jobs, systematically limits output. The union, he confessed, could probably improve productivity by 40 percent without half trying.

The GE situation is typical of industrial America. It cries out for some constructive social bargaining — not just "quality-of-work-life" programs, but an explicit bargain in which unions work to improve productivity, and companies stop trying to achieve a "union-free environment," as the National Association of Manufacturers calls its union-busting project. A few good model projects of industry-union collaboration that produced positive-sum gains could have a substantial demonstration effect.

Such projects also require government involvement, for they require resources beyond those available to one union or one company. Even if unions agree to labor-saving changes in work rules, the labor that is saved needs someplace to go. Given the weak condition of American unionism and the current offensive by management to rid enterprises of unions, it is hard to imagine a resurgence of the labor movement without the intervention of government. That, of course, is what happened in the 1930s, when John L. Lewis and the CIO used friendly labor legislation to sign up workers with the slogan, "President Roosevelt wants you to join the union."

The American labor movement will either regroup and adapt, or it will become a kind of relic, which is seen as antithetical both to economic progress and to fairness. The paradox — and in the mid-1980s it seems almost insuperable — is that labor must first become more powerful before it can become more statesmanlike. "Class solidarity" seems an outmoded and quite un-American idea. But the American model of pragmatic, nonideological unionism has proven very vulnerable to economic downturns. Recessions serve to remind skeptics that wage earners who are not independently wealthy, regardless of the color of their collars, really do share powerful common interests that are difficult to advance without a powerful, cohesive labor movement. The image of a labor movement as merely a constituency for wage increases is much too narrow. Strong labor movements are far more important as constituencies for positive efficiency/equality gains.

A friendly national administration could use tripartite social bargaining to breathe new life into the labor movement and encourage a less adversarial, more constructive form of industrial relations. However, the kind of labor solidarity that ultimately permits labor restraint does not begin in Washington but in the labor movement itself. It thrives in a benign political climate, but it cannot be created by governments. It is significant that the most successful of Europe's social democratic parties were invented by labor movements — not vice versa.

> It should be the policy of governments . . . never to lay such taxes as will inevitably fall on capital; since by so doing, they impair the funds for the maintenance of labour, and thereby diminish the future production of the country.
>
> — David Ricardo,
> *On the Principles of Political Economy and Taxation*

5

TAXES

IT IS AN ARTICLE OF FAITH to the laissez-faire mind that high taxes are bad for economic growth. If heavy taxation is used as the instrument of egalitarian policies, productive investment declines; once again, equality is the enemy of efficiency. To the extent that taxes are necessary at all, one especially should shun taxation of capital and of the income from capital — for that depresses the incentive to accumulate and reinvest wealth. So said David Ricardo, and so say Ronald Reagan, Margaret Thatcher, Milton Friedman, and George Gilder.

It therefore becomes awkward for modern conservatives to explain why the industrial nations with the highest postwar growth rates include several with relatively heavy tax burdens and more redistributive social policies. Even more surprising, from the perspective of classical economics, the two worst performers, the United States and the United Kingdom, place relatively low tax burdens on capital; while the top two performers, Japan and West Germany, have the highest and second highest reliance on capital taxes, respectively. Japan, with fairly low tax rates overall, nonetheless has the highest corporate tax revenues of any industrial nation — about 5 percent of GNP — and moderately high taxes on investment income.

A detailed comparison of the specific tax systems of different countries soon resolves the paradox. Germany and Japan enjoy high savings rates and low real capital costs for industry. They save much of their GNP and they have institutions very efficient at channeling savings to productive investment. As we saw in Chapter 2, German and Japanese industrial investment is financed substantially with cheap, debt capital. Thus, despite high rates of taxation on capital, real after-tax costs of capital for German and Japanese industry are low. Just as important, their capital costs are highly *stable*. German interest rates hardly fluctuate. In Britain and America, even with all our tax concessions, real capital costs are much higher, and they fluctuate wildly, which makes long-term corporate planning and investment more perilous. Because German and Japanese taxes on capital are higher but more efficiently structured, they don't seem to impair productive capital formation; so the tax collector can take a relatively bigger cut without undermining the dynamism of the economic system.

Germany, in particular, has a relatively simple tax code with few loopholes. Investment decisions are motivated more by real economic considerations and less by the search for tax shelter. In Germany, tax preferences equal less than 10 percent of tax collections. In the United States, tax preferences (loopholes) on individual and corporate income taxes now equal about 87 percent of tax collections. That is, the tax base that we forgo through loopholes is almost as large as the one we tax. Thus we Americans (and the British) have tax systems with more liberal tax preferences, but substantially higher nominal tax rates. These two characteristics go together; the many loopholes require that the remaining tax base be taxed at a high rate. This is fine for the investor who finds a shelter but not so good for the investor who pays the full official rate. Not surprisingly, extensive effort in Britain and America goes into finding tax shelter. The system is "efficient" for the shelter industry, not for the economy.

Conceivably, selective tax subsidies could be the instrument of economic planning. One could imagine a tax system with carefully targeted tax preferences designed to lower the cost of capital for particular key industries. That, as it turns out, describes the Japanese system, where MITI's priorities largely determine which industries enjoy temporary tax relief. But in the United States, the multiple tax loopholes do not reflect a coherent program to target investment to the most productive uses; rather, they reflect which business lobby had the most influence in Congress in a given legislative year. Many, if not most, of the preferences, in fact, steer capital into uses that nobody could defend as productive.

This characteristic of the British and American tax systems — high nominal rates and almost random distribution of costly tax preferences — was compounded by the Thatcher and Reagan tax programs. The post-1978 changes in British and American tax law provide a useful lesson in how inequity and inefficiency can be mutually reinforcing. Since it is owners of substantial wealth who benefit disproportionately from tax preferences on capital, it follows that such preferences make the tax system less egalitarian. Even worse, the particular tax preferences wrought by Reagan and Thatcher also managed to aggravate the distortion of capital investment, at a cost to economic efficiency.

It is understandable why the resurgence of laissez-faire economics, with taxation as the special villain, had particular appeal in Britain and America. First, our economies had bogged down. Both countries suffered not only slower growth rates than continental Europe and Japan throughout the postwar period, but also steeper-than-average declines in economic performance after 1973. Second, in both Britain and America effective tax rates on the nonwealthy during the 1970s rose substantially faster than the overall tax burden. For example, between 1969 and 1980, individual income taxes in the United States rose 37 percent, only one point more than GNP. But they rose more steeply on the middle class than on the rich. "Bracket creep" effectively increased the income tax burden of middle-class wage earners, who were pushed into ever-higher tax brackets by inflation. (An individual already in the top bracket stays there, no matter what the rate of inflation.) Between 1953 and 1974, direct taxes paid by the average-income family doubled, from 11.8 percent of income to 23.4 percent of income, while the tax burden of a family with four times the average income went from 20.2 percent to 29.5 percent, an increase of less than half. Between 1969 and 1980, social security taxes increased by 92 percent. And since social security taxes apply to only the first $35,700 of wages, the major portion of this increase was on the nonwealthy. During the same period, corporate income tax collections fell 14 percent, and capital gains rates were cut by 20 percent.

A good way of appreciating the excessive taxation of British and American wage earners is to compare the total tax load with the tax burden on an average production worker, in different nations. In 1974, the total U.S. tax level was 27.5 percent of gross domestic product, placing the United States 14th out of 17 major industrial nations. Only Switzerland, Japan, and Australia had lower overall tax levels. But the United States ranked 8th highest in the tax burden on an average production worker. In the same way, Britain's overall tax level placed it 10th of the 17 nations, but the tax load on an average production worker was 5th.

This comparison actually understates the regressivity of the American system, for in most of Europe the average citizen gets more back from the government for his taxes through free health care and generous family allowances. In eight European countries, family allowances add at least 6 percent to the wage income of the average household. In France, Italy, Austria, and Belgium, family allowances increase wage income by over 9 percent. American taxes also went heavily to finance military outlays that return no tangible economic benefit to the consumer. Thus, the average American taxpayer paid more and got back less than his counterparts elsewhere.

Politically, the shift of the tax burden onto the average British and American taxpayer led to a perverse ideological windfall for laissez-faire economics. In reality, Britain's *total* tax level was below average for industrial countries and America's was near the bottom; also, both nations had little growth of public spending during the 1970s. However the increasingly regressive *distribution* of taxes led ordinary British and American taxpayers to conclude that tax levels must have been soaring at a time when economic growth was stagnating. The heavy tax burden on *ordinary people* reinforced the illusion that taxes had killed growth.

Ironically, too, though the laissez-faire ideology was effectively marketed to ordinary nonwealthy voters as a remedy for burdensome taxes, wage earners in both countries ended up with an even bigger share of the tax load after enactment of the Reagan and Thatcher programs. Thus, an increase in tax inequity helped serve the conservative crusade against the egalitarian welfare state.

Contrary to the conservative view, however, low levels of taxation, maldistribution of tax burdens, and restraint of public spending were not the keys to economic performance during the past decade. If

Government Spending and Gross Domestic Product, 1973–1979

Country	Annual Growth Rate of Government Spending as Percentage of GDP, 1973–81	Government Spending as Percentage of GDP, 1981	Average Annual Growth Rate, 1973–81
Japan	6.6	34.0	3.2
Italy	4.2	50.8	3.0
France	3.3	48.9	2.8
Germany	2.3	49.3	2.4
United Kingdom	1.8	47.3	1.6
United States	1.6	35.4	2.6

Source: Author's calculations, using OECD data.

anything, the opposite held true. As the chart shows, the three large industrial countries with the best growth rates, Japan, Italy, and France, had the most rapid growth of public spending. Britain, with slow public-sector growth, was the worst performer. The United States had below-average public-sector growth, and about average economic growth.

TAXES IN THE UNITED STATES

The American tax system, pre-Reagan, consumed a lower fraction of total GNP than in any other large industrial country save Japan. America had the slowest rate of public-sector growth of any nation, including Japan. Before the Reagan revolution, our tax system was hardly punitive to the rich. Though the nominal rate schedule of the personal income tax was steeply graduated, the progressivity was largely undermined by the extensive tax preferences. For the well-to-do, capital gains were taxed at preferential rates as well. For low-income people, regressive sales taxes and social security taxes added up to surprisingly high rates. Taking the tax system as a whole, despite nominal elements of progressivity, the effective tax burden was roughly proportional to income for about 80 percent of the population. That is, it scarcely redistributed income at all.

In the debates about tax policy during the 1970s, the taxation of capital and of income from capital posed the sharpest equity and efficiency issues. Tax reformers looked at the taxation of capital and saw wide loopholes that rendered the whole tax system less progressive. Business groups looked at the same tax provisions and saw deterrents to productive investment. Both, as it turned out, were right. The system was inequitable *and* inefficient. And the remedy worsened the malady.

Capital Gains

The biggest tax preference benefiting the wealthy is the tax treatment of capital gains. Until 1978, half of "realized" capital gains (e.g., the gain on the sale of a stock) was exempted from taxation. "Unrealized" capital gains (the increase in the value of a stock that is held) were not subject to tax at all. For business groups worried about capital formation, this was plainly inefficient; tax-avoidance strategy locked the investor into his current portfolio, while more deserving uses of capital went begging. If you keep your moldering shares of AT&T, you never have to pay tax on your capital gain, no matter how high their paper value rises. Sell them to invest in something else, and you are socked with a big capital-gains tax. The system invited tax-free accumulation of wealth in a manner that gummed up the free flow of investment capital.

But people nonetheless sold stock; and when they did, the IRS taxed only 50 percent of the capital gain. For tax reformers, the 50 percent exclusion of capital gains was a long-standing target, since it sheltered a substantial portion of the income of the wealthy from taxation and allowed many wealthy people to enjoy tax rates lower than those of wage earners. For a high-income earner in the 40 percent income-tax bracket, capital gains were effectively taxed at only 20 percent — less than the income-tax rate of a factory worker. The capital-gains preference is heavily skewed to the very wealthy. This year, it will save taxpayers about $26 billion, with about 60 percent of the savings going to taxpayers with more than $100,000 of reported income.

During the early 1970s, tax-reform advocates attempted to repeal the 50 percent capital-gains preference. They failed. However, in 1976, the high-watermark year for tax reform, they did succeed (temporarily), in reforming the capital-gains treatment of *inherited* stocks and bonds. Under the old law, if grandson inherited a stock from grandfather, the IRS generously ignored all the appreciation that occurred during grandfather's lifetime. If grandfather bought some IBM at $20 a share and left it to grandson when it was trading at $100, grandson could sell it at, say, $101 and pay tax on only a dollar of gain. The increase in value during grandfather's lifetime was tax free. This represented a huge loophole that enabled substantial inherited wealth to avoid taxation. It cost the Treasury about $5 billion a year, nearly all of it in forgone taxes on people who could well afford to pay.

In the 1976 tax reform legislation, Congress provided that the original acquisition price of the stock would carry over after it was inherited. The tax-reform lobby had closed a $5 billion loophole and made the tax system more equitable. It was a notable victory, and reformers began planning their assault on the 50 percent capital-gains preference itself. But their timing proved disastrous.

During the 1970s, inflation had distorted the effect of taxes on capital investment. Through most of the seventies, the inflation rate was high and the stock market was in the doldrums. An investor who had purchased a stock for $100 in 1973 and sold it for $150 in 1979 was outperforming the Dow Jones average; but inflation rendered his nominal 50 percent gain a real economic loss. The IRS, however, did not recognize the inflationary loss, only the nominal gain. So a tax was levied on a $50 gain that was really a loss. Even the 50 percent exclusion only partly compensated for the inflation penalty.

In this climate, talk of repealing the capital-gains exclusion understandably horrified the business groups, who geared up for an all-out defense of the existing law. By the end of 1978, the legislative mood had so changed that not only did the old law escape unscathed, but Congress increased the exclusion from 50 percent to 60 percent, repealed the 1976 reform on inherited gains before it even took effect, and lowered the top marginal rate on wage and salary income from 70 percent to 50 percent. Further liberalizations in the 1981 Reagan legislation reduced the maximum capital-gains tax to just 20 percent of the gain.

Of all the tax cuts enacted since 1978, reduction of the capital-gains tax was seemingly the most defensible from an efficiency perspective, for inflation clearly had made the capital-gains tax more punitive than Congress had intended. But the remedy did not really solve the problem, and instead gave windfalls to investors who didn't deserve them.

If the problem is the impact of inflation on nominal capital gains, then the solution is to exclude the portion of the gain that represents inflation. But Congress's actual remedy — a bigger exclusion and a cut in effective *rates* — lowered capital-gains taxes on all investors, those hurt by inflation and those not. It is also the case that many capital assets are held for only a relatively short time, say, one year, and the effect of inflation on the erosion of the capital value is minimal. Now that inflation has subsided, the wealthy legally avoid taxes on most capital gains, and the Treasury is out some $50 billion a year.

Moreover, Congress might have cut capital-gains taxes selectively, to encourage capital to flow to productive uses. But in response to the massive lobbying campaign, Congress ordered *all* capital-gains taxes cut — on sales of houses and land, and on speculative investments in gold, jewelry, and antiques. The seller of a house (or of commercial real estate) who enjoyed a windfall created only by the inflationary market of the seventies, gained yet another windfall not of his own making through the tax cut.

In the debates over capital-gains liberalization, proponents claimed that lowering capital-gains rates would have a marvelous "unlocking" effect: Owners of stock who had been sitting on appreciated shares for fear of paying capital-gains taxes could suddenly become active investors, supplying capital to optimal uses, such as genuine risk taking. Capital markets would benefit, and the whole economy would gain from the improved investment flows. Martin Feldstein, who later became President Reagan's chief economist, predicted, in the fashion of Arthur Laffer, that a cut in capital-gains tax rates would actually increase tax collections, because it would lead to so much more buying and selling of shares.

Opponents responded that a rate cut would perhaps lead to a one-time selling off of old shares, but that afterwards investors would simply buy and sell stocks according to their usual economic calculations — with the difference that they would now enjoy more after-tax wealth. The opponents were right. Stock sales rose in 1979, the first full year of the big capital-gains tax cut, but declined in 1980, despite a 17 percent increase in the New York Stock Exchange index.

Dividends and Interest

A second aspect of the American tax system that seemingly punishes productive investment is the taxation of income from capital, namely, dividends and interest. Conservatives have long complained that capital income in the United States is taxed twice. If you earn a thousand dollars and place it in a savings account, you pay income tax on the earnings and you pay tax again on the interest. Dividend income is also taxed twice, in a different sense. Corporations pay corporate income tax on their total profits; then the individual owner of a share pays tax again when the same corporate profit becomes part of his taxable personal income, as dividends.

Some countries selectively exempt interest income from taxation, in order to promote personal savings (see Chapter 2). But as we have seen, this is seldom an efficient way of increasing net savings. Moreover, the double-taxation argument is unconvincing as it applies to interest on savings, for there is also double taxation of income that is not saved: A wage earner pays income tax on his paycheck, and the earnings are taxed a second time through the sales tax when they are spent. If he invests his savings in a home rather than in the bank, he will be taxed again through the property tax.

The double-taxation argument has more merit when it is applied to the corporate income tax. It is true that in order to give an investor in, say, the 30 percent bracket a real after-tax return of 7 percent, a corporation must earn a profit of nearly 20 percent. Here is the arithmetic: Corporate profits are taxed at 46 percent (46 percent, in theory; effective rates are below 20 percent, thanks to loopholes). A before-tax profit of $1000 equals an after-tax profit of only $540. If this is all paid out to shareholders as dividends, then it will be taxed again as personal income, at, say, 30 percent. That reduces the $540 further, to $378. Presumably, this system depresses the return on invested capital, and thus reduces the incentive to invest. This, in turn, depresses capital values, and thus the stock market. There is also a more subtle harm done to economic efficiency, because an incentive is created for corporations to retain their earnings, in which case they are taxed only once. Capital markets would operate more efficiently if corporations passed along all of their profits to shareholders, and then had to compete in the market for new investment capital, rather than relying on retained earnings.

Here again, however, the most efficient remedy is not the least egalitarian one. The best solution to the double-taxation problem is to integrate the corporate and personal income tax. There are several basic ways to accomplish this, which have been used by different countries.* Since holdings of stock are highly concentrated among upper-income people, most ways of eliminating double taxation lower tax rates on rich people and make the tax system less progressive. Yet a bargain that repealed inefficient tax preferences and at the same time moderated double taxation of profits could improve both equity and efficiency. Germany, which gives individual shareholders a credit for taxes on profits already paid by the corporation, nonetheless manages to have a more progressive tax system overall. One approach, so-called full integration, would simply regard all corporate profits as belonging to their shareholders, who would be taxed accordingly, as if the corporation were a partnership. The corporate income tax would be eliminated, except as a withholding device, and all shareholders would be taxed according to their overall tax bracket. This would make the corporate income tax more progressive and would increase pressure to pay out dividends. Although this approach is probably the fairest and most efficient solution to the double-taxation problem, there is little enthusiasm for it in business circles.

---

*The methods include: (1) a tax credit or exclusion for shareholders based on the tax already paid by the corporation; (2) a reduction in the corporation's tax liability for dividends paid out; (3) a split-rate corporate tax, with paid-out dividends taxed at a lower rate; (4) a "full-integration" system, in which all corporate profits are taxed as if they had been passed along to the shareholders. See Joseph Pechman, *Federal Tax Policy*, pp. 170–79.

Inflation and the Corporate Income Tax

In the 1970s, the same inflation rates that distorted the taxation of capital gains played havoc with the taxation of corporate profits. As machinery and equipment wear out, companies may take a tax deduction that supposedly equals the economic loss. That is, if a steel mill has a useful life of ten years, under a straight line depreciation accounting system, the company deducts from its taxable income one tenth of the mill's original cost each year. But in an inflationary economy, its "value" is hard to set. A mill that cost $100 million in 1975 may cost $500 million to replace in 1985. Therefore, the annual deduction of only $10 million (based on 1975 prices) understates the true economic loss to the corporation as the mill wears out.

Just as the solution to inflated capital gains is a bookkeeping adjustment for inflation, the solution to understated depreciation is a formula that takes inflation into account. It is possible for accounting systems to be based on replacement costs. But the business lobbies in the late 1970s pressed instead for wholesale liberalization of depreciation formulas. Congress was persuaded to abandon the idea that depreciation deductions should have any connection to the true useful life of a physical asset. Although a different approach was available, which would have given a company an annual write-off equal to the real decrease in a machine's value, business groups convinced Congress and the Reagan administration to accept an accelerated depreciation formula known as the "Accelerated Cost-Recovery System," which was little more than a disguised repeal of most of the corporate income tax.

The Accelerated Cost-Recovery System eventually became part of Reagan's 1981 tax act. Under ACRS, instead of depreciating plant, machinery, and equipment as it actually wears out, corporations use arbitrary "cost-recovery periods": 15 years for most structures, 5 years for most machinery, 3 years for cars, light trucks, and research-and-development equipment.

This change in depreciation formulas had both equity and efficiency consequences. It provided massive tax write-offs for business — far in excess of any shift needed to offset inflation. Thanks to the new deductions, corporate tax collections were projected to drop by half a *trillion* dollars by 1989, and at an accelerating rate. Corporate income taxes accounted for about 23.4 percent of federal tax revenues in 1960. By 1970, this had fallen to 13.5 percent. By 1981 the corporate tax share was down to 10.2 percent and was projected to drop further, to just 7.1 percent by 1987. Expressed another way, corporate taxes fell from 6.5 percent of GNP in 1951 to 4.2 percent of GNP in 1966, to 2.7 percent of GNP in 1975 to 1.7 percent of GNP in the mid-1980s. The effective tax rate on corporate profits has declined from 49 percent in the early 1950s to about 35 percent before the Reagan tax program took effect, to below 20 percent in the mid-1980s. In fiscal year 1981, before the new tax law took effect, the corporate income tax produced $61 billion of revenue. In FY 1983, corporate tax revenues declined to $35 billion, the lowest level in real dollars since 1942, when the economy was one fourth its present size.

Conservatives like to argue that since corporations are fictitious creatures, corporate taxes eventually must fall on consumers anyway. But most economists believe that a substantial share of corporate taxes fall on corporate stockholders, who are mainly well-to-do. To the extent that taxes on the wealthy are cut, either others must pay that share, or government services must be cut accordingly.

The supply-side rationale for corporate tax cuts contends that the reduction in taxes so stimulates productive investment that it more than makes up for any loss. But if anything, the efficiency consequences of the 1981 ACRS were even less defensible than the equity effects. If one wanted to slash corporate income taxes, an across-the-board cut in rates would have been far better than what the business lobbies convinced Congress to do.

Before the ACRS system was adopted, there was not a huge variation in the effective tax rates on different industries. In the 1960s, the effective tax rate on returns from investment in different industries varied between a low of 25 percent and a high of 34 percent. With ACRS, average effective tax rates on different types of new investment vary from a high of nearly 50 percent to a low of *minus* 194 percent. The depressed auto industry is one that seemingly might deserve special subsidy; yet under the vagaries of ACRS, new investment in autos is taxed at an effective rate of 47.7 percent, while investment in crude oil — currently glutted — is taxed at just 2.3

percent and the paper and wood products industry enjoys a negative tax rate of 14.2 percent.

A negative tax rate simply means that the tax write-off on an investment is so lucrative that the after-tax rate of profit exceeds the before-tax rate — a company has more shelter than tax and can apply the shelter against other profits. Under ACRS, nearly all investments in assets with a useful life of less than five years are taxed at a negative rate. Thus the ACRS system arbitrarily distorts the flow of investment capital, which must have efficiency costs.

Ironically, on the eve of the Reagan tax changes, a 1981 Federal Reserve Board study, *Tax Policy and Capital Formation,* found that the *prior* tax treatment of capital distorted investment patterns:

> While finding that the overall rate of capital formation is probably adequate, this study concludes that the existing capital stock is misallocated, probably seriously, among sectors of the economy and types of capital, primarily because of distortions caused by inflation and U.S. tax laws. . . . As a result capital is not applied to its most efficient uses. . . . The cost to the nation has been lessened productivity growth and reduced business output.

The effect of the 1981 Act was to worsen the distortion.

The 1981 depreciation changes produced such windfall write-offs that many corporations found that they had sheltered all of their profits and still had some unused tax shelter to spare. This led to a new form of paper entrepreneurship, known as "tax leasing."

Tax Leasing

The 1981 tax act permitted companies with excess tax shelter to create a fictitious lease of property, as a way of selling the shelter to other companies. In this manner, many companies added to their net profits by selling tax shelter, while other companies reduced their tax liabilities by buying it. For example, General Electric, with $1.6-billion profit in 1981, bought enough tax breaks to avoid any taxes and managed to get a $100-million refund on previous taxes. On the other side of the ledger, LTV Corporation, with profits of $504 million, sold $100-million worth of tax losses. The biggest buyer of tax losses was the petroleum industry. In the auto industry, money-losing Ford and Chrysler sold paper tax losses, while profitable GM was a net buyer. The outcry (and the revenue loss) was so great, that tax leasing was repealed by Congress in 1982. Had it stayed on the books, it would have cost the Treasury an estimated $80 billion a year by decade's end.

Real Estate

The 1981 changes in the tax code also created a bonanza for tax-sheltered real estate. Since the Revenue Code of 1946, which permitted accelerated depreciation, tax shelter has been an important ingredient of real-estate development. As in the case of an industrial machine, tax law permits the owner of a building to deduct a fraction of the building's capital value each year on the assumption that it is wearing out. But in the case of real estate, the building's actual value is typically *going up*. This creates an immense tax shelter, because the paper loss may be deducted from other taxable income. Although a portion of the excess deductions are "recaptured" by the IRS when a property is sold, the excess depreciation is taxed at capital-gains rates rather than at ordinary income rates.

Tax considerations are so central to real-estate development that the owner of a commercial property typically does extremely well even if he loses money on the property's rental income. The combination of tax deductions, substantial "leverage" (tax deductions may be taken even on capital borrowed from the bank), and the anticipation of capital appreciation more than makes up for the lack of profit from rental income. For example, let's assume that the owner of a $1,000,000 building has an $800,000 mortgage at 12 percent interest. The interest ($96,000 a year) is tax deductible; depreciation provides another $66,666 a year in tax write-offs. If the owner is in the 40 percent income tax bracket, the cash value of those deductions is $55,066, which can offset rental income; and the capital appreciation is taxed (at a lower rate) only when the property is sold.

Tax-sheltered treatment for real estate was originally justified as a kind of disguised subsidy for housing. In the 1960s, when the government was willing to offer rent supplements and subsidized mortgages to private developers of low-income housing, the combination of direct subsidies and tax subsidies enabled developers to make substantial profits, without risking much, if any, of their own money. Over a million such housing units were built. But as it turned out, this system was an invitation for developers to build shoddy apartment buildings. In the early 1970s, with default rates on privately built, publicly subsidized apartment projects soaring, President Richard Nixon temporarily suspended the subsidy program. When Congress rewrote federal housing legislation in 1974, much of the direct subsidy was gone but the tax shelter remained. Developers successfully resisted an attempt in 1976 to limit their ability to use artificial depreciation losses on one building as tax deductions against other income. By 1981, commercial real estate received virtually the same preferential tax treatment as rental property.

In the 1981 tax legislation, the combination of lower capital-gains rates and more liberal depreciation formulas substantially increased the tax-shelter value of real estate. It is now possible to depreciate a building with a true useful life of 50+ years in just 15 years, and to take the bulk of the deductions in the first six years.

This tax advantage has caused money to pour into real estate. Under one popular device, the limited partnership, a developer sells ("syndicates") shares in a project to absent partners who are usually individuals seeking to shelter high wage and salary income, such as doctors or lawyers. The typical tax shelter syndication deal allows them to recover about twice their cash investment in about 5–6 years through avoided taxes. For example, if a doctor with a $150,000 income would otherwise pay $70,000 in federal income taxes, an investment of $200,000 in a real-estate tax shelter might buy $100,000 a year in tax write-offs, which would reduce his taxable income to $50,000, and his tax liability to perhaps $15,000. Thus, over a five-year period, a $200,000 investment more than pays for itself. The effective "return" is 40 percent a year.

Tax-shelter syndications were common even in the 1960s, mainly to build housing. But since the 1981 tax revisions, the big boom has been in commercial office buildings. Nonluxury rental housing is a riskier economic enterprise, especially in the absence of direct government subsidies. If the same tax shelter is available on commercial properties, most profit-motivated developers will choose the office building. Since 1981, investment in rental housing has been flat, while tax-sheltered syndication deals for commercial development have set new records. According to data filed with the Securities and Exchange Commission, investment in publicly marketed real-estate syndications increased from $1.6 billion in 1981, to $2.5 billion in 1982, to $3.4 billion in the first nine months of 1983 — and this during a period when industrial investment actually declined.

What is wrong with this subsidy? In the first place, capital is a scarce commodity. If tax policy steers capital into the development of office buildings, there is less capital for other uses; or other users of capital must pay higher costs. In the entire debate about productivity and capital supply, it was never claimed that the United States was falling behind its industrial competitors because of an insufficient supply of office buildings and shopping malls! A piece of commercial real estate is an investment sheltered from the global competitive economy. Indeed, if one were considering candidates for subsidy, one might identify rental residential housing and competitive manufacturing industry as deserving cases, but it would be hard to make a special case for commercial office buildings.

Second, there is a good deal of evidence that too much tax-shelter partnership money is chasing a limited number of suitable properties. For many prospective limited partners, the perfect tax-shelter investment is an existing, prime office building that is fully tenanted. An established building is less risky than a new one. The result is that existing buildings are suddenly more valuable because of their tax-shelter possibilities. This does not add to the supply of buildings, but raises prices of existing ones. Under recent changes in the tax law, it is also possible for tax-deferred IRAs to invest in real estate, which further bids up its market price.

A 1983 report by the influential Real Estate Research Corporation warned, "Because deals are now layered in complex ways that segment ownership and tax benefits among disparate investors, individual partners can end up having attractive tax shelter from projects that actually don't make very good economic sense . . ." The report added that the flood of tax-shelter money pouring into real estate was a classic case of too much money chasing too little product.

Exaggerated shelter often steers capital into projects that would be unlikely to raise capital on purely economic grounds. In 1983, the brokerage house Bear, Stearns set the record for tax shelters when it purchased a subsidiary of Metromedia that owned 45,000 billboards, which were then offered as a $450-million tax shelter to investors.

Moreover, in tax-sheltered real-estate deals, it is common for the syndicators, accountants, and tax lawyers putting together the deal to skim off 25–30 percent of the total investment. That is, of the capital raised, only 70–75 percent goes into the actual building. This represents complete economic waste, of the sort usually attributed to *public* bureaucracies. When we add it all up, this form of real-estate tax shelter lowers the tax liability of the most affluent members of society (inequity), by steering their investment dollars into uses that the market otherwise would not dictate (inefficiency.)

The Parable of the Racquetball Club

A very posh racquetball club near my home is a good metaphor for the whole problem. The club is located in an old brick building, once a nineteenth-century mill, which has been renovated handsomely by a developer. As a building over 40 years old, the mill qualified under the 1981 tax amendments for a tax credit equal to 25 percent of the renovation costs. That is, the developer gets a cash subsidy from the government equal to one fourth of his costs. In addition, the developer depreciates his investment under an accelerated formula that gives him artificial tax losses to offset other income or to syndicate for cash. No expense was spared in renovating the building. The developer has tastefully rebuilt the interior with exposed brick, brass, hardwoods, and sleek glass. Luxury commercial tenants occupy the upper floors, while the racquetball club is off the lobby. Club membership fees are surprisingly low. Or rather, their low price is not surprising at all, since it reflects a substantial subsidy by other taxpayers. Arguably, this subsidy helped to turn the wheels of commerce; it got an old building restored, and the club members are beneficiaries only incidentally. (Arguably, I am the Queen of Rumania.)

Consider the distributive effects. Here is an affluent clientele enjoying a reduced rate on a luxury facility, thanks to subsidies in the tax code. The same tax preferences also serve to lower the taxes paid by other affluent people, in their role as investors. For symmetry, one could even imagine an investor joining his own club — and reaping subsidy both ways, as he polished his backhand. Imagine the outcry if Congress directly appropriated cash subsidies for members of racquetball clubs.

Further, consider the contrast between this luxury club and the ragged condition of public recreation facilities for the nonrich. In economic terms, if our luxury club were instead developed as a town recreation center built with public dollars it would produce the same physical asset, the same construction jobs, the same contribution to GNP, and the same stimulus to aggregate demand. In theory, public projects have bureaucratic overhead costs that are a drag on economic efficiency; but as we have seen, a private tax-shelter syndication deal wastes 25–30 percent in overhead. As a society, we are disinvesting in public recreation facilities, because we lack the tax dollars. But in one real sense we lack the tax dollars because they have been spent subsidizing the private clubs. We don't even build YMCAs, because land costs have been bid up, and nonprofit organizations can't play the tax-shelter game as effectively as for-profits, and the after-tax cost of capital thus is lower for for-profits than for nonprofits. Thus, ordinary people who need the recreational facilities lack the purchasing power to *join* the private clubs. Ordinary wage earners who need the tax relief lack the capital to *invest* in the tax-sheltered clubs.

Thus the rich get both the subsidized club and the tax relief, while the poor get neither. It would be no less efficient — and far more equitable — for government to close the loopholes, keep the tax revenues, and spend the same subsidy building gyms for the nonrich. The illusion that subsidizing the rich is more "efficient" is purely an artifact of the present tax code. Whom to subsidize, if anyone, is nothing but a political choice. Subsidies that flow from tax preferences often have extreme distributive bias, but the bias is rarely made explicit or addressed as a conscious policy choice.

Death and Taxes

None of the industrial democracies, not even Sweden, has high levels of taxation on wealth (as opposed to income). In the United States, the main form of wealth taxation is the property tax. In the nineteenth century, many states applied the property tax to stocks, bonds, bank accounts, farm animals, and even household furniture. Today, however, such "intangible" property wealth is exempt, and the property tax is mainly a tax on real estate.

A property tax, in theory, could be a progressive tax, since wealthy people tend to be the owners of lavish property wealth. But in fact, the nonwealthy tend to spend a higher portion of their earnings on housing, which makes the property tax effectively regressive. Moreover, because the property tax is collected locally, poor communities with relatively low per-capita property wealth are forced to tax themselves at a higher rate in order to obtain comparable per-capita revenues for public services. So the property tax is doubly regressive.

A few countries attempt to tax wealth directly. Sweden levies a tax on net worth, but the top rate is 2.5 percent, and little effective redistribution is accomplished. The main form of wealth taxation employed by most nations is the taxation of large inheritances. Interestingly, however, the vast bulk of inherited wealth escapes taxation in every single industrial democracy.

As we have seen, there are scant efficiency grounds for exempting large inheritances from taxation. Unless one imagines that the desire to amass wealth is whetted by the pleasing prospect of one's heirs spending it, there is little reason to believe that death duties depress personal incentive. Yet despite stiff nominal rates of tax on large inherited fortunes, no industrial democracy succeeds in taxing them at more than token rates. In a tax system riddled with loopholes, estate taxation has the most loopholes of all — loopholes that have no justification in either economic theory or tax theory. A cynic might suspect the political influence of the very wealthy.

In recent years, American tax law has taxed large inheritances at nominal rates as high as 77 percent. Yet nobody with the wit to hire an accountant need have his bequests taxed at even a fourth of that. The array of generation-skipping trusts, *in vivos* gifts, private foundations, and the other devices of tax avoidance are such that great fortunes may be passed along with a minimum of taxation.

In 1979, on the eve of the Reagan presidency, George Cooper, a Columbia University law professor expert in the dark arts of estate planning, wrote a learned and wry book titled *A Voluntary Tax?* From case studies of tax-avoidance devices used by the very rich, Professor Cooper concluded that it was easy to reduce effective tax rates on inherited wealth to the range of 5–10 percent. Punning on the usual cliché, Cooper observed, "It may be that the real certainties of this world are death and tax *avoidance.*"

In that year, only about 1.7 percent of all estates were paying any tax at all, and estate and gift taxes were accounting for about one percent of federal revenues. Nonetheless, at about the same time, the capital-formation crusaders began demanding relief from burdensome inheritance taxes. In a well-orchestrated lobbying stunt, a legitimate concern of small family businesses and family farms was made the stalking horse for a larger assault on the inheritance tax. For the proprietor of a family farm, there was a real worry that inheritance taxes levied against the inflated cash value of a farm might be so burdensome that the farm would have to be sold to pay the taxes. A farmer might not be able to pass the farmstead along to his sons and daughters.

Out of solicitude for the family farmer, Congress eventually rent a much broader hole in the larger inheritance tax, never a very watertight fabric in the first place. Besides giving special treatment to small family businesses and farms, Congress raised the exemption and lowered tax rates on *all* inheritances. When the new tax law is fully effective in 1986, only 0.3 percent of estates will be subject to tax. Professor Cooper might remove his question mark; the estate tax is now a truly voluntary tax.

No country taxes inherited wealth at very high rates; but surprisingly, the country with the highest effective rates turns out to be Japan. The Japanese government gets about 2.7 percent of its revenues from estate taxes; the rate schedule is low, but there are few avoidance devices. Japanese tax law solves the farm problem neatly by exempting bona fide family farms from estate taxation, while at the same time taking a dim view of tax-shelter farmers.

Proponents of more effective taxation of inherited wealth bump up against the political influence of that wealth. In his 1964 lectures, published as *Efficiency, Equality and the Ownership of Property,* the English economist Sir James Meade compared three alternative mechanisms for the realization of a broadly egalitarian society: trade unions, income transfers, and wide diffusion of property. The first approach, a "Trade Union State," Meade argued, is relatively inefficient because it will be inflationary; strong unions will use their power to bargain for excessive wage increases. (As an Englishman, Meade doubtless had in mind British trade unions — probably the world's most self-interested and fractious; he never raises incomes policy as a positive-sum social bargain.) Meade's second ideal type, a redistributive welfare state, he warned, also incurs efficiency costs: "a really substantial equalization of individual incomes" through taxes and subsidies would require a steeply progressive tax system, "and such highly progressive income taxation is bound to affect adversely incentives to work, save, innovate, and take risks."

Meade's solution — and it is a very attractive one — is what he calls "a Property-Owning Democracy." For Meade, the most efficient and inherently superior way of promoting equality is to broadly diffuse property wealth. It is an ideal most consistent with the tradition of Lockean liberalism — a tradition that makes American egalitarians suspicious of state-engineered redistribution. Meade wrote:

> Extreme inequalities in the ownership of property are in my view undesirable quite apart from any inequalities of income which they may imply. A man with much property has great bargaining strength and a sense of security, independence, and freedom . . . He can snap his fingers at those on whom he must rely for income; for he can always rely for a time on his capital. The propertyless man must continuously and without interruption acquire his income by working for an employer or by qualifying to receive it from a public authority. An unequal distribution of property means an unequal distribution of power and status even if it is prevented from causing too unequal a distribution of income.

Meade's notion of the good society, then, is one where public policy seeks to broadly diffuse wealth. This is admirable enough, and he is surely correct in saying that a more equal distribution of property relieves the pressure on trade unions, taxes, and income transfers as the agents of *re*distribution. If every citizen is a property owner, then citizenship has the sturdiness of Jefferson's yeoman peasantry. Unlike Milton Friedman, however, Meade doesn't believe that laissez-faire will bring us back to an egalitarian form of democratic capitalism in the bye and bye, for wealth tends to concentrate. He sees a role for redistribution here and now, but of property rather than income.

Central to Meade's scheme is a reform of inheritance taxation. As an economist, Meade argues (correctly) that inheritance taxes are less destructive of the incentive to earn and accumulate than income taxes. You can't take it with you. As a technician, Meade then goes on to describe the mechanics of reforming Britain's system of estate and gift taxation, which is as loophole-ridden as America's.

The trouble, of course, is what Meade himself observed earlier in his own argument: *An unequal distribution of property means an unequal distribution of power.* Society's wealthiest, who can be induced to go along with all manner of paternalist safety net schemes, can be counted upon to resist mightily when the redistributive state goes after them where they live. As long as very rich people have the wit to hire lawyers, there will be big loopholes in estate taxation. And as long as there are big loopholes in estate taxation, there will be very rich people.

The Bottom Line

The Reagan tax and spending program took from society's poorest and gave to society's richest. When the cuts in social programs, the shifts in the tax burden, the reductions in corporate and capital-gains taxes, and the increase in payroll taxes are all added together, here is the result:

In 1983, the combined effect of inflation, social security tax increases, and personal tax cuts added up to an exceptionally good deal for the well-off. Taxpayers with incomes over $200,000 enjoyed a 16 percent tax cut. Taxpayers earning over $100,000 got a 12 percent tax cut. Taxpayers with income of $50–100,000 got a 5 percent cut, while taxpayers earning $30–50,000 saved just 2 percent. With less than $30,000 of income, you broke even or lost. Taxpayers in the $10–15,000 range ended up with 5 percent tax increases, and taxpayers earning less than $10,000 had a 21 percent tax hike.

On the spending side of the equation, about 60 percent of the savings in the Reagan budget fell on the poor; the average family with income of less than $10,000 lost $360 in government benefits. According to the Congressional Budget Office, in fiscal year 1985 the disparities will be even greater. Taking the combined effects of tax changes and spending changes, households with income over $80,000 will gain an average of $8930. Households with $10,000–$20,000 will lose an average of $60. Households with $10,000 or less will lose $440.

Unmistakably, equality was sacrificed for the sake of efficiency. But consider this: The total impact of the Reagan tax cuts on capital lowered the effective cost of capital to American industry by an estimated 1.2 percent. Unfortunately, the Laffer curve did not work as advertised. Lower tax rates did not produce more tax revenues. They produced deficits. The unprecedented peacetime deficits prompted fears of renewed inflation, which in turn caused the Federal Reserve Board to clamp down on the money supply. During 1981 and 1982, tight money raised real interest rates (the difference between nominal rate and the rate of inflation) to crushing levels of 7–9 percent. In short, the tax subsidies more than canceled themselves out. The deficit-driven increase in interest rates far exceeded the value of the tax cut. Industry would surely be better served by lower real capital costs, even if the price were higher taxes.

When the long-awaited economic recovery began in mid-1983, it had an oddly Keynesian flavor. All during 1982, the supply-side incentives did not cause business to invest, because there was slack demand for their products. No matter what the tax benefits, businessmen do not increase investment when existing plant is operating at 60 percent of capacity and customers are not buying. Finally, in mid-1983, as the Federal Reserve Board allowed real interest rates to fall, demand picked back up. It was fueled mainly by the huge $200-billion federal deficit. The deficit would have been no less stimulative had the tax breaks gone to the poor rather than the rich. The deficit would have contributed not one whit less to aggregate demand had it been the result of government social spending rather than the private consumption of the well-off. So steep was the supply-side recession that only in late 1983 did national output return to 1981 levels.

BRITISH TAXES

Much of the Reagan tax program was anticipated by the British tax system: Not just by Mrs. Thatcher's post-1979 blend of tax cuts for the rich and welfare cuts for the poor, but by Britain's long-standing policy of levying high taxes on wages and giving substantial tax shelter to unproductive wealth.

In this century, Britain has consistently had the lowest rate of economic growth of any major industrial nation. Although conservatives are quick to ascribe the British disease to trade unionism and the welfare state, British slow growth long antedates the postwar era of social entitlements. As the first industrial nation, Britain's industry matured — and stagnated — early. British dominance of manufacturing was already losing ground to Germany, France, Japan, and the United States in the late nineteenth century. As we have seen, British stagnation was severe, even in the booming 1920s. Between

1960 and 1973, Britain's economic performance was somewhat improved, but, even so, Britain gained less from the postwar boom than any of her major competitors.

The explanation for the British malaise varies with the ideological hue of the explainer. Britain's overall tax burden is not a particularly plausible culprit, for it is below average. Many left-wing critics blame instead British financiers' long-standing habit of exporting capital abroad rather than developing dynamic manufacturing industry at home. As the economist and Labour M.P. Stuart Holland observes, British manufacturers are renowned at locating manufacturing plants overseas. Holland calculates that British overseas industrial production is 215 percent of domestic British industrial exports, compared with 38 percent in Japan and 37 percent in West Germany. Nicholas Kaldor, a leader of the Cambridge school of economics, likes to remind his Tory colleagues that during the early twentieth century, British capital exports were as high as 10 percent of GNP, while net investment in domestic industry was zero, at a time when effective income-tax rates were 3 percent. Low taxes are no miracle ingredient for industrial dynamism.

Another favorite candidate to explain Britain's poor performance is the traditional low social esteem of "trade" as a profession unsuitable for gentlemen — surely a problem that long antedates the welfare state. In a conservative variant of the argument that Britain is hostile to business, Robert Bacon and Walter Eltis contend that too much of the British economy takes either the form of public services or nationalized industries, neither of which generates profits. The absence of profits, in turn, leads both to a shortage of investment capital and, in more human terms, to a feeble entrepreneurial culture. But other nations with bigger public sectors manage somehow to have far more profitable industry.

Britain has particular difficulty translating savings into productive investment. Even during the 1960s and early 1970s, when personal savings rates were steadily rising, investment in domestic productive industry was falling. As domestic and foreign markets for British manufactured goods eroded, the problem worsened. British capital investment per employed worker is now below half the level of Germany, Sweden, France, Japan, or the United States. Investment per worker began to increase only after Britain idled 12 percent of her labor force — not a very good solution.

The roots of the British disease are surely multiple; but the contemporary British tax system deserves special attention; Britain supports its welfare state on a very regressive tax system. As Britain's most astute tax critics, John Kay and Mervyn King, observe in their classic, *The British Tax System,*

> There is justice both in the left-wing criticism of the [British] tax structure for its failure to shake concentrations of wealth and privilege, and in the right-wing criticism that it deprives people of the returns of effort and initiative. The present system has given us the worst of both worlds, with maximal disincentive effect for minimal redistributive impact.

As Kay and King suggest, the British tax system tends to punish productive economic activity, at both the top and bottom of the income-distribution ladder. For the wealthy, wage and salary income is taxed at high nominal rates; but tax avoidance is easy and it tends to reward speculative and unproductive investment. For the poor, who are heavily dependent on the social wage, the "poverty trap" problem is extreme; as earnings rise, transfer income is reduced, more than pound for pound. In effect, wages are taxed at a marginal rate as high as 287 percent. In other words, a breadwinner loses £2.87 in higher taxes and lost social benefits for every additional £1.00 of earned income.

Taxation and the Poverty Trap

The distinguishing characteristic of British taxation is an income tax with a very high "basic rate," of 30 percent. Wage earners begin paying that steep rate of tax when they earn as little as £48 a week. In addition, they pay another 9 percent in social security payroll deductions, for a total tax rate of 39 percent. Additional payroll taxes cease when income reaches £235 a week, at which point the marginal tax rate drops back to 30 percent. So a professional or executive earning, say, £300 a week (about $475) actually pays a far lower marginal tax rate than a low-wage manual worker. Only at about the 90th percentile of income do marginal tax rates begin rising again.

The poverty trap only exaggerates the disparity. It results from the interaction between means-tested social benefits, which fall as wages rise, and a tax system that taxes the working poor at 39 percent. As a breadwinner's income rises, family allowances, income supplements, rental assistance, free school meals, property tax relief, et cetera, all begin phasing out. With a weekly wage of £60, a married man with two children pays net taxes of about £9 a week, and is entitled to social benefits adding another £49 a week, for a total net income of £100. A coworker can earn double the gross pay, £120 a week, but will pay higher income tax and collect almost no means-tested benefits. His take-home pay after taxes and benefits will be about £104. Thus, when we factor in the loss of social benefits, an increase in gross earnings from £60 to £120 will be "taxed" at a marginal rate of about 93 percent — far higher than the tax rate on the highest paid millionaire. The disincentive against seeking promotion, or working longer hours, is almost total.

For the millionaire, however, there is a proliferation of tax preferences available to reduce his effective tax on earned income far below the top nominal rate of 60 percent. Prior to Thatcher, marginal tax rates on investment income were nominally as high as 98 percent. But as Kay and King observed, "Anyone who paid an effective rate on his investment income of anything resembling 98 percent should have sought competent advice."

Most, of course, did just that. According to British Treasury data, rare is the wealthy Briton who pays even 40 percent on his investment income. And unfortunately for British productivity, most of the tax preferences available to the wealthy steer capital to nonproductive sectors of the economy. Thus, the problem is a more extreme version of our own: The same tax subsidies that reduce tax fairness also diminish the efficiency of capital investment.

A basic strategy for tax avoidance is to convert income to capital gains by investing it, since the top capital-gains rate is only 30 percent. But the easiest source of a capital gain is an investment in real estate or in a bond with a low coupon rate, rather than in Britain's depressed industry. Contrast, for example, the tax treatment of a real estate investment with the purchase of shares of common stock. If you buy a piece of property, the main anticipated benefits are the prospect of a capital gain plus tax shelter that can be used to reduce other taxable income. In the case of the common stock, the main reward is current earnings, which are fully taxed.

Sheltering Inefficiency

Wealthy people in Britain are also able to shelter their wealth in a bewildering array of trusts and other tax-sheltered investment schemes. Farmland enjoys special tax treatment. So does life-insurance savings: the Inland Revenue reduces a taxpayer's income-tax liability by up to 17.5 percent of premiums paid.

As in America, residential housing is a major tax shelter. Interest on mortgage loans up to £25,000 is tax deductible. Inflation has eroded the value of this deduction, but it is relatively more valuable than in the United States, because interest on other consumer borrowing is not tax deductible. Not surprisingly, housing prices have been bid up for their value as both an inflation hedge and a tax shelter. Though the percentage of the British population owning their own homes has been stable at about 50–55 percent for decades, more and more net wealth is held in real estate. Mortgage debt has increased as a share of net personal wealth from 19 percent in 1957 to nearly 40 percent in the late 1970s. During the same period, the share of wealth held in common stocks fell from 22 percent to 10 percent.

The British government also provides exceptional tax advantages to persuade the public to buy government bonds. Persons over 55 are entitled to buy inflation-indexed bonds, which are guaranteed a rate of return in terms of real purchasing power. Small savers are offered a variety of tax-exempt bond plans. The big institutional investors, life insurance companies and pension funds, are also heavy buyers of government bonds, which are less risky than industrial investments. Moreover, the government designs steeply discounted bonds with low current yields, to attract wealthy investors seeking to convert current income into tax-sheltered capital gains. Thus the government conspires in tax avoidance, as it outbids more productive uses for capital investment.

"Tax Exhaustion"

The system of accelerated depreciation of corporate investments, the centerpiece of the 1981 Reagan tax package, is actually a British import, dating to 1973. British tax treatment of corporate investment provides a convenient ten-year experiment in the value of such deductions. The results lend little support to the supply-side school.

In 1973, as inflation rates took off, British corporations found themselves in a serious tax squeeze owing to the effect of inflation on their accounting systems. Much as in America in the late 1970s, this concern was parlayed into a wholesale assault on the corporate income tax. The Tory government, then under Prime Minister Edward Heath, first devised a tax-relief scheme to discount the inflationary increase in the taxable value of inventories and later invented what is still the world's most liberal system of accelerated depreciation. Since 1974, British corporations have been permitted to deduct from their taxable profits the entire cost of a capital investment in a single year. As a result, according to the International Monetary Fund, Britain has the lowest effective taxation of capital of any major nation.

The result has not been what the government hoped. The main effects have been to distort patterns of corporate investment and to eliminate the corporate income tax as a major revenue source. The corporate share of British government revenues has declined from about 9 percent in the late 1960s to just 3 percent today. In recent years, dozens of large and highly profitable British corporations have paid no corporate income tax, including British Ford, Rio Tinto Zinc, Courtaulds, Allied Breweries, the Imperial Group, Dunlap, and British Esso.

This tax subsidy has *not* stimulated capital investment. The ratio of industrial investment to gross national product has declined; the decline accelerated after 1979 as unemployment rose. However Britain's one-year tax write-off law did lead to massive investment in the skills of accountants. One side effect was the creation of a leasing industry, allowing banks with high taxable profits to hold title to a piece of industrial machinery on behalf of a company that has already written off all its tax liability. This device allows the bank to reduce its own taxes and to pass along some of the savings to the customer. No new investment is created by this maneuver, just lower taxes for the bank and for other high-profit industries. Depreciation write-offs reduce the nominal corporation tax rate of 52 percent to about 15 percent, and even less for most banks.

A new, unintentionally ironic term has crept into British corporate accounting jargon: *tax exhaustion*. It means that a business has exhausted all of its tax liability — it pays no taxes — but still has paper write-offs that it can't use. According to the London *Economist,* the accumulated value of unused tax write-offs now exceeds £30 billion. Tax leasing has permitted banks to soak up some unused tax subsidy, but if the British government were to allow companies to buy and sell tax benefits (as American law did for one year in 1981), it would eliminate the corporate income tax entirely.

The result of this perverse system is that effective tax rates on different kinds of investments vary wildly, with no relationship to their true economic utility. *The Economist* calculates that a pre-tax return of 10 percent can have an after-tax return of as little as 1.7 percent or as much as 25 percent, depending on the source of the funds, the tax bracket of the investor, and whether it qualifies for a one-year write-off. Entrepreneurial energy that could go into real enterprise goes into the manipulation of paper. When effective tax rates are very high, they may indeed depress incentives. But when they are low, lowering them further accomplishes little. "Tax exhaustion" not only exhausts revenue; it exhausts the value of the incentive.

At this writing, the Thatcher government is weighing a proposal to go back to a system based on true economic depreciation.

Thatcherism

The Thatcher government, beginning in 1979, anticipated the Reagan program in some respects, but not in others. Both Reagan and Thatcher subscribe to the capital-supply doctrine that lower taxes on the well-off are necessary for capital formation. In her first budget, Mrs. Thatcher reduced the top nominal tax rate on personal income from 83 percent to 60 percent. To compensate for the revenue loss and to reward saving over consumption, the basic rate of the value-added tax (VAT) was increased from 8 percent to 15 percent; the policy of applying a higher VAT rate to luxury goods was abolished, making the VAT that much more regressive. Payroll deductions for social security (also regressive) rose from 6.5 percent to 9 percent.

Despite a slight reduction in the overall ratio of taxes to income the effective tax burden on the average worker rose from 44 percent to 48 percent. Taxes were cut for the rich, while social benefits were cut for the poor. According to the British Institute of Fiscal Studies, a typical executive earning £45,000 got a tax cut worth £6000 a year, while an average worker lost over £750, in higher taxes and lower benefits, or 21.5 percent of his real income.

In that respect, the parallel between the Thatcher and the Reagan programs is almost exact. But unlike President Reagan, Prime Minister Thatcher takes seriously her rhetoric about monetarism and balanced budgets. Although the Reagan administration in its first year promised balanced budgets and appointed monetarists to key policy positions, Reagan was nimble enough to jettison both tight money and budgetary balance when they got in the way of a recovery.

British monetarism, however, led to an obsession with one technical indicator of the money supply, called sterling M3. Efforts to reduce the growth of British money supply, so defined, led to a policy of tighter and tighter money, which made Britain's recession longer and deeper than any other nation's. Tight money and high interest rates made British exports that much less competitive. Even the temporary windfall of North Sea oil revenues was converted from a blessing into a curse, because the resulting balance-of-payments surplus overvalued the pound still further. Unlike Mr. Reagan, whose huge deficit at least stimulated a Keynesian recovery, Mrs. Thatcher remained doggedly committed to budget balance. The British deficit was held to about 3 percent of GNP, less than half the U.S. level.

By 1983, Thatcher, like Reagan, could point to an impressive decline in the rate of inflation, but it was the most Pyrrhic of victories. British unemployment was over 13 percent — the highest rate of any major nation. Since the Industrial Revolution, Britain had always exported manufactures to pay for imports of raw materials. By 1981, Britain was a net importer of industrial goods.

Thatcher's policy of tight money, fiscal austerity, wage discipline, and reverse redistribution produced a vicious circle of unprecedented economic contraction. Gross domestic product fell 7½ percent in two years; manufacturing output dropped 20 percent. Although recession eventually took the steam out of inflation, in Thatcher's first year inflation was superheated by high interest rates and consumption taxes, causing prices to rise by 21 percent. The drop in British industrial output from the end of 1979 to the end of 1980 was the most abrupt one-year decline in modern British history — a one-year fall in manufacturing output of fully 15 percent. This compares with the worst year of the Great Depression, 1930–31, when industrial production declined by 6.9 percent, and the worst single year of the nineteenth century, 1878–79, when it fell by 5.5 percent.

Despite the supply-side incentives, investment capital did not flow into British industry, because demand had gone flat. The world's most liberal tax incentives on investment could not alter that, nor could a redistribution of the personal tax burden from rich to poor.

WEST GERMAN TAXES

The tax system in West Germany offers a striking contrast to those in Britain and the United States. To begin with, the public sector in West Germany is slightly larger than in Britain and substantially larger than in the United States. In 1980, German taxes consumed 42.8 percent of GDP, compared to 40.4 percent in the United Kingdom and 32.7 percent in the United States.

But despite this higher overall tax burden, Germany has also enjoyed a higher rate of economic growth and a far lower rate of inflation, both before and after the 1973 oil shock. Germany's growth rate averaged 4.5 percent between 1960 and 1973, compared to 4.1 percent in the United States and 2.8 percent in Britain. Even between 1974 and 1980, Germany's growth rate averaged 2.4 percent, far better than that of either Britain or the United States. Germany's unemployment rate was effectively zero throughout the 1960s and early 1970s, at a time when U.S. unemployment was above 5 percent. Until the 1981–83 recession, German unemployment remained below 3.7 percent. German inflation has also been well below that of other industrial nations, averaging just 4.3 percent between 1965 and 1981. After the first oil shock, German inflation briefly peaked at 7 percent, but soon settled back to the 3–5 percent range. In the great stagflation of the late 1970s, German unemployment *and* inflation both stayed well below British and American levels, confounding the Phillips curve.

Simpler Taxes

Given the usual conservative claims about low taxes and high capital formation, it is intriguing that West Germany has reconciled a robust economic performance not just with high taxes, but with high taxes *on capital*. As we have seen, several factors are at work: a monetary policy aimed at keeping interest rates low and stable; a system of industrial relations that trades labor influence for labor peace; and a system of industrial finance that relies heavily on debt capital. But the German tax system is also worth a close look.

West Germany has a moderately progressive income tax, which provides about 38 percent of total revenue; corporate income taxes provide about 5 percent — midway between the British and American share. But social security taxes provide 35 percent, much higher than in Britain or the United States — and corporations pay the preponderance. (Employer contributions now equal about 20 percent of total revenues. Professor Jack Wiseman suggests that the high *fixed* corporate taxes on payrolls and the relatively low *variable* taxes on corporate profits serve to reward the most efficient producers.) Value-added taxes and other consumption taxes account for another 25 percent — about the same as in Britain but, again, much higher than in the United States. German tax law rewards consumer saving and discourages consumer borrowing; Germany taxes investment income at lower nominal rates but offers far fewer loopholes that stimulate unproductive entrepreneurship in tax evasion. West Germany, in short, comes closer to what tax-reformers keep advocating (in vain) for the United States: a tax system with lower rates, fewer loopholes, and less distortion. The result is a fiscal system that accomplishes more redistribution at less pain to economic efficiency than in Britain or America. Taken as a whole, the final distribution of income in West Germany is slightly more nearly equal than Britain's and substantially more nearly equal than America's. The egalitarian outcomes are accomplished first by full employment and high wages and second by generous entitlement programs. The tax system by itself is not the principal source of redistribution.

West German Corporate Taxation

Since 1953, West Germany has taxed corporate profits at a "split rate" — initially, profits distributed to shareholders were taxed at 15 percent, while retained earnings were taxed at 51 percent. The value of a split rate is that it encourages corporations to distribute their profits, which presumably makes capital markets operate more efficiently. In 1977, this approach was further refined. Under the present "imputation system," the corporation pays a tax of 36 percent on behalf of the shareholder. The shareholder is then permitted to offset a portion of that tax against his personal income-tax liability. Thus, shareholders pay a relatively low rate of tax on their dividend income. Corporations, however, now pay a higher nominal rate on profits that they retain, 56 percent compared to 46 percent in the United States. In practice, this 56 percent tax on retained profits is reduced somewhat by a variety of selective tax incentives. Most of these are carefully targeted tax subsidies to promote investment in particular industries or regions, such as West Berlin or the areas along the East German frontier. All told, these subsidies added up to about 10 billion DM, in 1980, or only about $4 billion — so the effective corporate tax rate is higher in West Germany.

This form of selective tax subsidy, however, differs markedly from its British and American counterparts, which tend to be broadly gauged measures that reward investment indiscriminately and sometimes perversely. The American investment tax credit is a flat credit against the corporate income tax, no matter whether the investment is a piece of advanced capital equipment or a redecoration of the executive suite, no matter where the investment or what the industry. The investment tax credit will cost American taxpayers $29.1 billion a year in 1985. There is no such credit in German tax law.

Similarly, while Britain and America have extremely liberal depreciation allowances that bear scant relationship to the actual wearing-out of capital goods, West Germany has no accelerated depreciation. In fact, German tax law stipulates that corporations must treat depreciation for tax purposes exactly as they treat it in their internal accounting. In Britain, 100 percent of the cost of a new investment may be deducted from taxable income in the first year. In Germany, where depreciation formulas closely correspond to economic depreciation, the first-year deduction averages about 25 percent.

The results are no tax subsidy for capital investment and no tax-shelter–motivated distortion of the economically efficient pattern of investment. Scholarly comparisons of the taxation of capital in different nations have consistently reported that West Germany has a much steeper effective tax rate than the two worst performers, the United States and Britain. A 1981 study by an International Monetary Fund economist found that in the United States and Britain most industrial investment had what amounted to a negative tax rate, i.e., a subsidy. An investment earned a higher profit after taxes than before taxes. Germany, like Japan, had a positive tax. A somewhat more comprehensive 1983 study, made by economists Don Fullerton and Mervyn King under the auspices of the National Bureau of Economic Research, compared the taxation of capital investments in the United States, Britain, Sweden, and Germany and reached the same conclusion.

In the study Fullerton and King took into account inflation, nominal tax rates, tax credits, and depreciation formulas. They found that the effective marginal tax rate on new industrial investment was 48 percent in Germany, 37 percent in the United States (before the Reagan program), 36 percent in Sweden, and just 4 percent in Britain. Looking only at investment in new machinery, which looms so large in the supply-side view of the sources of productivity growth, Britain's effective tax rate is minus 37 percent, Sweden's is effectively zero, the U.S. rate is a positive 18 percent, and the effective tax in Germany is a stiff 45 percent. Contrasting the gap between the effective tax rates on industrial investment and the effective personal income tax rates, King and Fullerton noted that the effective rate on investment in Britain is a full 40 percentage points below the average marginal personal tax rate; while in Germany it is actually several points above the personal rate.

Professor Fullerton, incidentally, is a strong exponent of taxing consumption, on the ground that the gain to growth outweighs the loss to equity. Professor King is also a consumption tax advocate and a well-known critic of the effects of inflation on capital taxation. Both men are otherwise sympathetic to the view that light taxation of capital is beneficial for economic growth. They conclude:

> The results are surprising to say the least. If we rank the countries by their average annual growth of GDP, we obtain exactly the same order as when we rank by effective tax rates. Germany has the highest overall effective tax on income from capital *and* the highest growth rate. The U.S. is second in both categories and Sweden is third. The U.K. has the lowest overall effective tax on income from capital *and* the lowest growth rate.

What are we to make of this? It appears that high taxation of capital is just the ticket to stimulate capital formation! This result *is* surprising. It is possible, King and Fullerton aver, that perhaps the slow-growth countries have "reacted to their slow growth by providing more investment incentives." But that doesn't really wash, for Britain's ultraliberal depreciation formulas have been on the books for ten years, and things keep getting worse. Even before the Reagan amendments, the United States had the world's second most liberal tax incentives, and they didn't seem to help.

The reality, I suspect, is that other real economic factors matter a good deal more than tax levels. If the customers are buying, the labor force is productive, and real interest rates are low, industry will invest and pay taxes out of its profits. If not, even negative tax rates won't make much difference in the rate of investment. They will, of course, make a substantial difference in the distribution of a country's overall tax burden.

JAPANESE TAXES

The recent practice of Japan worship by Westerners recalls the tale of the blind men of Hindustan and the elephant. Methinks, say the classical economists, that Japan's secret is a high savings rate and a small public sector. Oh no, reply the industrial policy advocates, Japan's secret is economic planning. Wrong, say the trade unionists; Japan's secret is lifetime employment and economic security for the work force. Wrong again, say the cultural revisionists; Japan's secret is a close-knit, conformist society schooled in paternalism, discipline, and self-denial. It wouldn't work here. You don't really want to sing the company song and sleep on a mat. Do you?

I have sympathy for the revisionist view. But the fact remains that Japan has a prodigiously dynamic economy, with a high rate of net savings and economic growth. To Westerners accustomed to associating the modern idea of equality with a welfare state, a paradox is that Japan apparently manages to combine a relatively small public sector and a pro-business regime, with a broad though somewhat privatized welfare system, an egalitarian income distribution, and an extremely progressive tax code.

I will be the first to agree that culture is a big factor in economic development. Japan's system of corporate paternalism and industrial planning-by-consensus is almost feudal. It has costs to individualism. Its applications for American society are surely limited. Yet Japan above all serves to make the case that different social bargains alter terms of tradeoff between equality and efficiency.

Japanese taxes as a share of GNP are smaller than the OECD average, but not by all that much. If you factor-out military spending, which Japan keeps below one percent of GNP, and if you factor-in Japanese demographics, which allow for a much lighter pension burden, then the Japanese fiscal picture is not all that different from the other advanced industrial nations.

Demography, Taxes, and Welfare

To pursue demographic differences for a moment, the Japanese welfare state is enjoying a brief fiscal free ride, because its population is relatively young. In 1980, only 9 percent of Japan's people were over 65, compared to 14–15 percent in Britain, France, and Germany. Old-age pensions are by far the costliest item for any welfare state. According to the OECD, pensions consume 65–70 percent of all social outlays in the industrial nations. Contrary to popular misconceptions, Japan's national pension system is as generous as any. Japanese "replacement ratios" (the ratio of pensions to wages) are already comparable to those of the most advanced European welfare states. A Japanese who retires — and Japanese may take full retirement at age 60 — will get a pension that equals about 44 percent of his best earning year. But the Japanese population will continue to be younger than the Western average until 1990, at which time Japanese social security taxes will have to rise or the retirement age be postponed, or both. Further, the Japanese pension system only dates to 1961, so it also has the advantage of being actuarially "immature" — that is, the large working populaton pays taxes into it, but pensioners have not been contributing for enough years to draw maximum benefits out of it. The relatively small elderly population also lowers Japan's health-care outlays. In other words, in a few years, Japanese tax levels will be very close to European levels. In the meantime, however, Japan's payroll deductions for social security are lower than average, and its overall tax burden is indeed lower, too.

Breaking the Rules

The supply-side school can take some comfort from Japan's relatively low total tax level. But interestingly, the *composition* of Japanese taxation violates the laissez-faire prescription for economic growth in just about every respect. Japan has high taxes on capital (astronomically high compared to Britain or the United States), low taxes on consumption, steeply progressive taxes on personal income (with generous tax relief for low-income earners), and even fairly high inheritance taxes. And the Japanese economic performance doesn't seem to suffer at all.

Consumption taxes, for example, are very much in vogue. If you tax consumption rather than income, that is supposed to reward saving and punish spending. Many conservative economists are actively promoting either a value-added tax or an expenditure tax as an improvement on the income tax. Taxing consumption, however, also leads to a far more regressive distribution of taxes, since the rich invariably save more than the poor; fair distribution is sacrificed to efficiency.

Or is it? Japan, as we have all read, leads the world in savings rates. But oddly, it has neither value-added taxes nor retail-sales taxes, though it does tax manufacturers' sales of some products. In effect, Japan's taxation of consumption is about tied with the United States for last place in the industrial world. Yet Japan has the highest savings rate and we have the lowest.

Corporate Taxes

Japanese taxation of capital investment would bring tears to the eyes of a classical economist. Corporate income taxes account for about 6 percent of national government revenue in the United States, and just 3 percent in Britain. In Japan, the corporate income taxes account for fully 28 percent — and have consistently accounted for between 26 and 34 percent of central government income every year since 1960. As a result, Japanese corporations pay the world's highest effective tax rate on their profits. Even with Japan's low overall taxation rate, corporate income taxes equal about 5 percent of GNP, the highest of any nation.

Like Germany, Japan uses an imputation system, in which retained profits are taxed at a higher rate (42 percent), distributed dividends are taxed at a lower 32 percent, and the individual shareholder receives a tax credit for taxes already paid by the corporation. In addition to the national corporate income tax, there are also municipal corporate taxes, which can raise the total tax rate for big firms to over 60 percent. Far fewer corporate tax deductions are available than in the United States or Britain, and one sees less paper entrepreneurship motivated by tax avoidance. Effective corporate income tax rates on big companies are said to exceed 40 percent — double the American effective rate. One 1976 study placed the average effective rate at 33.2 percent, and it was criticized as unrealistically low.

According to a comparative study by the Congressional Research Service, when local "enterprise taxes" are added in, the total tax rate on manufacturing in Japan is an incredible 50.5 percent, compared to a total state and local tax rate on comparable manufacturing profits of 27.7 percent in the United States.

As in Germany, allowable tax deductions for depreciation are supposed to reflect true economic depreciation, not serve merely as an artificial tax subsidy. Machinery is typically depreciated over a 10- or 11-year useful life, compared to 3 to 5 years in the United States and one year in Britain. Japan does allow some corporate tax incentives but only to serve narrow, well-defined purposes. For example, the government currently permits accelerated depreciation write-offs for investments in certain energy-saving technology and in pollution control. Companies may transfer a small portion of their profits to tax-free reserves. However, as a general rule, the Japanese system prefers to use direct subsidies that MITI can target and tightly control, rather than broadly diffused subsidy entitlements via the tax code. Interestingly too, while many other nations have been widening tax loopholes intended to stimulate industrial investment, Japan has tightened up its corporate tax system. For example, accelerated depreciation for export industries was abolished in 1972. Ten years ago, selective tax subsidies were far more common. In 1983, corporate tax loopholes cost the Japanese treasury only $1.1 billion, or about 3 percent of corporate tax revenues. In the United States that same year, corporate tax loopholes cost $1.67 for every dollar raised in corporate taxes.

Precise comparisons between Japanese and American effective corporate tax levels are next to impossible, because our systems are so different. Accounting standards differ. And because Japanese corporations rely so much more heavily on debt financing, profits as a percentage of sales are lower to begin with. However, according to the Japanese finance ministry, total revenues from the corporate income tax equaled 9497 billion yen in 1983, nearly half of estimated corporate profits.

Personal Income Taxes

Japan has a personal income tax with a steeply progressive rate, which can be as high as 75 percent. Japanese income taxes, however, do allow substantial personal exemptions and deductions. Taxpayers may elect to have interest and dividend income taxed at a 25 percent rate, even if their total income would otherwise place them in a higher tax bracket. Long-term capital gains, up to a total limit of yearly stock transactions, are not taxed at all. While these systems of preferences for the well-to-do clearly erode the progressivity of the Japanese income tax, the system is even more generous with tax exemptions for the nonrich, which makes the system as a whole substantially more progressive than the British or American. Basic exemptions are sufficiently liberal that the bottom third of the work force pays no income tax at all, while professionals earning the equivalent of $40–50,000 a year typically pay a real rate of about 40 percent. Elaborate American-style personal tax shelters are almost unheard of.

As we observed in Chapter 1, when the public sector is relatively small it is somewhat easier to maintain an effectively progressive tax system. But in the Japanese case, this outcome is also the result of deliberate policy choices. Since the corporate income tax brings in almost as much money as the personal income tax, the pressure is taken off direct taxation of wage earners as a revenue source. When the American public sector was as small as the Japanese is today — before 1974 — our tax system was far less progressive, nonetheless.

Just to complete the Japanese affront to the supply-side school, it is also worth noting that Japan has the world's highest effective inheritance taxes, which last year accounted for 2.7 percent of the Japanese government budget, compared to less than one percent in the United States and the United Kingdom.

The Japanese tax system is highly elastic — that is, one percent of economic growth reaps more than a one percent increase in tax revenues. The Japanese public sector has grown far faster than average during the past twenty years, though it started from a very low base. The tax system is so elastic that the government has been able to expand public programs, maintain something close to budgetary balance, and still have money left over for tax refunds nearly every year.

Japanese Lessons

Japan, like West Germany, combines high effective tax rates on corporate capital with preferential treatment of personal capital investment. Both nations have steeply progressive taxation of personal wage and salary income, which translates into a more effectively progressive tax system. But apparently, the efficiency costs are minimal.

Joseph Pechman of The Brookings Institution and Keimei Kaizuka of Tokyo University observe in their study of Japanese taxes,

> There is no evidence that these relatively high marginal rates have any effect on the working habits of persons who are subject to them. Anybody who observes business life in Japan cannot fail to be impressed by the tempo of hard work that seems characteristic of virtually all members of the economic community.

Pechman and Kaizuka, taking note of the central importance of debt capital in the Japanese economy, add, "Access to credit is much more important to the business innovator than preferential tax treatment, at least in the initial stages of his work."

What is it about Japanese and German taxation that produces positive-sum equality/efficiency gains? I can't prove the case algebraically, but I will venture some educated guesses.

First, in comparison with the American and British, both the German and Japanese systems are more straightforward and produce less distortion in capital flows. When distortions occur, they are deliberate and narrowly targeted. Second, both systems are more consistent. It is more likely that similarly situated taxpayers will have similar tax liabilities. Third, the absence of loopholes, especially in the case of Germany, allows a system that can be effectively progressive without using absurdly steep rates. Very few Germans and Japanese pay real tax rates in excess of 45 percent, but most well-to-do people pay effective rates above 30 percent.

But it would be wrong to conclude from this discussion that we should therefore emulate the details of German or Japanese taxation. For the most important conclusion is that taxation doesn't matter all that much. Public opinion in the United States has been assiduously cultivated to believe that tax rates on capital investment and on rich people in general are a central determinant of economic growth. If this comparison proves anything at all, it proves that they aren't. Tax concessions are vastly overrated.

Political conservatives have focused on tax reduction as an economic growth strategy for three reasons. First, it is self-serving; it saves rich people lots of money. Second, it comports with their ideological allegiance to laissez-faire economics. And third, tax incentives are less intrusive to business-as-usual than any other form of government planning. They are self-executing; a firm decides where to invest and collects its tax subsidy automatically. Unlike direct subsidies or government loans or the other instruments of affirmative planning, tax concessions involve no scrutiny by any government planner other than an occasional IRS audit.

Other nations are less enamored of tax concessions as a primary means of economic development, because they are less ideologically fearful of the other instruments of economic planning. The relative economic dynamism of Germany and Japan, seen in the light of their tax systems, suggests that government can claim a fairly high share of GNP without destroying the economic engine, so long as marginal tax rates are not ridiculously high and so long as the tax system does not inadvertently invite unproductive tax-shelter activity.

Germany seems to prove that the public sector can tax and transfer as much as 45 percent of national income without disrupting personal motivation and economic growth, as long as individual tax rates are not confiscatory. People who are doing well can live with effective personal income tax rates of 40 percent. Japan seems to prove that as long as business is brisk, corporations can coexist with equally high rates of tax. Both countries suggest that if tax concessions for capital formation are necessary at all, it is more sensible to target them very narrowly and to reward personal investment rather than corporate investment. But since both nations rely on debt finance so heavily, personal dividend income is not all that important in any event.

Their tax systems serve to indicate that whatever the secret of Japanese and German success, it isn't low taxes, flat taxes, or tax preferences aimed at capital investment. Far better candidates would be financial systems that engender high savings rates and low capital costs, and social systems that produce a high degree of cohesion and cooperation. As long as the goose has a healthy diet, the tax man can continue collecting a lot of golden eggs.

The pursuit of equality is a mirage. Opportunity means nothing unless it includes the right to be unequal.
— Margaret Thatcher

6

WELFARE

THE EVOLUTION OF THE WELFARE STATE reflects an ongoing conflict between two incompatible systems for distributing income: need and market. Socialism is based on the distributive principle "to each according to his needs." Market capitalism distributes according to wage income and private property — to each according to initiative, inheritance, and luck. The social democratic welfare state that has developed since the 1930s represents an uneasy compromise between the distributive criteria of market economics and those of socialism. Most personal income and nearly all private wealth are still allocated according to market principles. Whatever prizes one can gain from the market system through wage income and property wealth largely determine one's social status and personal well-being. But the modern state tempers the market's extremes in several respects — through taxation, income transfers, and social services. In at least some spheres of human life, the criteria of need and citizen entitlement have substantially replaced the criterion of private means. Thus, in most of Europe, one has a right to medical treatment based on one's medical needs, not one's private purse. In Europe and America, children have a citizen entitlement to public education, even if their parents have not paid a penny in property taxes.

Need, of course, is a very slippery concept. If nothing else, cash-in-hand has the virtue of being unambiguous. When private purchasing power dictates what commodities and services are provided, no other criteria are necessary. The market simply creates supplies of services or goods in response to the demand. But if "need" is the determinant, all sorts of difficult issues arise. Who decides what needs are to be served and according to what standards? Everyone "needs" a nice place to live, but what is a reasonable social minimum? Everyone can benefit from a college education, but how many shall receive one, and at whose expense? Need is also relative. Conservatives never tire of pointing out that America's working "poor," with their televisions, private autos, and Big Macs, would be rich indeed in the America of a century ago, or in much of the world today. But that insight isn't very useful, for a democratic society requires a common political community; and despite its mass consumption our society remains one of vast extremes.

WELFARE AND EFFICIENCY

The idea of having the government provide income support to the "needy" is not an innovation of the welfare state. Ever since the Elizabethan poor laws, governments have made special provision for the destitute. Before the modern welfare state, however, poor-relief typically erected an inferior class of citizenship. Those who sought relief found themselves stigmatized, pauperized, and with fewer rights than others. They flung themselves on the mercy of the state — and wound up in the workhouse. Today's welfare mothers, who are increasingly subjected to investigations and "workfare" requirements, would recognize the dilemma.

In theory at least the welfare state, unlike the English poorhouse, considers the social safety net a right of citizenship, not of pauperism. But the state still looks largely to the market as the engine of growth. Democratic welfare capitalism, therefore, finds itself having to reconcile two irreconcilables: how to provide for special needs without isolating or stigmatizing the needy; and how to assure freedom from want, without excessively encouraging freedom from work or otherwise wrecking the market system. The most "efficient" solution — means-tested public assistance — is in practice inequitable if not iniquitous. Targeting aid to the "truly needy" tends to isolate the poor in separate programs and erodes the political constituency for equality. It creates a welfare-state culture that is not just means-tested, but mean-spirited. But the more equitable solution — broad citizen-entitlement programs — is expensive and in some respects inefficient.

The Ideal of Universalism

Welfare states, particularly those of Northern Europe, have gone a substantial way toward establishing need as a distributive criterion, by providing for certain needs as entitlements of citizenship. Minimum pensions provide a social guarantee against poverty in old age. The state furnishes cash family allowances based on the size of the family. Medical care is made available throughout Western Europe as a citizenship right, for citizens of all ages. Education in most of Europe is free, from primary school through graduate school. None of these benefits requires the recipient to humble himself before the state or to prove dire distress.

The idea is that universal entitlement to these basics is not only decent social policy, but serves to reinforce a sense of community and solidarity. Being treated in the same medical clinic or sending one's children to the same day-care center or school — regardless of one's personal resources — is inherently egalitarian. When the middle class shares basic public services with the poor, the middle class demands high quality and dignified treatment; the middle class is also reminded that poor people are human. Thus does universalism in public services cement the political constituency for egalitarian social policy.

But the welfare state is a kind of sand castle. As the benefits are piled higher, it continuously erodes. As the welfare state becomes larger and more universal, it becomes less redistributive. Admittedly, it redistributes from workers to pensioners and from childless couples to large families and from the healthy to the sick, but when everybody is paying high tax rates to support all of these services, the welfare state doesn't accomplish much redistribution from rich to poor. A basic family allowance that gives everybody a thousand dollars per child is expensive for society, but it fails to eliminate poverty. Beyond a certain point, it is not possible to have both universalism based on citizenship and also redistribution based on need. Moreover, as long as private income and wealth are initially created and distributed by market criteria, the better-off will keep trying to defend their relative status. The welfare state can provide public education, basic pensions, and basic health care, but the well-to-do can use their private resources to purchase private education, private cosmetic surgery, private psychoanalysis, private pension plans. More and more benefits are job-related, which means that the better-off receive better benefits. In most of the West, the "private welfare state" is heavily tax-deductible; so in effect, the public welfare state is subsidizing its own erosion. The dilemma is political as well as fiscal: If the state prohibits private competition for certain basic services, then it stands accused of interfering with personal liberty. But if it encourages privatization of welfare, then the constituency for comprehensive public services steadily erodes.

In sum, the welfare state is always playing catch-up. In the social democratic compromise, the market keeps generating inequalities, and the welfare state keeps trying to compensate after the fact. As one Swedish observer graphically puts it, social policy is the "charwoman [of the capitalist system] who sweeps aside or looks after the human waste that the economic system itself is constantly generating."

Roots of Inefficiency

For conservatives, of course, it is not the market system that causes the waste, but the welfare-state appendage. According to the conservative critique, social welfare is a drag on economic efficiency in two distinct respects. First, it allows people the luxury of not having to provide for their own economic needs; thus, it misallocates resources and breeds improvidence. Second, because politicians pander to electoral majorities, the welfare state grows ineluctably, eventually overburdening the private economy, the ultimate source of real wealth.

A survey of the different models of the welfare state suggests that the conservative claims are at best too sweeping. The argument that socialization of welfare necessarily leads to waste and improvidence is the easier claim to refute. There is very little practical evidence that free medical care or free public education or even social provision of old-age pensions leads to a squandering of the service or a slackening of personal effort. Significant variations of detail reflect the balance of political forces in the design of particular programs. If anything, social democratic Europe rations its education and medical services more parsimoniously than does capitalist America. As for improvidence, the industrial West enjoyed twenty years of unparalleled growth *after* most of the major institutions of the welfare state were established.

One's basic place in society continues to be determined primarily by one's private resources. The welfare state may make it possible to subsist as a vagrant — or a poet — without quite starving, but a doctor or a lawyer continues to enjoy far more income and status; if we believe with the economists that economic "maximization" is a primary determinant of human motivation, *homo economicus* continues to strive for relative well-being and status beyond the social minimum, even in the welfare state.

Yet, because of the fundamental conflict between the logic of market distribution and the logic of distribution according to need or citizenship, the welfare state has ample problems. The second conservative allegation — fiscal excess — must be taken more seriously. During the postwar period, all of the Western welfare states have indeed expanded enormously. Once needs are defined as society's responsibilities, it is always possible to identify more of them. We can always think up more uses for education or for health care, more personal catastrophes that deserve social remediation. Once services are priced substantially below their cost, the social demand for them will tend to outrun society's ability to pay. In a system of voluntary charity, *The New York Times* can stop at the Hundred Neediest Cases, and Nancy Reagan can draw the line at a few Korean orphans. But the universalistic welfare state must treat all comers.

With some welfare states now allocating as much as 60 percent of national income, this growth trend is surely near its fiscal limits. And during a period of slow economic growth the limits of the welfare state must be the subject of intense social bargaining and political conflict, as they are throughout the West today. With cuts in services comes more erosion of political support. Yet before one condemns the welfare state out of hand as inherently unstable or inherently ruinous fiscally, one must get down to cases. In reality, the different welfare states of the industrial world offer a wide range of approaches to the provision of social services and the redistribution of income, some of which are extremely efficient in their own terms, others of which are terribly wasteful.

In this area of political economy as in others, it is not true that efficiency is best served by inequality. On the contrary, the least efficient welfare systems are typically found in minimalist welfare states, where private markets are imperfectly harnessed to social purposes; where the state provides entitlements but fails to set effective rules; where the poor are isolated and in separate (and unequal) systems of income support, and social service is confused with social control. The more encompassing social programs are frequently the most successful. The main message of this chapter is that universalism in social services — broad citizen entitlements that serve entire populations — tend to be more efficient as well as more equitable. The trick, admittedly, is to rein in the tendency toward fiscal excess, without undermining the welfare state's quality or its broad middle-class political constituency.

FROM WORKHOUSE TO SOCIAL CITIZENSHIP

The idea of universal citizen entitlements is a fairly recent one. Before the 1930s, two older traditions governed the state's relationship with social needs: poor relief for the destitute; and later, social insurance for the middle class.

Poor Relief

The poor laws of Elizabethan England differentiated between the "deserving poor" (widows, orphans, cripples) who were worthy of Christian charity — and able-bodied vagrants. In the evolution of relief schemes, the charitable impulse clashed with society's need to discipline labor. If poor relief offered anything more generous than the barest subsistence, why should the laboring classes continue to work? Laborers, warned Bernard Mandeville in his famous *Fable of the Bees,* "have nothing to stir them up to be serviceable but their wants, which it is prudence to relieve but folly to cure." The original

Poor Law of 1601 required each parish to provide for its poor. As Britain industrialized and social dislocation swelled, the disciplinary aspect became more explicit in the new poor laws of the nineteenth century. Cash aid to the poor gave way to "indoor relief" — service in a workhouse — deliberately designed to be unpleasant and stigmatizing in order to discourage dependence and enforce wage labor. "I wish to see the Poor House looked to with dread by our labouring class," wrote one member of the Poor Law Commission, "and the reproach for being an inmate in it extend downward from father to son . . ."

Social Insurance

In the late nineteenth century, as organized society took more responsibility for individual misfortune, the model of poor relief was complemented by new systems of social insurance. As suffrage was broadened to the industrial working class in the late nineteenth and early twentieth centuries, the first stirrings of modern welfare statism continued to serve manifestly contradictory purposes. In the design of social insurance for industrial workers (pensions, workmen's compensation, health insurance), the motivation was partly charitable, partly a desire to rationalize labor markets, and partly a plain need to compete with the appeal of socialists. Otto von Bismarck, the first great conservative architect of the welfare state, believed in state paternalism as a strategy for winning worker allegiance to the Prussian crown. In Bismarck's original scheme, worker health and pension benefits were, in effect, a gift from the benevolent state. However, his more liberal contemporaries argued that workers and employers, in accord with market principles, should finance benefit plans with their own contributions; the state should merely play the role of a giant insurance company. The financing of Bismarck's welfare state ultimately reflected both approaches. The pension system of 1889 combined worker and employer contributions with a subsidy from the imperial treasury.

As the modern welfare state has evolved in this century, it has retained several tiers. The affluent have continued to purchase the elements of a private welfare state — pensions, annuities, private health care, private schooling. For the wage-earning middle class, the welfare state erected institutions of social insurance to insure against unforeseen calamities — Beveridge called them "interruptions": ill-health, temporary unemployment, industrial accidents, the death or disability of a breadwinner, and poverty in old age. But the poor, especially in England and America, remain dependent on the older system of poor relief.

Safety Nets or Citizen Entitlements

The liberal, Anglo-Saxon version of the welfare state insures against the vagaries of the market, but it does not seek to equalize incomes per se, or to depart from the general principle that social status should be based primarily on private earnings. As T. H. Marshall sagely described social insurance under liberal auspices,

> It raised the floor-level in the basement of the social edifice, and perhaps made it rather more hygienic than it was before. But it remained a basement, and the upper stories of the building were unaffected. And the benefits received by the unfortunate did not flow from an enrichment of the status of citizenship.

The difference between social insurance and citizen entitlement seems subtle, but it is crucial. A universal entitlement belongs to a citizen as a matter of right, regardless of private means. An insurance benefit is "earned" — it depends upon the premiums that you have paid into the insurance fund. To collect unemployment insurance you first need a work history. Your benefit level is governed by your previous wage. Thus, much of the welfare-state system reflects rather than alters market outcomes, and this is particularly pronounced in Britain and the United States. Benefits based on social insurance are more consistent with market capitalism since they do not operate at cross purposes with market-determined income distribution. Social insurance provides for unforeseen calamities; it also redistributes income over the life cycle, but it does relatively little to alter the wage-based inequalities of the market system.

Since the big increase in income-support programs, beginning in the 1930s, the English-speaking welfare states have followed this "social insurance" model. Though there is some general subsidy by the state, the design is essentially *contributory,* and *minimal,* rather than redistributive. The famous Beveridge report of 1942, which became the broad model of the postwar welfare state, carefully linked universal coverage with this "insurance principle." Beveridge saw the abolition of means tests and the insurance principle as two sides of the same coin. If everybody paid into the system on a more or less flat basis, everybody would feel they had earned the right to take from it when needs arose. "Benefit in return for contributions, rather than free allowances from the State, is what the people of Britain desire," Beveridge wrote. "Payment of a substantial part of the cost of the benefit, irrespective of means, is the firm basis of a claim to benefit irrespective of means." The moderate left and many trade unionists saw the insurance principle as a bulwark against attempts to undo the system during periods of conservative rule. A mere government program could always be repealed. But an insurance scheme, into which people had paid premiums, would be tampered with only at political peril.

In countries that are fundamentally wedded to individualistic values, "social insurance" has been a politically useful myth. The idea that social-security old-age pensions are merely a form of insurance makes such programs appear less socialistic than they really are. In the United States, most defenders of social security have fought to maintain the insurance model, because it reinforces the broad political constituency for the program; most Americans look upon social security as an earned right rather than a social wage that redistributes private income. In fact, old age pensions under social security are substantially redistributive, and not just from the working population to the retired population. According to one study, social security redistributes four times as much income as the progressive income tax. But because the ideological support for egalitarianism is much thinner in America than the support for retirement security, the insurance myth persists. As one scholar of American social security, Martha Derthick, observes, the less social security has become like an insurance program, the more its defenders have insisted on the insurance principle.

Beyond Beveridge

Beveridge's own model sought to provide income security in four broad areas: insurance against unemployment, against ill health, against death or disability of a breadwinner, and against inadequate income due to low wages or family size. Contributions were to be paid at a flat rate; benefits were to be adequate to assure subsistence; they were to be administered nationally, and universally available as a matter of right. Beveridge repeatedly pointed out that his scheme was not intended to redistribute income among social classes; rather, it was to insure against unforeseen misfortune.

In practice, however, the principle of universality collided with the principle of adequacy. The flat benefits were universal all right, but they were not enough to live on. In Britain, the Labour government of 1945–51 created the institutions of the modern welfare state; but as it was refined during the 1950s under conservative auspices, neither family allowances nor old age pensions were funded at sufficiently generous levels to keep recipients out of poverty, and the old, means-tested welfare state crept back in. British child allowances are currently about $7 per week for each child — not nearly enough to lift large families out of poverty. By 1981, 42 percent of single parents and 38 percent of elderly widows were dependent on "supplemental" means-tested benefits. As unemployment rates increased, more and more of the unemployed have exhausted their entitlement to unemployment compensation as a citizen wage (which is limited to six months), and have been thrown back upon the means-tested "welfare" component of the system. At this writing, supplementary (means-tested) benefits for the long-term unemployed are costing Britain £4.5 billion a year — more than double the outlay for unemployment insurance. Only in the area of health care did Britain succeed in establishing a truly universal system, which served the broad middle class as well as the poor, with equal standards and with no means tests.

MODELS OF THE WELFARE STATE

In a comparison of advanced welfare states, we find the United States at one extreme and the more social democratic nations of Northern Europe at the other. In the United States, the very term *welfare* is associated with wasteful aid for the (undeserving) poor. Opinion polls consistently show "welfare" as our least popular public program. The United States has a less universalistic model in two key respects. It spends less on social aid — about 12 percent of GNP compared with over 20 percent in Northern Europe; but overall spending levels are not the test of an effective welfare state. More important, poor relief in the American system is fragmented and isolated. The social benefits that do reach the poor in the United States are more heavily means tested — and America's version of means testing is more adversary, isolating, and punitive.

Welfare USA

Our two principal programs aimed at relieving poverty — Aid to Families with Dependent Children and food stamps — are means-tested programs. Our Medicaid program, also means tested, is the only such separate medical program for the poor in the industrial West. By default, we have created a "system" of nursing-home care for the aged in which middle-class people pay exorbitant rates to for-profit nursing-home entrepreneurs — and then when private resources are consumed and the patient qualifies as a pauper, the nursing home begins billing Medicaid. This is precisely the antithesis of social citizenship; instead of the poor being accorded the dignity associated with the middle class, equality of treatment is achieved by making the middle class undergo pauperization.

Unlike most of Europe, we have no general program of family allowances; instead, we subsidize the expense of child-rearing by means of tax exemptions. This approach is distributively regressive, since a $1000 tax deduction gives a high-bracket family more tax subsidy than a low-bracket one. A very low-income family, with no tax liability to shelter, gets nothing. We also use a tax credit to subsidize the costs of day care, rather than offering a comprehensive day-care program. The very limited subsidized day-care centers that do exist are part of "poverty programs," and restricted, by definition, to the poor. In housing policy, tax subsidies for homeownership are available as a matter of right for the middle class and the wealthy, but there are no housing cash allowances for the poor. A separate program of housing for the poor exists, but not as an entitlement; it has been funded so minimally that only about one family in ten that qualifies for subsidized housing actually lives in a subsidized house. (Since 1974, the United States has had a very limited housing voucher program, in which the government pays part of the family's rent. This does help overcome the isolation of the poor, but many private landlords will not participate in the program.)

In effect, the American welfare state perpetuates the older distinction between "deserving poor" and undeserving poor. Under the Social Security Act, an orphan is deserving, while a bastard is deemed undeserving. A minor child with a deceased father collects a government benefit that substitutes for a portion of his late parent's lost income. The benefit comes as a matter of right, under the Social Security "survivorship" program, with no means test. It does not matter whether the family has money in the bank, or how the mother spends her social life. However, if the child is "dependent" because his father is absent or unknown, his case comes under a different provision of the law. The mother is treated as a fallen woman rather than a deserving widow. In order to collect a "welfare" check under Aid to Families with Dependent Children, the mother must demonstrate that she has no substantial savings, no earned income, and no man assuming the role of a spouse.

European Universalism

At the other extreme are the welfare societies of Northern Europe, with a full panoply of universal income-support and social-service programs. Until the slump of the 1970s, the more socialistic of Europe's social democratic welfare states succeeded admirably in providing income support either through wages or through citizen entitlements, so that very few people landed in the secondary, means-tested system. As long as there was full employment, unemployment compensation was a minor expense. Family allowances and cash subsidies for basic commodities like housing largely solved the problem of low household income for working families. Increases in basic citizens' pensions for the elderly largely eliminated poverty in old age.

As noted, welfare states try to socialize needs and to equalize personal resources both through cash grants and through provision of common services. In general, the ideal of universal entitlement based on Marshall's "social citizenship" is somewhat easier to accomplish through socialization of a *service,* such as education or health, in which everyone is in the same system and charges are nominal. Substantially equalizing income through *cash transfers* — without either stigmatizing the needy or bankrupting the state — is a much trickier business.

Old-Age Pensions

Pensions are by far the costliest single item of the welfare state. For advanced industrial nations generally, old-age pensions consume about 65–70 percent of total social outlays. For the United States, which has no general health insurance or family allowance programs, pensions account for about 75 percent. The pension burden has grown substantially in recent years for several distinct reasons. First, the retired population has increased enormously; people are retiring earlier and living longer. Second, birth rates are declining, leaving fewer workers to support pensioners. Third, most countries have deliberately increased the real value of pensions, as a strategy to eliminate poverty in old age. Finally, every Western country indexed pension benefits, usually to consumer prices, during a period when prices grew faster than wages.

After World War II, most of Europe built its retirement system in the Beveridge image. The War and the Nazi occupation had shattered Europe's prewar economic and social systems. In the first postwar decade, the task of economic reconstruction went hand in hand with a commitment to economic security. Immediately after the War, parties to the left had substantial influence throughout Western Europe, either as the party of government or as coalition partners. Even where conservatives governed, as Christian Democrats or as nationalists, they usually shared the left's commitment to economic security programs. In this climate, the idea of a basic citizen's pension enjoyed wide appeal. Throughout Western Europe, the scattered remnants of prewar pension programs were consolidated into unified national pension systems.

It soon became apparent, however, that Beveridge-style, universal, flat-rate pensions were not adequate to provide a decent living standard for the elderly. By the 1960s, most countries had added supplemental pension schemes that reflected earnings histories. In the most successful of these programs, the basic citizens' pension is sufficient to provide decent living standards even to those retirees with very low earnings histories. Better-paid workers receive more generous supplementary pensions based on their lifetime contributions, but everybody is in the same system, and the system enjoys broad allegiance. Most important, the guarantee of a decent living standard is provided as a matter of right. Very few pensioners are thrown back into the old, means-tested system of poor relief. Thus, market factors still influence the distribution of income in old age — high-wage workers can look forward to more comfortable retirement than low-wage workers — but there is substantially less inequality for the retired population than for working-age people.

According to an OECD survey of income-support programs in the mid-1970s, Germany provided the most generous system of income replacement in old age; the average social security pension equaled 51 percent of the average wage. The average for Common Market countries was 27 percent. The United States ranked second to last; the average U.S. pension under social security equaled just 18 percent of the average wage. For Britain, the figure was also below average, 22 percent. Just as significantly, Germany used its pension system to bring up the level of the poorest elderly people, without subjecting them to the indignity of a means test. Germany accomplished this, even though the ratio of German workers to German retirees is one of the lowest among all advanced industrial countries — about two workers to each retiree.

Thanks to a broadly distributed and fairly generous general pension system, fewer than 3 percent of elderly Germans receive supplementary means-tested allowances. For Britain, the figure has hovered between 25 and 30 percent. In the United States, where old-age pensions are more redistributive than in Britain, some two million old people — 7 percent of the total — still depend on means-tested aid, and another million are poor enough to qualify, but haven't applied.

According to one study comparing German and U.S. income-maintenance programs, Germany spends nearly three times what we do on income support (27.5 percent of GNP versus 10.5 percent), but more than a quarter of U.S. outlays are means-tested, compared to just 3 percent of German outlays. America's greater reliance on means-tested benefits should not be confused with generous treatment for the poor. Although the United States spends more than Germany on means-tested "welfare" (2.8 percent of GNP versus about 1 percent), it has far more welfare recipients dependent on such benefits, so the aid that each recipient receives is far less than in Germany.

Today, the Swedish pension system probably tops Germany's as the most generous and the most redistributive. The citizens' pension currently provides a basic benefit, as a matter of right, equal to about

$4000 a year for an individual, and about $7000 for a couple: 27,974 Skr and 49,053 Skr as of January 1983. Additional supplemental social security pensions based on earnings go as high as about $14,000 for a couple. Sweden is another country in which very, very few old people require supplemental, means-tested aid.

Most of Northern Europe has the same commitment to universalism in old-age pensions, with roughly the same results. By the mid-1970s, means-tested poor relief accounted for less than 5 percent of total social outlays in Sweden, Austria, Norway, Denmark, Belgium, and Germany. In Sweden and Denmark, it accounted for only about 1 percent. In the United States, means-tested poor relief equaled over 26 percent of total social outlays.

Means testing, American style, is not just an administrative device to "target" aid to the neediest. It is very destructive of the logic of social citizenship; means testing requires pauperism as a condition of assistance, which is an effective means of discouraging the needy from applying. As we have seen, in most of Europe all old people receive a minimum citizen's pension, even if they have not contributed a sou into the state retirement fund during their working lives. If their contributions were substantial, they get higher pensions. The system in the United States works in the opposite way. People do not get a basic pension, *unless* they qualify as paupers. Old people receive social security pensions in rough proportion to their contributions; and then if they have too little total income to live on, they may apply for additional means-tested aid. But in order to get such aid (Supplemental Security Assistance), they must first deplete their savings and other personal assets (other than a house and a car) to no more than $1500. They may have life insurance only sufficient to pay burial costs. In effect, they become wards of the state, not free citizens.

Family Allowances

It is rather more difficult to equalize purchasing power for people of working age without recourse to some kind of income test, for circumstances and needs differ much more than for the elderly. The three major causes of poverty among families are inadequate wage or salary income, unemployment of the breadwinner, and large families. As I have stressed in other contexts, full employment and an egalitarian wage structure are the most effective strategy of equalizing household income for the population as a whole. But there are still whole classes of families, such as families headed by women, who will often require special assistance.

The difference between universal family allowances and the American "welfare" program — Aid to Families with Dependent Children — is that AFDC is means tested. It is welfare for "them," not for "us." Although every European family-allowance system supplements the general allowance with means-tested aid for the neediest, such aid exists as part of a universal system that benefits most families. It carries nothing of the stigma or the punitive aura of AFDC in the United States.

At present, universal family allowances exist in Austria, Belgium, Canada, Denmark, France, Germany, Italy, the Netherlands, Norway, Sweden, and the United Kingdom. Formulas vary, but the typical benefit is on the order of $500 per child per year. In the case of a large, poor family, family allowances can equal 20–25 percent of total household income; in France and Belgium, they average about 14 percent of the median industrial wage. Though supplemental social assistance exists in all of these countries, basic family allowances are given to middle class as well as to poor families and are taxed as ordinary income. Typically, over 90 percent of families with children receive some aid. In most countries, benefits are disproportionately large for families with more than three children.

For Europe as a whole, family allowances consume one to two percent of GNP, and in France and Belgium, the share exceeds two percent. While the United States uses tax deductions as a substitute for cash subsidies, Sweden, Norway, and Denmark have repealed tax allowances based on family size and use only cash transfers.

France, oddly enough, has Europe's most generous family allowance system. This is somewhat surprising, for during nearly all of the postwar period, France was governed by conservative administrations. And not until the Mitterrand cabinet of 1981 did a left government come to power with an effective majority. The French affinity for family allowances, however, is long-standing, and more nationalist than socialist. In the years after 1870, the French birthrate fell precipitously, from about a million live births a year in the 1860s, to about 600,000 a year on the eve of World War I. French nationalism during this period spawned a strong pro-natalist movement.

Family benefit funds were established on a regional basis as early as 1918, and consolidated into a broad national program that was expanded substantially by the Popular Front government of 1937–38. Today, families with two or more children collect family allowances averaging over $2000 a year; in the case of families with a single wage earner, benefits are increased. For a family of four, the total family allowance is equal to about one fourth of the average worker's wage. For a low-income family with two wage earners and four children, family allowances can increase the family's purchasing power by fully 50 percent.

The value of a family allowance is that it comes as a matter of right, whether there is one parent in the home or two, and whether or not the head of the household works. This provision actually encourages a single mother to work if she can, for by working she does not lose her benefits and can increase her real income. AFDC, on the other hand, operates perversely. It is usually available only when the female head of household does *not* work: this creates an incentive for AFDC recipients to stay out of the work force as long as possible. It also creates an incentive for bureaucrats to coerce them into the work force in order to save the state money. Moreover, since AFDC is generally available only when the father is absent, it also serves to break up families.

Until the Reagan administration, the perverse aspects of AFDC were somewhat mitigated by an "income-disregard" formula, which allowed recipients to take jobs and lose only a portion of their welfare grants. Welfare recipients could keep the first thirty dollars a week of earned income and one third of the remainder. This enabled the working poor with very low incomes to qualify for partial welfare benefits, and it also gave welfare recipients incentives to find part- or full-time jobs. In 1981, the Reagan administration repealed the provision as a cost-cutting measure.

Even in a system as generous and universal as the French, flat-rate family allowances by themselves cannot succeed in raising all families out of poverty without straining fiscal resources to the breaking point. Throughout the industrial West, the two-income household has become the norm for the middle-class family. Yet at the same time, the incidence of divorce and single parenthood has risen dramatically. Most of the increase in poverty in the past decade, in the United States and elsewhere, has been in female-headed households. Given the need for two incomes to provide decent living standards, the difficulty of raising a family alone, and the concentration of women in lower-wage occupations, families headed by women are likely to be substantially poorer than two-income households. Universal family allowances are very useful for equalizing incomes of "traditional" large families. But female-headed households present income insufficiency of a different order of magnitude.

In France, the proportion of families receiving supplementary, income-tested aid gradually increased, from 14 percent in 1970 to 35 percent in 1976. This departs somewhat from the ideal of flat-rate universal benefits. Yet means testing in the European context is far less demeaning and destructive of citizen rights than its American counterpart. In most of Europe, an income-tested program simply means that you must have a low total income in order to receive benefits. You are not required to deplete your savings, submit to bed checks, or enroll in a make-work program to earn your keep. And the program is administered by the same agency that serves other citizens.

Housing Allowances

Cash housing allowances provide the other major form of income support for European families. These are typically based on family size and family income — thus, they are available to all moderate-income families; housing allowances are typically tied to family need but not means tested in the sense of isolating the poor. In the more generous of Europe's welfare states, they equal 15–20 percent of the average worker's wage.

Sociologists Alfred Kahn and Sheila Kamerman, comparing cash transfers in eight industrialized nations, considered the effect of each major transfer program on the disposable income of different types of families. They found that family allowances and housing allowances, taken together, can be considered a single system of income support that guarantees families with special needs a standard of living not far from that of more conventional families, with a minimum of indignity. A single parent with no job in France collects a combined family allowance and housing allowance package equal to about 79 percent of the average worker's wage. In Sweden, the figure is 94 percent.

The Swedish system provides a housing allowance of 1500 Skr per year, per child (about $210); there is an income ceiling, but there is no stigma attached to the program. The French system is similar. About one third of all Swedish families with children benefit from the housing allowance program, and about one quarter of French families.

Pensions, housing allowances, and family allowances together consume more than three fourths of social security expenditures in most advanced countries. In addition, European nations provide a variety of other income-transfer programs — income support for workdays lost to illness, disability benefits, and cash maternity and paternity benefits.

Unemployment Compensation

The other fairly expensive income-support program is unemployment compensation. Large outlays for unemployment benefits, of course, are an indication of the welfare state's failure, not its success. During the 1950s and 1960s, when most of Europe was near full employment, unemployment benefits were primarily used to support workers experiencing brief spells of joblessness or to maintain income during troughs in the business cycle. As late as 1970, unemployment compensation consumed less than half of one percent of GNP in most major industrial nations. The United States, despite lower benefit levels, nonetheless incurred higher costs, because of our far higher rate of unemployment. As European unemployment rates rose in the late 1970s, total unemployment compensation outlays have grown to an average of 1 to 2 percent of GNP, and are above 3 percent in the countries with very high unemployment rates and generous welfare formulas, such as Belgium, the Netherlands, and Denmark.

Unemployment compensation in every major Western country is paid as a form of social insurance, not as poor relief. No means test or exhaustion of private assets is required in order to receive it. The system is designed to maintain unemployed workers at close to their customary standard of living while they look for a new job. In Western Europe, unemployment compensation benefits average about 70 percent of the average production worker's wage. In some countries, such as Sweden and Denmark, the benefit ratio is as high as 90 percent. In the United States, unemployment compensation replaces 30–40 percent of the average wage, depending on the state.

But the unemployment compensation system was not designed for prolonged high unemployment. In every system, benefits eventually run out, usually after a year or two. Unemployment compensation benefits run for as little as six months in Britain, to as much as nearly three years in France and Denmark. After the benefits have run out, workers must fall back upon the second tier of the welfare state — means-tested social aid. In most of Europe, thanks to fairly generous family allowances and housing allowances, workers whose unemployment compensation runs out do not suffer the precipitous drop in living standards that they would experience in the United States in a similar situation, although high-wage workers do end up with substantially less real income.

The problem has become far more serious as increasing numbers of the unemployed have been without work for extended periods. Between 1975 and 1982, long-term unemployment (12 months or more) as a percentage of total unemployment rose from 36 percent to 60 percent in Belgium, 17 percent to 40 percent in France, 10 percent to 21 percent in West Germany, 11 percent to 32 percent in the Netherlands, and 14 percent to 33 percent in England. Only in the full-employment countries of Norway, Sweden, and Austria have long-term joblessness and government outlays for unemployment compensation stayed low.

The principle of universalism, with provision of income support as a citizen right, is being strained to its breaking point by long-term high unemployment. With more people out of work, fewer employed workers are paying into the system. Tax rates on the employed must be steadily raised to support the deadweight burden of the un-employed. Resentment grows, and a wedge is driven between the working voter and the jobless. Even so, Europe does a far better job of keeping the poor and the middle class within one system than the United States and Britain do. European welfare states are both more generous with their benefits and more devoted to a sin-gle standard of treatment. The Danish-American sociologist Gösta Esping-Andersen compared several welfare states in terms of how much income was replaced by five "safety net" programs. The results were:

Country	Income replacement percentage	Income replacement times percentage of work force eligible
Sweden	78	71
Austria	70	61
Denmark	68	61
Netherlands	68	59
Norway	66	63
West Germany	63	55
Belgium	59	49
United Kingdom	53	46
Japan	53	33
France	47	38
Canada	46	37
Italy	44	32
United States	42	25

Source: Gösta Esping-Andersen, "Politics Against Markets: De-commodification in Social Policy," monograph (Stockholm: Swedish Institute for Social Research, 1981).

Even as demographic and economic changes have required more of a reversion to income-tested transfers than under the Beveridge ideal, countries like Sweden, Norway, Denmark, Austria, West Germany, and France have carried them out within the framework of a unified system, with a minimum of indignity and no pauperization.

Universal Services: Health Care

The ideal of universalism is easier to attain in the provision of social services. Probably the clearest example is health care. With the exception of the United States, virtually every industrialized country guarantees equal access to medical care as a citizen right, either through a compulsory state insurance system or through a national health service in which most medical personnel are direct employees of the state. Socializing health care involves more than a distributional change in who receives services; it involves a major power shift. The relative political strength of doctors, private hospitals, and private insurance companies must be reduced substantially in order for socialized health care to function efficiently.

As life spans have increased throughout the West, health care presents a particular problem of potentially unlimited demand. The longer people stay alive, the more society incurs costs of the very expensive medical treatment required to artificially prolong life of the very old. Applying every available medical technology to every patient would consume more than 100 percent of GNP. As the total cost of health care spirals, the issue is not whether to ration medical care, but how. In most of the Western countries, health care is now rationed according to other criteria than market demand.

Socialized health care has both efficiency and equality benefits. The equality gains are obvious enough: the poor receive roughly the same medical care as the rich. But a comprehensive health-care system turns out to be more efficient as well. Britain, with the most completely socialized health system in the West, now spends the lowest fraction of GNP on health care of any major nation. There are frequent complaints of excessive waits for elective surgery and other inconveniences, but British citizens live slightly longer than Americans, on average, and our overall health conditions are comparable.

Despite the claim of many conservatives that public-sector providers are the source of public-sector growth, the socialized British health system has had a far slower growth rate than the more market-oriented American system. Rudolf Klein, a prominent student of the British National Health Service, has observed, "In the NHS, the incentives to providers have been to lower expectations, not to raise them. In contrast to fee-for-service systems, providers do not benefit from increased demand; on the contrary, they simply increase their own workload."

The United States, with about 50 percent of its health costs paid through the public sector, has managed to create a very poor equality/efficiency bargain. In our form of public-private partnership, the private profit motive drives costs, and the government pays much of the bill. Hospital and medical care in the United States is based on fee-for-service billing and third-party reimbursement. Doctors and hospitals charge patients based on what services are rendered, and third parties — private insurance companies or government Medicare and Medicaid — pay the bills. Most doctors and many hospitals act like any other profit-maximizing actor in a market system. Thus there is every incentive to maximize expensive treatment modes, to overbuild hospitals, use expensive technology that generates lucrative reimbursements, and to avoid less profitable public-health approaches. After a brief effort to regulate costs through such devices as "peer review" panels and "certificate of need" reviews for proposed new hospitals, regulation has been rolled back in the Reagan years.

In addition, corporations are seeing hospitals and medical practices as lucrative profit centers. For-profit hospitals are now the fastest-growing portion of the hospital sector. Even prepaid group health plans (Health Maintenance Organizations), which were invented as alternatives to for-profit medicine, are now being organized and marketed by profit-making concerns. The free market is often held out as an efficient system for keeping costs low, because of competition to please the customer. But it would be hard to think of a less appropriate sphere for market economics than health care. In the medical system, decisions are primarily made by providers, not consumers; and the patient is seldom likely to change doctors or hospitals in order to shave costs, when his life may be at stake. For-profit hospitals, statistically, are more costly than nonprofit hospitals. They tend to shun charity cases, since such cases lower their profit margins. Thus, we combine inefficiency — inflated health costs — with inequality: a two-track health system for the rich and the poor.

Although the practice of third-party reimbursement is often held responsible for inflating costs, the particular American system of reimbursement by *private* insurance companies with scant public control over charges seems to be the most inflationary mix of all. A comparison between the Canadian and U.S. health systems provides an almost laboratory case in point. Canada's provincial health-insurance systems, like ours, use third-party reimbursement. You go to the doctor, and the insurance system pays the bill. But in the United States, the insurer might be Blue Cross Blue Shield, or Prudential, or Medicare, or one of hundreds of others. In Canada, there is only one insurer — the provincial health plan. Each patient simply pays the bill with a credit card, and the insurance system reimburses the provider. As a result, Canadian hospital administrative costs are about one sixth those of American hospitals. Moreover, with one unified system, the state has a much easier time regulating rates, procedures, and fees. In the early 1970s, when Canada first adopted its comprehensive plan, it was spending about the same total health outlay as the United States: roughly 7.3 percent of GNP. Since then, health-care costs in Canada have stabilized at about 7.5 percent of GNP, while in the United States they have soared to the 9–10 percent range.

Universalism and Ideology

The failure to achieve a universal health entitlement program in the United States is emblematic of the fragmented American welfare state generally. With the exception of free public education (a "welfare state" idea that antedates even the American Republic), the idea that middle-class people and poor people should get common, free services, somehow goes against the individualistic American grain. When George McGovern, in his hapless 1972 presidential campaign, proposed a "demogrant" of $1000 per person per year as a kind of universal family allowance, he was ridiculed; the proposal did more to discredit his candidacy than any other single campaign theme.

A 1971 bill providing a universalistic and comprehensive system of child-care centers aimed at enrichment rather than mere custodial care was vetoed by President Nixon as wasteful and antifamily. Said Nixon in his veto message, "For the Federal government to plunge headlong into supporting child development would commit the vast moral authority of the national government to the side of communal approaches to children over against the family-centered approach." Instead, Congress legislated a tax incentive — an individualistic (and fragmented) alternative that permitted middle-class people to make private child-care arrangements and take a tax credit for them, while the poor were left with largely unsubsidized makeshift arrangements. The idea that there might be something inherently valuable about having children from different social classes in the same system had little appeal. That idea is at the very center of the European social democratic welfare state.

And yet, even in laissez-faire America, the state finds itself deeply involved in family life — only in America the state's main role is picking up the pieces of family failures rather than helping to shore up healthy families. Alfred J. Kahn and Sheila B. Kamerman say in their fine book on European social services, *Not For the Poor Alone:*

> What the Europeans apparently know but what many Americans do not perceive is that social services may support, strengthen, and enhance the normal family — and that failures in social provision may undermine our most precious institutions and relationships. The issue is not whether or not government will intervene. It will. The question is whether it will intervene for enhancement and prevention or to respond to breakdown, problems, and deviance alone? . . . Whether programs foster dependency depends on how they are administered and the nature of the entitlements. Are they beneficence, charity, given upon condition of subservience to those defined as weak? Or are they rights, seen as meeting widespread need, delivered with dignity, to a user who is seen as citizen, taxpayer, and policymaker?

There is deep ideological support in America for the proposition that only the "truly needy" are worthy of public support. Ignoring two hundred years of free public education, most Americans think there is something illogical or wasteful about having the state provide free, comprehensive services to the middle class. The logic and ideology of universalism are alien to most Americans, as something socialistic — which of course it is.

A visitor to Western Europe cannot fail to be impressed with the simple humanity of European social services. The services that exist are not so different from those that exist here — day-care centers for children, halfway houses for the mentally ill, home care and "meals-on-wheels" programs for elderly shut-ins, school lunch programs, subsidized housing, and, of course, health clinics.

The difference is that the European services include everybody in one system, while ours tend to be a patchwork, with one system of services for the officially certified Poor, and another system for paying customers. In the United States, the poor people's service tends to be understaffed, overcrowded, burdened with demeaning conditions, and often just plain nasty. And a middle-class person experiencing sudden adversity thinks twice before submitting to the shame of the charity system. Because subsidized services are designed mainly for the poor, and because the poor are an unpopular constituency, these programs tend to be poorly operated.

Home Care

Almost any category of social service illustrates the value of a comprehensive, one-class system. Consider the example of home care for elderly shut-ins. Elderly people often are able to live at home if they can have some assistance from a homemaker. In the United States the availability of a homemaker subsidized by some agency or other depends on where the elderly person happens to live and what he or she earns. If you are certifiably destitute the local welfare department usually provides assistance, depending on its state of funding. If you are not quite destitute, you may get help, depending on whether you happen to live in a jurisdiction affluent enough to have a local program. But there is no citizen entitlement to such assistance. As a result, many elderly people lead drearier lives, and many others are shunted to institutional care far earlier than necessary, which is much more expensive to society.

In contrast, here is how the Danes do it: Every elderly Danish citizen who is incapacitated is entitled to homemaker services, such as shopping, preparing meals, cleaning, helping with dressing, undressing, and personal hygiene. Home help care is free to pensioners who have no other income; others with independent incomes pay according to a sliding scale. If more care than six hours is required by the person's condition, no additional charge is imposed for extra hours. And everybody, rich or poor, is in the same program. Danish authorities figure that this approach produces a net savings, because it keeps so many people out of nursing homes. There is also a net contribution to the dignity, mobility, and autonomy of old people. In short, there is more equality *and* more efficiency.

Most of Western Europe offers variations on the same theme. In Sweden, homemaker assistance is provided through the local municipal Home Help Service. Workers assist not only the elderly, but the severely handicapped, the blind, the mentally ill, and families in need of temporary assistance because a parent is ill or incapacitated. Unlike homemakers in the employ of American welfare agencies, who are typically low-paid and untrained domestic workers, Swedish homemakers in the employ of the municipal government are required to go through a 160-hour training program and are paid "middle-class" wages. Note that the Swedish solidarity wage policy complements the national commitment to human services. Home care is a more valued profession than in the U.S. because it is paid decently. As in Denmark, the program is universally available, and fees are on a sliding scale. Even for relatively affluent clients, the program is subsidized. With upwards of 87,000 employees (about 2 percent of the total Swedish work force), the program is a centerpiece in Sweden's national policy of promoting autonomy and mainstream treatment for the handicapped and the aged; it is also a substantial source of jobs. In addition, Sweden provides its large elderly population with a full spectrum of housing alternatives, ranging from normal apartments, scattered among housing for the younger population, to apartments specially equipped for those of limited mobility — with communal kitchens, on-site social services and recreation programs, and special hardware.

In the Netherlands, the system is quite similar, but it is run through nonprofit agencies rather than the state. The program, nonetheless, is a citizen entitlement, with most of the cost being paid by the Dutch government. For Americans fearful of "bureaucratic" welfare programs, one revelation is that these European programs are highly decentralized and tailored to local conditions. A universalistic system is fully compatible with operation by a local town government or a nonprofit agency. In practice, the Swedish or Danish or Dutch home helpers are far more responsive than their American counterparts. One reason is that resources and coverage are adequate. Bureaucratic rationing sets in when resources are thin, not when they are ample. According to Kahn and Kamerman, Sweden has one home-health aide for every 260 citizens; the Netherlands, one per 380; the United Kingdom, one per 667; and Denmark, one for every 760. In the United States, there is one per 7000, and in many areas the program doesn't exist at all.

In-kind, universalistic services — such as homemaker assistance for the old, day care for the young, services to the mentally ill — are terribly important in assuring a model of the welfare state that renders useful service to the entire population. Compared to the big-ticket items like public education and health care, they consume a relatively small fraction of total state budgets. For 1983–84, Sweden spent a total of 2.544 billion Swedish kronor on all social services in the home, including special transportation and home-nursing care — less than 1 percent of national government budget outlays. The United States, incidentally, spends about the same fraction of GNP on domestic labor. In America, this outlay goes for household servants hired to clean and cook for the most affluent 5 to 10 percent of the population. In Sweden, it goes to help the aged and the incapacitated to maintain some dignity. Which approach is more equitable? Which is more efficient? To ask the question is to answer it.

The European models of home care and universal medical service are the best refutation of the claim that the welfare state fosters dependency or is inherently bureaucratic. In reality, the American model of isolated state charity for the certified poor is far more destructive of autonomy and liberty. In our system, the market is the main source of income, but there are a few "windows" of income support through which the needy can petition for aid. The aid is usually inadequate to the need. It is not surprising that the few windows are overwhelmed, and that the relations between the welfare workers and the clientele quickly become adversarial rather than constructive.

Michael Lipsky, a political scientist, has written compellingly of the human costs of the isolation and chronic inadequacy that characterize the American welfare state.

> Workers on the front lines of the welfare state find themselves in a corrupted world of service. The worker is continually torn between mobilizing client energies and rendering the client docile, between advocating on a client's behalf and minimizing client services . . .
> One of the better kept secrets of the [American] welfare state is how wide and deep is the demand for human services generally . . . but resources are chronically inadequate to the demand . . . Workers find that the best way to keep demand within manageable proportions is to deliver a consistently inaccessible or inferior product. Public programs cannot charge fees, but they can set "prices" by inflicting indignities . . .

Thus, concludes Lipsky, welfare programs, American style, are

> trapped in a cycle of mediocrity. The better the program and the more responsive it is to the needs of citizens, the greater will be the demand for the service. The larger demand forces the agency to limit service artificially or to impose costs on clients in the absence of a pricing mechanism that would otherwise ration service. The imposed cost of inferior quality or difficulty in receiving services continues until, in the extreme, the agency is returned to the previous equilibrium of indifference to client needs.
> It is one thing to be treated neglectfully and routinely by

> the telephone company, the motor vehicle bureau, or other
> ... agencies whose agents know nothing of the personal circum-
> stances surrounding a request. It is quite another thing to be shuffled,
> categorized, and treated "bureaucratically" (in the pejorative sense)
> by someone from whom one expects at least an open and sympathetic
> hearing.

And, one might add, when the issue is not a phone bill, but one's
mental health, physical incapacity, or the needs of one's children.

An American who has grown up with only one model of the
welfare state can conclude all too easily that shabbiness and bureaucratic ill treatment are the inevitable hallmark of government
social programs. A classical economist might explain smugly that
this result is simply the predictable consequence of overriding market
demand and supplying a service priced below its cost. But as we have
seen from the European examples, this Peter Principle of diminishing
quality does not apply to systems where services are better financed,
provided to rich and poor in the same system, and where markets
are not permitted to generate such initial disparities in the first place.

The middle-class welfare state never quite reached critical mass in
the United States. And in the 1980s, the isolation of the poor in their
own means-tested programs is increasing in both England and America. President Reagan, in his profession of concern for the "truly
needy," concentrated his social-program cuts on the working poor —
those whose incomes are just above poverty levels. In recent years,
Medicaid and food-stamp income ceilings have been lowered; income
support has been withdrawn from the working poor; and requirements have been increased to prove dire distress before social services
are available. This, naturally, drives a wider wedge between the poor
and everyone else, and makes it that much more demeaning to apply
for public assistance.

Richard Titmuss, in his classic 1955 essay on the future of the
welfare state, "The Social Division of Welfare: Some Reflections on
the Search for Equity," warned that the welfare state was already
fragmenting into three parts: a social-service state, aimed primarily
at the poor; an "occupational welfare state" made up of private
"perks" that better-off people obtained through their jobs, and a
"tax welfare state," made up of tax deductions primarily valuable
for the well-to-do. After thirty years, this characterization describes
the British and American welfare states all too well. The ratio of tax

expenditures to direct expenditures is rising in both countries. The ratio of private, job-based pensions to public social security pensions is also on the upswing. Expenditure on tax subsidies for middle-class mortgages has overwhelmed direct spending on housing for the poor and the elderly. An upper-middle-class executive, who pays private college tuition for his children, enjoys first-class medical care thanks to his tax-free corporate health insurance plan, drives a tax-deductible company car, retires in style on a tax-sheltered company pension, and perhaps lives securely in a tax-sheltered exclusive building policed by private guards, enjoys substantial subsidy, but none of it visible. He wonders what his tax dollars are accomplishing — other than coddling the undeserving poor.

"Privatization"

Significantly, a big theme of both British and American conservatives is "privatization" — the idea that public services will be provided more efficiently if they are contracted out to private-sector providers; or better yet, services should be subsidized by means of tax incentives or vouchers — with specifics left to the initiative of private suppliers and demanders. Private rather than public institutions providing health, education, and welfare will supposedly lead to more competition, more efficiency, and more freedom of choice. So goes the argument. This remedy contains one part ideological faith in market solutions, and one part cynicism. In many areas, such as health care, the market is an inappropriate and inefficient means of providing service. At best, leaving social services to the market will produce very different distributive outcomes. Those with private resources will get services, and those without the means to pay will simply do without.

The idea that the certified poor could be given vouchers is fine in theory, but in practice the isolation of the poor into a separate category undermines the willingness of the middle class to pay for the program. For every principled conservative who consistently supports vouchers for the poor as an alternative to public social programs, the right has ten David Stockmans warning that the idea is unfortunately too expensive. That is why universalistic public programs aimed at all income groups are the best guarantee of high-quality, egalitarian services based on need.

LIMITS OF WELFARE CAPITALISM

Perhaps the most puzzling thing about the welfare state is how little redistribution it manages to accomplish. Even when 30–60 percent of national income is taxed, redistributed, and spent, final income distributions are not so strikingly different from initial ones. If taxation and free provision of services do incur efficiency costs — even minimal ones — one might legitimately inquire whether all the taxation and income transfer is worth the bother.

Most studies of income distribution and the welfare state suggest the following conclusions: First, wealth remains distributed much more unequally than income. In America, the top 20 percent of people have 43 percent of the income but 80 percent of the wealth. This is simply a function of the vast inequalities of property wealth that characterize market capitalism — and the refusal of any present democratic society to impose confiscatory taxes on private wealth. As long as the richest households control the vast bulk of private wealth, that wealth will keep generating disproportionate concentrations of private income.

Second, full employment and an egalitarian wage structure are inherently a more potent source of equality than taxes and income transfers, for there are limits to government's ability to redistribute. Universalistic income-support programs cannot by themselves undo vast inequalities of earned income — in part because they transfer money to the middle class as well as to the poor, and in part because very high tax rates are indeed inefficient. Finally, relatively little redistribution is accomplished through services. Some services, like public works, roads, sanitation, police, the armed forces, and so on, are not intended to redistribute; while others, like public higher education and mass transit, actually redistribute slightly from the general population to the affluent; and still others, like health care, are consumed more intensely by the middle class. Nonetheless, universal services foster a kind of egalitarianism that is hard to quantify.

Concentrated Wealth

Concentration of wealth varies somewhat among countries; and during the past fifty years, the share held by the very top of the wealth distribution — the richest 1–5 percent — has diminished slightly while the upper-middle class — the top 25 percent — has gained relatively. But the bottom half of society still owns virtually no net wealth other than social security entitlements: practically no stocks and bonds and very little private savings or net real estate wealth. In general, the property wealth held by the bottom 40–50 percent of society is canceled out by debts.

In the United States, the top 1 percent of the population owns 60 percent of corporate stock and fully 35–40 percent of all net wealth. The top 10 percent have 65–70 percent of all net wealth. The bottom half of the population have just 1 percent of all the net wealth, which includes 0.1 percent of corporate stock and 1.8 percent of privately owned real estate. The distribution of wealth is less unequal in the more advanced welfare states, but not by all that much. In Sweden, with the most egalitarian wealth distribution, the top 1 percent owns about 15 percent of net wealth. That is a good deal of inequality for a fairly socialist country. However, Sweden has made impressive equality gains since 1920, when 1 percent of the population owned 50 percent of the wealth.

In Britain and the United States, wealth distribution has become somewhat less unequal, but the progress has been far slower. In Britain, the top 1 percent owned 60 percent of the wealth in 1924. By 1960, that had fallen to 33.9 percent; however, wealth distribution has hardly changed since 1960. The top 10 percent owned 88 percent of all wealth in 1924; in 1972, they still owned 72 percent.

In the United States, wealth holdings have become more dispersed, but again, there has been relatively little change in the past three decades. The share of wealth owned by the richest half of 1 percent declined from about 41 percent in 1922 to 19 percent in 1953. By 1972, the share had *increased*, to 21.9 percent. It dropped again in the mid-1970s, but is apparently increasing again today.

The Dutch economist Jan Pen uses a graphic metaphor to convey the extent of wealth inequality that still exists in the Western democracies. Imagine a parade of people, he suggests, in which everyone's physical height is proportional to his or her individual wealth. A person of average wealth is represented by a person of normal height. The entire population is arranged in a parade with the poorest (the smallest) at the front and the richest marching last. The parade passes by a reviewing stand over the course of a single hour. For the first several minutes, there is a vanguard whose heads are buried several feet in the ground; they have negative net worth — they owe more wealth than they own. Then, for almost twenty minutes, the people who pass by are invisible; they own no net wealth. At about half past the hour, we begin seeing some dwarfs — people about six inches tall, whose wealth is household furniture, a car, and perhaps a small savings account. Pen notes: "But a new surprise awaits us here. *We keep on seeing dwarfs.* Of course they gradually become a little taller, but it's a slow process." Only at about twelve minutes before the hour do we begin seeing people of average height, for more than three quarters of the population have fewer assets than average.

In the last few minutes, writes Pen, "giants loom up . . . a lawyer, not exceptionally successful, eighteen feet tall." And then, in the last few seconds, people so tall that we can't see their heads . . . Corporate managing directors a hundred yards tall . . .

> The rear of the parade is brought up by a few participants who are measured in miles . . . their heads disappear into the clouds. . . . The last man, whose back we can see long after the parade has passed by, is John Paul Getty. . . . His height is inconceivable: at least ten miles; perhaps twice as much.

How Much Redistribution?

Income is distributed more unequally in the United States than in most other Western nations, both before and after taxes. With a flatter tax system and a more meager program of income transfers, U.S. public spending has relatively little effect on the final income distribution.

Highly unequal wages provide a second explanation of why final income remains so unequal despite high levels of public spending. The Swedish solidarity wage policy remains the exception. In Britain and America, earned income became more unequal during the 1970s. As we saw in our discussion of labor (see page 170), American wage income polarized during the past fifteen years. In general, the share of the bottom fifth of American family income, before taxes and income transfers, increased by nearly one third between 1929 and 1947 (from 3.5 percent of the total income to 5.0 percent of the total); it increased slightly until the late 1960s, and then has been decreasing since. The increase in government spending during the 1960s and early 1970s more or less compensated for the widening inequality of earned income; but since the late 1970s both market trends and public policy have been widening the inequalities.

In Britain, despite the welfare state, shares of earned income have remained astonishingly constant for a hundred years. Professor A. B. Atkinson, the dean of British income distribution scholars, reported that during an 87-year period, while the median weekly earnings of British workers increased from slightly over one pound to £37, the distribution changed scarcely at all.

Even in welfare states more comprehensive than ours, programs of income support selectively assist certain groups rather than transforming the entire distribution of income. The most dramatic effect is on the elderly, who receive about two thirds of all transfer payments. In the United States, the effect of real increases in social security pensions has been to substantially reduce poverty among the elderly. In 1959, fully 35 percent of elderly people in America were living in poverty, compared to 22 percent of the population as a whole. By 1981, the percentage of elderly poor was down to 15 percent — virtually identical to that of the rest of the population. Social security is a substantial source of income to the elderly, providing 39 percent of all cash income to the elderly, but fully 76 percent of the income to the elderly *poor*.

The equalizing effect of social transfers on the nonelderly is less dramatic. Even in the most advanced welfare states, such major income-transfer programs as family allowances and housing allowances add up to only 3–4 percent of GNP, much of which goes to middle-class families under universalistic programs; private income remains vastly greater than social income, and wealthy households still retain many times the purchasing power of poor ones.

Nonetheless, gross statistics on pre- and post-tax income distribution can be misleading. Income-support programs do make a significant contribution to the resources of needy families. Even in the United States, where total income support for the poor equals less than 3 percent of GNP, poor people have such a small share of national income to begin with that this additional amount has a major impact. According to one respected scholar of income distribution, Timothy Smeeding, transfers increase the total income of the poorest fifth of the population by about 24 percent. That relatively small contribution has been sufficient to cut the U.S. poverty rate almost in half. According to a study by economists Sheldon Danziger and Robert Plotnik, cash transfers reduced the 1965 poverty rate from 21 percent to 15.6 percent. By 1978, transfers had an even more dramatic effect: they reduced poverty from 20.2 to 11.4 percent.

Unfortunately, several other trends are combining to wipe out the recent progress toward greater income equality in America. Demographically, the increase in persons living alone — especially older people — and the increase in female heads of households — tends to increase pretransfer inequality and personal hardship. We have also seen how wage and salary income are becoming more unequal. As the Princeton economist Alan Blinder observes, "Because of powerful demographic forces, we have been swimming upstream in terms of reducing income inequality; just to have held our own was an achievement."

Since 1981, however, the policy of the U.S. government has been to swim downstream and exacerbate the forces making for greater inequality. Income-support programs aimed at the needy were cut by $13.8 billion, or about 14 percent, between 1980 and 1984, while the tax burden was redistributed from rich to poor. According to an extensive study by the Urban Institute, real disposable income among the poorest one fifth of American families will have fallen by 9.4 percent between 1979 and 1984 — from an average of $7946 to $6833. For the richest fifth of families, real income remained virtually constant. Moreover, effective tax burdens for the richest one fifth of families, taking all kinds of taxes into consideration, remained stable, while taxes on the poorest fifth increased by 23 percent.

Austerity with a Human Face

The welfare state everywhere is in a period of retrenchment. The Western nations went through a period of nearly a decade in which political systems were unwilling to face up to economic stagnation. Instead, safety-net programs took up the slack, and government deficits were expanded to their limits. It is doubtful that the expansion of public spending can continue without beginning to have serious real economic effects. When a budget deficit is 2 or 3 percent of gross national product, and there is a high rate of private saving to finance the deficit, the impact is negligible. When the deficit is 10–15 percent of GNP, public debt begins to mount, government borrowing competes with productive investment, and soon the interest on the debt becomes the largest single category of public spending. That course is no longer supportable.

During the boom years of the 1950s and 1960s, Europe's economy roared along even though public spending was already in the range of 30–40 percent of gross national product. The welfare state seems to reach a natural limit when public spending approaches about 50 percent of GNP. Beyond that point, tax rates on the entire population become so high that little redistribution is accomplished, and private energies turn to tax avoidance. There is far greater payoff in equalizing primary incomes and assuring full employment.

As different countries are limiting their public outlays in the 1980s, there are very significant differences in how spending is being limited. In Sweden, wage levels generally have been cut by about 6 percent, but the lowest paid workers have received the most favorable treatment. In France, the Mitterrand government has reduced total social spending but raised the minimum wage, minimum pensions, and family allowances for the poorest families. In Holland, where pension benefits are indexed to wage levels, the entire society has taken a 3 percent cut. Only in Britain and the United States has austerity fallen disproportionately on the poor.

There is no doubt that the ability of the welfare state to counter the inequalities of the laissez-faire market has its limits. Who bears the cost of adjusting the welfare state to hard times, and how social criteria might be substituted for market criteria in the investment of capital and the distribution of wages — these are also matters not of positive economics, but of political choice.

As long as egalitarians assume that public policy cannot contribute to economic equality directly but must proceed by ingenious manipulations of marginal institutions like schools, progress will remain glacial. If we want to move beyond this tradition, we will have to establish political control over the economic institutions that shape our society. This is what other countries usually call socialism.

— Christopher Jencks

The average American worker is convinced that the government could screw up a two-car funeral.

— Douglas Fraser

EPILOGUE: POLITICS

THIS BOOK, thus far, has sought to establish that many models of economic distribution and economic performance are possible; that efficiency and equality coexist in all manner of relationships; that equality/efficiency bargains involve social choices; and that distributions of economic resources reflect distributions of political power. We have also seen that Northern Europe, on the whole, has done better than the United States during most of the postwar era at maximizing both equality and efficiency. And we have seen that a well-organized labor movement — ideologically sophisticated but institutionally restrained — is a key ingredient in this social model, as a broker, a constituency, a counterweight to market-distribution, and a locus of power.

Two questions remain: Can the Northern European model of the social democratic welfare state survive a long period of slow growth, either economically or politically? And is there any likelihood that the United States can develop social mechanisms that improve equality/efficiency bargains, given our history, our political institutions, our individualist ethic, and our industrial-relations culture?

Social Democratic Futures

European socialists use the phrase *American exceptionalism* — the fact that the United States, uniquely, never developed a class-conscious work force, an ideological trade-union movement, or a politically influential labor or socialist party. Although one can debate the details, the list of reasons is not hard to identify. The granddaddy of this literature, a 1906 book by the German economist Werner Sombart titled *Why Is There No Socialism in the United States?* begins with the memorable line, "The United States of America is capitalism's land of promise." And, of course, it is.

As a kind of latter-day Teutonic Tocqueville, Sombart went on to identify the other key factors, in an analysis that is richly detailed and still fitting for our own day: In America, said Sombart, opportunity has retarded class consciousness. Nativism substitutes for worker solidarity; ethnic division gets in the way of labor organizing. The frontier is an escape valve. The two-party system undermines radical third parties. Since liberalism and universal manhood suffrage came early to the United States, political liberty was not the fruit of class struggle. The "civic integration" of American workers is impressive; their living standards are high. Sombart meticulously tallied wages and household budgets of workers in Pennsylvania and Upper Silesia, New York and Breslau, and concluded that American workers had nearly three times the purchasing power of their German cousins.

For the American worker, wrote Sombart, Liberty and Equality

> are not empty ideas and vague dreams, as they are for the European working class; for the most part they are realities. . . . In his appearance, in his demeanour, and in the manner of his conversation, the American worker also contrasts strongly with the European one. He carries his head high, walks with a lissom stride, and is as open and cheerful in his expression as any member of the middle class. There is nothing oppressed or submissive about him.

In America, concluded Professor Sombart, "All socialist utopias came to nothing on roast beef and apple pie."

More recent scholarship has embellished this line of inquiry. The "end of ideology" literature of the late 1950s celebrated the fact that the American work force had surmounted the years of Depression with scant radicalization; that a flirtation with ideology ended when prosperity returned. A mirror-image socialist literature wistfully reaches similar conclusions. Racial divisions are identified as a major factor in the failure of American wage earners to unite and mobilize politically as they did in Europe. Indeed, the history of pre-1960 American social legislation is littered with provisions designed to keep blacks from benefiting. Minimum wage and social security long excluded farm workers and domestics, as the price of white Southern congressional support.

Moreover, American political parties divided along regional, ethnic, and interest-group lines, rather than ideologically or according to class. The party realignment of 1896 headed off the one radical party, the Populists, which had come close to becoming a major national force. Even the New Deal Democratic Party of Franklin D. Roosevelt was more a coalition of regional, ethnic, and interest groups, than a clear ideological or class alliance. This tradition has created a political culture in which business is disproportionately strong and organized labor unusually weak.

I stress the key importance of labor's political mobilization, not out of a desire to romanticize the working class, or out of a Marxian vision of its historic role (most Marxists scoff at Western European social democracy). Rather, I emphasize labor as a political actor because a survey of social and economic policies in different nations suggests that labor — that is, wage earners organized and mobilized to articulate the self-interest of the nonrich — is invariably the indispensable political constituency for economic strategies that reconcile efficiency with equality.

The difficulty of maintaining egalitarian policies against the steady thrust of the market system toward greater inequality is immense. Big money retains a potent hold on the limits of the possible. In a liberal democracy, conservative parties frequently govern; they usually can be counted upon to reintroduce policies that frustrate universalistic income redistribution, weaken labor movements, separate the dependent poor from the working poor, and erode the political constituency for equality. Egalitarianism never quite reaches escape velocity.

In that respect, it is almost more appropriate to talk of a "Swedish exceptionalism" than an American exception. For Sweden is virtually the only country in the parliamentary West where Social Democrats held power long enough to refine economic institutions to match social goals. Thus, it is only in Sweden that we find major economic breakthroughs like socialized savings under the national pension system; a comprehensive active labor-market policy; a strong solidarity wage policy; a commitment to wage restraint for the sake of increasing investment; and most recently the Meidner plan for worker ownership. The more such institutions prove practical, the stronger is the public support for them. Although a conservative-liberal coalition did govern between 1976 and 1982, public support for universal social entitlements and income transfers was so well entrenched that the Swedish conservatives did not dare undertake any dismantling of the welfare state. Swedes are brought up believing in egalitarian values as firmly as Americans cherish political democracy. The Swedish electorate would no more sacrifice social health care than the American electorate would cast aside freedom of speech. And even so the Swedish labor movement has had some difficulty maintaining labor unity as living standards have begun to stagnate.

But Sweden is very, *very* atypical. One American student of Swedish socialism, Andrew Martin, in a seminal essay titled "Is Democratic Control of Capitalist Economies Possible?" calls attention to the difficulty of maintaining durable, countervailing influence by "political elites independent of business" in an economy that remains fundamentally capitalist. In the American context, the residual power of business creates a setting in which even "left of center" presidents go through a ritual of appointing Treasury secretaries and Federal Reserve Board chairmen reassuring to industry, and the fundamental test of soundness for most policies is whether they are good for business. Martin argues that the entrenched power of business in a market capitalist economy can be counterbalanced only if several conditions are present: a strong, ideologically coherent labor movement; a very high voting participation by wage earners; and a labor or social democratic party that is the party of government most of the time. Martin concludes bluntly, "In short, democratic control of a capitalist economy is not likely to be possible under most conceivable political circumstances."

For a time, during the 1950s and 1960s, it looked as if Keynesian full employment and the social guarantees of the welfare state were so well entrenched that they would be impregnable to periodic conservative rule. In the 1960s some observers concluded that democratic-left parties — the West German SPD, the British Labour Party, the American Democratic Party — had become virtually the "natural party of government." In a famous 1956 book, *The Future of Socialism*, the British Labour Party theorist C. A. R. Crosland predicted that the social democratic compromise was permanently established, invulnerable to episodes of Tory governance. He did not anticipate 13 percent unemployment and Mrs. Thatcher. As things turned out, the regular alternation between Labour and Conservative governments in Britain ultimately produced not so much a class entente as a stalemate, in which public spending steadily rose, but more fundamental economic reforms were consistently frustrated, and even the British working class gradually deserted the Labour party because it couldn't deliver. (Much the same phenomenon beset the Democratic party of the United States, as the blue-collar vote substantially deserted the Democrats in the 1972 and 1980 elections.)

The stagnation of Britain — slow growth, high unemployment, high public spending, and political fragmentation — is only an extreme case of a kind of social democratic deadlock afflicting most of Western Europe. The welfare-state bargain seems stuck in a political impasse. At projected rates of economic recovery, unemployment will stay at present levels. As unemployment rises, state expenditures are consumed supporting the idle and the poor rather than providing needed and more politically popular services on a universal basis. The voters are reluctant to see services cut, but they are resistant to higher taxes. Public spending is marooned on a plateau. In most countries, partisan allegiances on both ends of the political spectrum are weakening. Socialist governments can't move very far left, and conservative governments, even Mrs. Thatcher's, can't undo all that much of the welfare state — though they can preside over depressingly high unemployment. Ironically, it is the safety net of the welfare state that keeps the unemployment from becoming socially explosive. In country after country, the incumbent government escapes much responsibility for economic stagnation, because voters look at countries with politically opposite regimes and see the same stagnation; "world recession," rather than particular policies, is held responsible. Austerity politics are the order of the day, but in most of Europe they remain the politics of muddle through. Even France under Mitterrand can manage little better than austerity with a human face.

The roots of economic stagnation in the West are multiple and complex. Although the OPEC oil price increases are heavily implicated, OPEC is not the main villain. Productivity growth and rates of profit began slowing down throughout the West in the late 1960s, before the OPEC price rise. Clearly, the political viability of the welfare state has suffered on account of the economic slump; but it is not at all clear that welfare spending *caused* the slump.

According to one school of thought — shared by some Marxists and most conservatives — the welfare state is indeed the culprit: growth slowed down because excessive labor-bargaining power, redistribution, and public outlays squeezed profit margins and discouraged investment. For the Marxists, the slowdown is a sign of the contradictions of capitalism; for the conservatives, growth succumbed needlessly to welfarism.

According to another school — a more eclectic one, with which I identify — growth expired because the big economic spending boom fueled by World War II, by European economic integration, by mass consumer spending and the automobile age, slowly petered out; the OPEC price hike was merely the coup de grâce. Saturated consumer spending on the demand side and heightened global competition on the supply side — *not* the cost of the welfare state — were the main cause of a squeeze on profits and the main source of stagnation. In the second view, if growth can be ignited once more by a concerted decision to revive demand and restore full employment, the distributional issue is simply a matter of political choice. We can have an equitable society if we want one. The issue is whether the major Western nations will muster the political ability to revive a full-employment economy.

Therefore, the impasse of the social democratic model is more a political impasse than an economic one. Economic growth does not suddenly cease when public spending reaches 40 percent of GNP and old people enjoy secure retirements. Egalitarian Europe enjoyed a fine economic performance until world recession struck. Interestingly enough, the high-spending nations of Europe have maintained their rates of productivity growth, post-OPEC, rather better than the United States. Between 1960 and 1973, the fat years, labor productivity in manufacturing improved at an average yearly rate of 3 percent in the United States. After 1973, American productivity growth dropped to 1.7 percent a year. In Europe, growth of productivity averaged

5.9 percent a year before OPEC but was still 4.2 percent after 1973. In other words, Europe's productivity gains have been better during the recession decade of the 1970s than ours were during the boom years of the 1960s. The problem, however, is that productivity gains during a period of slow growth mean only that capital is substituted for labor. In other words, they mean rising unemployment, not rising living standards.

For most of the postwar period, social democratic Europe out-performed laissez-faire America. Since the pit of the 1982–83 recession, the United States has reduced unemployment somewhat faster than Western Europe, and at this writing our unemployment rate is in the 7–8 percent range while much of Europe's is over 9 percent. It is also evident that the United States during the 1970s generated new jobs at a faster rate than Europe.

This recent history has led to a new set of arguments on behalf of laissez-faire. American labor markets, it is said, are flexible, while social protections make Europe's labor markets rigid. Entrepreneurial America, therefore, is enjoying a faster recovery than Europe. European equality is finally undercutting European efficiency.

The reality, I would submit, is less fanciful. The United States generated so many new jobs in the 1970s mainly because we were so successful at substituting labor for capital as women and young people poured into the work force and wage levels fell. A study by the OECD found that of all industrial nations, those with the most wage rigidity achieved the highest productivity growth, for the obvious reason that high wages led employers to replace workers with machines that much faster. Productivity growth, of course, is good, but unemployment is bad. The only way out of the bind is to restore a high rate of overall growth of output and steadily to adjust working time.

If "flexible wages" are desired, in order to limit the rate of wage gains to real productivity gains, anarchic labor markets with erratic bouts of wage cutting and high unemployment are not the only available strategy for achieving labor flexibility. In the OECD study, the country with the most adaptable real wages was Sweden (the United States was third). But Sweden achieved its wage flexibility through finely tuned social bargaining; we achieved ours by trusting the market and letting the devil take the hindmost. If Sweden, with its elaborate protections, can achieve both full employment and more flexible wages than the United States, then another equality/efficiency claim is so much polemic.

Moreover, the 1983–84 recovery had little if anything to do with a docile labor force. The American economy began growing at a rapid clip in late 1983 for reasons that are entirely Keynesian: a $200-billion federal deficit stimulated aggregate demand. Any other nation that ran such a large deficit would have paid for it in a weakened currency. Yet because the dollar is the world's favorite reserve currency, the big American deficit and the resultant high interest rates had the paradoxical effect of attracting foreign money to our shores; foreign investors financed the American deficit, and the dollar grew stronger. This had the added effect of punishing Western Europe, which had to raise its own interest rates defensively and retard its own recovery. There is near universal agreement among economists of all persuasions that a recovery based on very big deficits, high interest rates, and temporary capital inflows cannot last very long.

Instead of a one-country recovery based on a perverse form of Keynesianism, the industrial West needs a common effort to restore balanced growth, based on lower real interest rates, coordinated fiscal policies, managed rather than laissez-faire trade, and joint measures to adjust labor markets. Only in that wider economic climate of high growth and full employment does the replacement of labor with capital bring broadly distributed social gains.

Europe's task in the 1980s, therefore, is to restore growth, not to dismantle its wonderful thirty-year experience of social and national peace. Growth will require a concerted program of economic expansion and new mechanisms to keep on generating jobs and purchasing power as the problem of physical production is increasingly solved by machines. Technologically, the Western economies are in a period of explosive innovation. Steelmaking, automotive production, aviation, electronics, agriculture, computers — all are becoming more efficient, both in their production technologies and in the products they offer consumers. Why, then, should we have to lower our living standards? What is the mysterious source of the economic loss? If productivity is increasing, why should we sacrifice services and wages?

The source of the loss is a systemic bottleneck that Keynes (and Marx) would recognize: competitive overproduction, and the failure of the system to provide enough employment and enough purchasing power. There is no failure on the supply side. The system has plenty of capital, plenty of production technology. The failure is a Keynesian one. But Keynes wrote in a time when there was far less global interdependence than there is today, and national strategies of stabilization and demand management were technically feasible. The times today demand adaptation of Keynesian insights and strategies across national frontiers, at a time, unfortunately, when Keynesianism is in disrepute and laissez-faire is in favor.

The economic giant of the midcentury who is newly rediscovered and lionized today is not Keynes, but Joseph Schumpeter, the prophet of entrepreneurship. A new burst of entrepreneurialism, it is said, will pull the Western economies out of their slump. What fetters the entrepreneurial soul? Only the welfare state. In Western Europe, neoliberal ideas imported from America are the fashionable ones. Envious looks are cast at Silicon Valley. Many Europeans think the way to emulate American entrepreneurship is to emulate American conservatism.

There are movements throughout Western Europe to "privatize" health care, to substitute job-related pensions for universal social security, to weaken trade unions. It is difficult to see how this will solve Europe's economic problems, but it could well revive the ghosts of nationalism and bitter class conflict that were seemingly laid to rest in the 1950s. It is ironic indeed that a Reaganesque America is a model to many Europeans; for we are a model of uneven development and social calamity. Schumpeter himself was the first to term market capitalism a system of "creative destruction." By throwing away social stability, Europe is more likely to buy central Harlem than Silicon Valley.

Historians looking back at the quarter century between 1948 and 1973 are likely to record that the social democratic epoch was a uniquely successful period of social harmony and economic growth. During nearly all of the postwar era prior to the 1981 recession, social democratic Western Europe outperformed laissez-faire America. Europe enjoyed both faster growth of productivity and of output, as well as a broader diffusion of material goods. It remains to be seen whether the 1980s have dealt the European welfare state a temporary setback, or a coup de grâce.

The current plight of European social democracy has heartened critics on both the left and the right: Marxists who argue that welfare capitalism cannot endure as long as the means of production are private, and conservatives who insist that redistribution must wreck the dynamism of the private market. This ideological *Schadenfreude* — joy at another's misfortune — is unseemly and unpersuasive. With all of its imperfections, the social democratic compromise is worth defending, intellectually and politically. It is far more untidy theoretically than either Marxian socialism or laissez-faire capitalism; but even with the post-1981 setbacks, the overall postwar record suggests that a social democratic society manages to leaven both the potential tyranny of the state and the potential tyranny of the market far better than either of the more doctrinaire alternatives. There is no convincing evidence that it was social democracy that killed economic growth.

But if Andrew Martin is right and the political preconditions for a durable social democratic economics exist only rarely, then Europe may be in for an extended period of stalemate and stagnation — and perhaps a nasty period of protracted social conflict as resurgent business elites preaching market economics attempt to seriously roll back the class detente of the welfare state. Moreover, the Western economies are now so closely bound together that one nation pursuing a different course cannot readily buck the tide. On the other hand, equity economics could be the instrument of renewed growth, if they gain sufficient political support.

American Futures

The United States presents an even more difficult case. At present, the political center has moved very far to the right. The limited solicitude for the poor that remains in our political system is directed at the "truly needy" and the social "safety net," rather than at broadly egalitarian approaches. Citizen entitlements are in universal disrepute as budget-busters.

I have tried to argue that equity economics can be sound economics; the problem is in animating and maintaining a constituency for it. Occasionally, even in America, the political system allows some anomalous breakthrough like social security retirement or Medicare or public higher education — which then becomes a highly esteemed part of the established order, despite its plainly socialist character. In Reagan's assault against the welfare state, the high ground turned out to be the most expensive and universal program of all, social security. There may be a lesson here.

If a strong labor movement is the linchpin constituency for progressive politics, American progressivism is in deep trouble. Labor today is weak, defensive, self-interested, and fragmented. To regain political influence and legitimacy, both with its members and with the general public, the American labor movement will need to operate in very unfamiliar territory. Using the power it has to bargain for wage gains is no longer possible. However, one can imagine a different sort of social bargain in which unions reassert their influence, but use it to improve the lot of the lowest paid; in which unions stop defining security in terms of work rules, but define security as the right to be retrained and reemployed in a full-employment economy. One could imagine a labor movement bargaining for work-place innovations and becoming the ally of productivity as well as of industrial democracy. To survive and to play the key role as a constituency for growth with equity, labor must simultaneously become more militant *and* more broadly legitimate.

A further obstacle to equity politics is that voting participation by the poor in America remains low by international standards, even after the Jesse Jackson campaign. Yet another obstacle is that American politics are nonideological, except on the business side, where they are steadily becoming more ideological. In short, both the faith in equality as an ideal and the constituency for equality are at a low ebb. One must go back to the 1920s to find a time when the political balance between left and right was so asymmetrical.

The political problem of the 1980s is how to break into a closed circle. The stagflation of the 1970s discredited Jimmy Carter's brand of liberalism, but the unemployment, the deficits, and high real interest rates of the 1980s may not discredit laissez-faire. High unemployment magnifies all of the cracks in what was once the Roosevelt coalition. It pits blacks, women, and young people looking for decent jobs against breadwinners who are unionized. It encourages communities to bid away their tax base in the hope of attracting some benevolent entrepreneur. It pits region and community against each other. High unemployment makes decent social policy seem wasteful economics. It plays off people needing services against people wanting tax relief. It creates a climate in which adequate medical care and pensions for the elderly are considered excessive burdens on the productive young.

Democratic Party politics remain nonideological because Democratic voters don't think ideologically and there is a weak constituency for explicitly egalitarian policies. The constituency for equality is weak because public policies continue to isolate the poor. Business is so dominant that mainstream Democrats are perennially seeking accommodations with economic elites rather than challenging them. Labor unions are fragmented, unpopular, and easy for business-oriented administrations to neutralize. Government, as the instrument of social justice, has little ideological support, even from its natural allies. The American political economy is so unsupportive of public programs that some government agencies probably *could* screw up a two-car funeral. Federalism, and interest-group rather than ideological politics, create a constituency for pork-barrel spending rather than structural change. Thus the economics of inequality, the politics of inequality, and the ideology of inequality are all mutually reinforcing.

Historically in America, the means of egalitarianism have been individual. Liberty and possibility — these were embodied in personal gain, not in social transformation. People were equal to the extent that they were equally free to pursue opportunity. That is why redistribution and social solutions to inequality go so deeply against the American grain. That is why ordinary wage earners have seen little reason to make common cause with society's losers. The flawed ideal of individual opportunity remains the potent force that it was in Sombart's day, despite a decade of declining opportunity.

At the same time, there is a powerful minor current in the American experience — a deep conflict that periodically erupts between the democratic promise of American individualism and the practical power of big money. The "money issue" that pervaded the nineteenth century — from Andrew Jackson's skirmish with the Bank of the United States to Bryan's Cross of Gold speech — was about wealth versus commonwealth. The occasional populist impulse, though far more inchoate than European socialism, is also about the opportunity of the ordinary American versus privilege. The New Deal was about restoring both economic opportunity and economic security, after the market system had failed on both counts. It did not accept the idea that security had to be sacrificed to opportunity. The Democratic Party at its most vigorous is a party of the common American, demanding that privilege get out of the way. That is not socialism, but at least it is an economics of the self-interest of the nonrich.

Historically, egalitarian policies made headway in America when presidents or presidential candidates helped to mobilize ordinary voters. Franklin D. Roosevelt substantially increased his 1936 victory margin over 1932 because record numbers of nonrich people saw in Roosevelt a reason to vote. It seems to me that the most likely way that egalitarianism might again break into the closed circle is if the nonrich begin to vote in large numbers; that in turn might bring to office an administration friendlier to egalitarian goals; that would give labor organizations the political space to regroup, as they did in the 1930s. And that might again make egalitarian politics and ideologies of collective well-being respectable.

In that respect, the renewed voting participation by minorities is encouraging; and so is the mobilization of women voters around issues of economic equity and self-interest. Women's demands for equal opportunity are not unrelated to the broader economics of equity. A politics of economic expansion predicated on full employment could unite and animate all of the disparate constituencies that once made up the constituency for the New Deal — just as the stresses of stagnation divide it.

Whether a newly mobilized egalitarian constituency causes a more venturesome leadership to materialize or whether a leader animates a constituency is almost beside the point. The relation of constituency to leadership to policy and ideology is always somewhat circular. But at least one can imagine different circles than the one we are stuck in today are possible.

It is distressing to imply that our closed circle can best be broken by a deus ex machina, by some sort of Roosevelt reincarnated. Would that ordinary people might simply grow indignant at the gross inequalities of American society and organize for progressive change. Would that economic resources and ideological energy were more symmetrically distributed; that think tanks were burgeoning on the labor left instead of on the corporate right, and that there were six thousand well-paid trade union economists and twenty corporate economists, instead of vice versa. Would that democratic politics began to revive "at the base."

That might yet happen; however, it is the subject of another book. This book is simply a description of practical social alternatives, of strategies for reconciling equality with efficiency. I have tried to suggest that injustice is not necessary economics; that the economics of equality can work, and often has worked, when the constituency for it is animated. The *politics* of equality — that is a little harder.

NOTES
ACKNOWLEDGMENTS
INDEX

NOTES

INTRODUCTION

page
1   "The political problem of mankind": John Maynard Keynes, *Essays in Persuasion* (New York: Harcourt, Brace and Co., 1932), p. 344.
     "Don't punish the rich": John Schreiner, *New York Times*, September 18, 1983, Sunday Business Section, p. 3.
     "In order to succeed": George Gilder, *Wealth and Poverty* (New York: Bantam Books, 1981), p. 144.
5   "Social citizenship": T. H. Marshall, *Class, Citizenship, and Social Development*, especially Chapter 4, "Citizenship and Social Class" (Garden City, N.Y.: Doubleday, 1964), pp. 71–134.
6   Other books: Michael Walzer, *Spheres of Justice: A Defense of Pluralism and Equality* (New York: Basic Books, 1983); William Ryan, *Equality* (New York: Vintage Books, 1981).

1. EQUALITY AND EFFICIENCY

10   "To approach the question": R. H. Tawney, *Equality* (New York: Harcourt Brace and Co., 1929), p. 29.

11   "In liberal thought": Charles E. Lindblom, *Politics and Markets* (New York: Basic Books, 1977), p. 46.

12   "The homage that vice": Philip Green, *The Pursuit of Inequality* (New York: Pantheon Books, 1981), p. 4.
        "Measures — so the argument runs": Tawney, *Equality*, p. 197.

13   J. K. Galbraith's "The poor need the incentive": his speech at the Harvard University Institute of Politics, May 22, 1982.

14   "The contrasts among": Arthur Okun, *Equality and Efficiency: The Big Tradeoff* (Washington: The Brookings Institution, 1975), pp. 1–2.

15   "Property is not theft": Tawney, *The Acquisitive Society* (New York: Harcourt, Brace and Co., 1920), p. 70.
        "The more you look": T. H. Marshall, *Class, Citizenship and Social Development* (Garden City, N.Y.: Doubleday, 1964), p. 95.

17   Windfall origin of most fortunes: Lester Thurow, *Generating Inequality* (New York: Basic Books, 1975).

18   "Large instant fortunes": Thurow, "The Redistribution of Wealth," *Working Papers*, Winter 1976, p. 23.
        "In fact, most of the ardent supporters": Okun, *Equality and Efficiency*, p. 41.

22   Positive tradeoffs: David R. Cameron, "Social Democracy, Corporatism, and Labor Quiescence," paper presented at Conference on Representation and the State, Stanford University, October 1982. The original article by Phillips was "The Relation Between Unemployment and the Rate of Change of Money Wage Rates in the United Kingdom, 1861–1957," *Economica* 25 (November 1958), pp. 283–99.

24   ". . . spread wealth": Hugh Heclo, "Spreading Wealth: An International Survey of Asset Promotion Policy," unpublished research report sponsored by The Brookings Institution, Cambridge, 1980.

26   British unemployment statistics: Sir William Beveridge, *Full Employment in a Free Society* (London: His Majesty's Stationery Office, 1944), p. 47.

27   "Appropriate fiscal and monetary policies": Paul Samuelson, *Economics,* fifth edition (New York: McGraw-Hill Co., 1963), p. 403. See Andrew Levison's fine discussion of this issue in his *The Full Employment Alternative* (New York: Coward, McCann & Geogeghan, 1980), pp. 78–80.

27   "Bastard Keynesianism": Joan Robinson, in *Essays on John Maynard Keynes*, Milo Keynes, ed. (Cambridge: Cambridge University Press, 1978), pp. 123ff.

28   "In the enforced idleness": Keynes, *Essays in Persuasion* (New York: Harcourt, Brace and Co., 1932), p. 344.

29   "Keynes, en une mot, c'est le Freud de l'economie": Michel Albert, *Le Pari Francais* (Paris: Editions du Seuil, 1982), p. 72.
      "Pyramid-building, earthquakes": Keynes, *The General Theory of Employment, Interest, and Money* (New York: Harcourt, Brace and Jovanovich, 1964; first published in 1936), p. 129.

30   Unemployment in the United States: Statistics from *Economic Report of the President*, 1982 edition (Washington: Government Printing Office, 1982).

31   "An occasional depression": Quoted in Otis L. Graham, Jr., *Toward a Planned Economy* (New York: Oxford University Press, 1976), p. 88.

32   "Now, when the war": William Beveridge, *Social Insurance and Allied Services*, American edition (New York: The Macmillan Company, 1942), p. 6.
      "When for any reason": Beveridge, *Full Employment in a Free Society* (London: HMSO, 1944), p. "B".
      "Idleness is not the same": Ibid., p. 20.

33   "[The labor market] should always be": Ibid., p. 19.
      ". . . even if an adequate income": Ibid.
      "Only if there is work for all": Ibid.

34   "The necessity of socialism": Ibid., p. 37.

35   "The essential list of liberties": Ibid., p. 23.

38   Family income distribution, percentage share:

Year	Lowest Fifth	Highest Fifth	Highest 5 Percent
1947	5.0	43.0	17.5
1957	5.1	40.0	15.6
1967	5.5	40.4	15.2
1977	5.2	41.5	15.7

Source: Derived from U.S. Bureau of the Census, *Current Population Reports*, Series P-60. See also Morgan Reynolds and Eugene Smolensky, *Public Expenditures, Taxes and the Distribution of Income, 1950, 1961, 1970* (New York: Academic Press, 1977); and Sheldon Danziger, Robert Haveman, and Robert Plotnick, "How Income Transfer Programs Affect Work, Savings, and Income," *Journal of Economic Literature* 19 (September 1981), pp. 975–1028.

39   Twenty percent source: Gavyn Davies and David Piachaud, "Social Policy and the Economy," in *The Future of the Welfare State*, Howard Glennerster, ed. (London: Heineman, 1983), p. 40.

40   Failure of welfare state to redistribute: Julian Le Grand, *The Strategy of Equality* (London: George Allen & Unwin, 1982).
      "If we want to redistribute income": Christopher Jencks in Le Grand, Ibid., p. 139.

42   On the tendency of welfare states to fiscal calamity: J. M. Buchanan and G. Tullock, *The Calculus of Consent* (Ann Arbor: University of Michigan Press, 1962); J. M. Buchanan and R. E. Wagner, *Democracy in Deficit* (New York: Academic Press, 1977); see also Samuel Brittain, *The Role and Limits of Government* (Minneapolis: University of Minnesota Press, 1983); Allen Meltzer and Scott F. Richard, "Why Government Grows (and Grows) in a Democracy," *The Public Interest* 51 (Summer 1978).
      Marxist view . . . "legitimation": James O'Connor, *The Fiscal Crisis of the State* (New York: St. Martin's Press, 1973).

43   Irrationalities seen as purposive: Richard Cloward and Frances Fox Piven, *Regulating the Poor* (New York: Pantheon Books, 1971).
      "In the 1960s": Ian Gough, *The Political Economy of the Welfare State* (London: The Macmillan Company, Ltd., 1979), p. 11.

44   "There is no obvious": Okun, *Equality and Efficiency*, pp. 23 –24.

45   "The privileged position of business": Charles Lindblom, *Politics and Markets*, pp. 173 and 88.

46   Public-sector expansion and growth rates contrasted:

Government Revenue as a Percentage of Gross Domestic Product

Country	1955–57	1974–76
Britain	28.6	36.0
France	30.9	37.2
West Germany	31.4	38.3
Japan	18.0	22.1
Sweden	26.2	47.0
United States	24.8	27.5

Source: *Public Expenditure Trends* (Paris: OECD, 1978).

Average Growth Rate of Gross Domestic Product, Per Annum		
Country	1965–73	1973–79
Britain	3.1	1.1
France	5.4	3.0
West Germany	4.3	2.4
Japan	10.7	4.1
Sweden	3.2	1.9
United States	3.7	2.4

Source: Derived from OECD *Economic Outlook*, various issues.

2. CAPITAL

51   Pioneering work: Edward Denison, *Accounting for Slower Growth: The United States in the 1970s* (Washington: The Brookings Institution, 1980).

53   Capital formation debate: For a more detailed account, see the author's *Revolt of the Haves* (New York: Simon and Schuster, 1980), pp. 230–77.

57   On who gained and lost from the Reagan program: "The Combined Effects of Major Changes in Federal Taxes and Spending Programs Since 1981" (Washington: Congressional Budget Office Staff Memorandum, April 1984); Benjamin A. Okner and D. Lee Bawden, "Recent Changes in Federal Income Distribution Policy," *National Tax Journal*, Vol. XXXVI, No. 3 (1983), p. 347; Frank Levy and Richard C. Michel, "The Way We'll Be in 1984: Recent Changes in the Level and Distribution of Income" (Washington: Urban Institute, 1983); Robert S. McIntyre and Dean C. Tipps, "Inequity and Decline" (Washington: Center on Budget and Policy Priorities, 1983).

59   Study by the New York Federal Reserve Bank: Robin C. De-Magistris and Carl J. Palash, "The Impact of IRAs on Savings," Federal Reserve Bank of New York *Quarterly Review*, Winter 1983–84, p. 24.
     Capital spending: *Economic Report of the President*, 1984 edition (Washington: Government Printing Office, 1984).

60   Pension statistics: Alicia H. Munnell, *The Economics of Private Pensions* (Washington: The Brookings Institution, 1982).

63   Very detailed study: John C. Carrington and George T. Edwards,

Financing Industrial Investment (London: The Macmillan Company, 1979).

65   Source for comparative savings data: Peter Sturm and Derek Blades, "International Differences and Trend Changes in Savings Ratios," OECD study (Paris: OECD, 1981).
Canadian savings rates: Gregory Jump, "Tax Incentives to Promote Personal Saving: Recent Canadian Experience," paper presented to Federal Reserve Bank of Boston Conference on Savings, Melvin Village, New Hampshire, October 6, 1982.

68   Comparative savings rates and distribution: Sturm and Blades, "International Differences."

70   "If you rely entirely": Author's interview with Anna Hedborg.

71   Technical literature: For a good example of the genre, see Franco Modigliani and Arlie Sterling, "Determinants of Private Saving with Special Reference to the Role of Social Security," Research Paper #1209 (Cambridge: National Bureau of Economic Research, 1981).

72   Corporate retained earnings: Sturm and Blades, "International Differences," pp. 6–9.
Japanese savings: Miyohei Shinohara, "The Determinants of Japan's High Savings Ratio and Its Behavior Pattern," paper prepared for International Economics Association conference, Bergamo, Italy, June 9, 1980.

74   Twenty percent rate of return: W. Krelle, "The Distribution of Wealth," University of Bonn, unpublished paper, 1980. Also Hugh Heclo, "Spreading Wealth: An International Survey of Asset Promotion Policy," unpublished research report sponsored by The Brookings Institution, Cambridge, 1980.

75   Feldstein's famous article: Martin Feldstein, "Social Security, Induced Retirement, and Aggregate Capital Accumulation," *Journal of Political Economy* 82 (September–October 1974), pp. 905–26; also Feldstein and Anthony Pellechio, "Social Security and Household Wealth Accumulation: New Econometric Evidence," *Review of Economics and Statistics* 61 (August 1979), pp. 361–68.
Critique of social security: Peter G. Peterson, "The Coming Crash of Social Security," *New York Review of Books,* December 2, 1982, pp. 34–39; Peter Ferrara, *Social Security: Averting the Crisis* (Washington: Cato Institute, 1982).

77   Congress's finest hour: Robert Kuttner, "Social Security Hysteria," *The New Republic,* December 27, 1982; also, the Final Report of the President's Commission on Social Security Reform (Washington: GPO, 1983).
On the history of social security: Martha Derthick, *Policymaking*

for Social Security (Washington: The Brookings Institution, 1979); and Robert W. Ball, *Social Security* (New York: Columbia University Press, 1978).

79   Martin Feldstein's technical error: Dean R. Leimer and Selig Lesnoy, "Social Security and Private Saving: New Time-Series Evidence," *Journal of Political Economy* 90 (June 1982), pp. 606–42.

80   Tax expenditure on private pensions: Alicia H. Munnell, *The Economics of Private Pensions* (Washington: The Brookings Institution, 1982), p. 44.
      Redistributive features of social security: Ball, *Social Security,* p. 23; and Henry Aaron, *Economic Effects of Social Security* (Washington: The Brookings Institution, 1983), p. 70.

81   Sweden statistics: *Growth or Stagnation: The Swedish Economy 1981–1985* (Stockholm: The Swedish Ministry of Economic Affairs, 1981), pp. 55 and 258.

83   Keynes, "Employment can only increase": *General Theory,* p. 98.
      Keynes, "There is no clear evidence": *Essays in Persuasion,* p. 282.
      Keynes, ". . . by the belief": *General Theory,* pp. 372 and 373.
      Keynes on social justifications for inequality and "communal saving": *General Theory,* p. 376.

84   Keynes, ". . . some coordinated act": *Essays in Persuasion,* p. 318.

85   German interest rates: *Danish Economic Review* (Copenhagen: Privatbanken), May 1983, p. 9.

86   John C. Carrington and George T. Edwards, *Financing Industrial Investment* (London: The Macmillan Company, 1979).
      Cost of capital: George Hatsopoulous, "The High Cost of Capital" (Washington: American Business Conference, 1983).
      Debt to equity ratios: "Report of the Committee to Review the Functioning of Financial Institutions" (known as the Wilson Committee) (London: Her Majesty's Stationery Office, 1980), p. 152.

88   Steel investment figures: *Wall Street Journal,* May 17, 1983, p. 34.

3. TRADE

91   "I was brought up, like most Englishmen": Keynes, "National Self-Sufficiency," *The Yale Review* XXII (June 1933), p. 755.

93   "Protectionism might mean a few jobs": *New York Times,* December 14, 1982.

94   Ricardo: See his *Principles of Political Economy and Taxation*

(1817), in *Works of David Ricardo,* Pierro Sraffa, ed. (London: Cambridge University Press, 1951).

95   Eli F. Heckscher: See his *Mercantilism* (London: G. Allen & Unwin, 1935). Bertil Ohlin: See his *Interregional and International Trade* (Cambridge: Harvard University Press, 1967).

96   "Japan's situation": Edwin O. Reischauer, *The United States and Japan* (New York: Viking Press, 1954), quoted in Bruce Scott, "Can Industry Survive the Welfare State," *Harvard Business Review,* September–October 1982.

101   "Suppose that in one year": Talk by William Branson at the "Stagnation in the West" conference, Center for Mediterranean Studies, Athens, June 2, 1983.

        Displaced New England workers: Barry Bluestone and Bennett Harrison, *The Deindustrialization of America* (New York: Basic Books, 1982), pp. 97–98.

        "Most modern processes": Keynes, "National Self-Sufficiency," *Yale Law Review* XXII (June 1933), pp. 760–62.

103   "Very few American workers": Michael Kinsley, "Keep Trade Free," *The New Republic,* April 11, 1983, pp. 10–12.

105   Havana Conference: William Ashworth, *The International Economy Since 1850,* second edition (London: Longmans, Green and Co., Ltd., 1962), p. 267.

107   On MITI and Japanese trade and industrial policy: Chalmers Johnson, *MITI and the Japanese Miracle* (Palo Alto: Stanford University Press, 1982); Ezra Vogel, *Japan as Number One* (Cambridge: Harvard University Press, 1981).

108   "For example, Coca-Cola": William Cline, "Reciprocity: A New Approach to World Trade?" (Washington: Institute for International Economics, 1982), p. 14.

109   "No other advanced economy": Gary Saxonhouse: "The Micro- and Macro-economics of Foreign Sales to Japan," in *Trade Policy in the 1980s,* William Cline, ed. (Washington: Institute for International Economics, 1983), p. 22.

        Paul Krugman's ideas on trade: See Paul Krugman, "Targeted Industrial Policies: Theory and Evidence" (paper delivered to Federal Reserve Bank of Kansas City conference on industrial targeting, August 1983), p. 34.

111   "A number of economists have noticed": See the discussion of Ricardian trade by Nicholas Kaldor, "The Foundations of Free Trade Theory," in *Studies in Economic Theory and Practice,* J. Los et al., eds. (Amsterdam: North Holland Publishing Co., 1981), pp. 214–21.

"How to sustain": John Zysman and Steven Cohen, "The Mercantilist Challenge to the Liberal International Trade Order" (Washington: U.S. Congress Joint Economic Committee, December 29, 1982), p. 62. ·

112 Steel strategy: Report of the *ad hoc* Steel Tripartite Advisory Committee (Washington, 1980).

114 Comments by Alan W. Wolff and Robert Herzstein: Interviews with the author.
Fred Bergsten comment: Interview with the author.

115 Harley-Davidson case: Report of the U.S. International Trade Commission, U.S.I.T.C. Publication No. 1342, February 1983.

116 David Morrissey comment: Interview with the author.

118 Japanese semiconductors: *The Effect of Government Targeting on World Semiconductor Competition* (Washington: Semiconductor Industry Association, 1983).

119 Houdaille case: Houdaille Industries, Inc., petition to the President of the United States (Washington: Covington and Burling petition), May 3, 1982.
Municipal research centers in Japan: Author's interview with Richard Copaken and Copaken's videotapes.

121 "The cheap [imported] shirt": Wolfgang Hager, "Protectionism and Autonomy: How to Preserve Free Trade in Europe," *Journal of International Affairs,* Summer 1982, p. 424.

123 Common Market Study: Michael Noelke and Robert Taylor, *EEC Protectionism: Present Practice and Future Trends,* Vol. 1 (Brussels: European Research Associates, 1981), p. 282.

124 EEC protectionism: Noelke and Taylor, ibid.

125 Japanese F-15s: Barry Bluestone and Seamus O'Cleireacain, "Towards Democratically Negotiated International Trade" (paper delivered to the "Stagnation in the West" international conference, Athens, June 2, 1983), Appendix 2, p. 2.

127 "Beggar-my-neighbor competitive deflation": *Out of Crisis,* Stuart Holland, ed. (Nottingham: Spokesman University Paperback, 1983).

130 "Europe's era" and "The effective entry": Noelke and Taylor, *EEC Protectionism,* pp. 23 and 27.

131 Pierre Defraigne comment: Interview with the author.

133 "Europe cannot give up": "The European Steel Policy" (pamphlet issued by the European Community, Brussels: 1982), p. 4.
Low-wage mercantilism: The purest exposition of this viewpoint is Bruce Scott's "Can Industry Survive the Welfare State," *Harvard Business Review,* September–October 1982.

4. LABOR

136   Joan Robinson's "If we are to enjoy": in *Essays on John Maynard Keynes*, Milo Keynes, ed. (London: Cambridge University Press, 1975), p. 129.

137   Demand-led recovery from the Depression: Jeffrey Sachs, "Real Wages and Unemployment in the OECD Countries," in *Brookings Papers on Economic Activity*, 1:1983, pp. 271–72.

138   "If unions raise wage rates": Milton Friedman, *Capitalism and Freedom* (Chicago: University of Chicago Press, 1962), p. 124.
        Works on the efficiency effects of labor corporatism include: David Cameron, "Social Democracy, Corporatism, and Labor Quiescence: The Representation of Economic Interest in Advanced Capitalist Society," paper delivered to Conference on Governability and Legitimacy in Western European Democracies, Stanford University, 1982; Gösta Esping-Andersen and Roger Friedland, "Class Coalitions in the Making of West European Economies," in *Political Power and Social Theory*, Vol. 3 (Greenwich, Conn.: JAI Press, 1982); Walter Korpi, *The Democratic Class Struggle* (London: Routledge and Kegan Paul, 1983); Peter Lange and Geoffrey Garrett, "Organizational and Political Determinants of Economic Performance, 1974–1980," Fourth Conference of Europeanists, Washington, D.C., October 1983; Leon Lindberg and Charles Maier, *The Political Economy of Inflation* (Washington: The Brookings Institution, 1984); Jeffrey Sachs, "Labor Markets and Comparative Economic Performance," from Sachs and Michael Bruno, *A Study of Stagflation* (Cambridge: Harvard University Press, 1984); Philippe C. Schmitter, "Interest Intermediation and Regime Governability in Contemporary Western Europe," *Organizing Interests in Western Europe*, Suzanne Berger, ed. (Cambridge: Harvard University Press, 1981); Harold Wilensky, *The "New Corporatism," Centralization and the Welfare State* (Beverly Hills: Sage Publications, 1976).

146   Statistical studies: Harold Wilensky, *The New Corporatism*, and David Cameron, "Social Democracy, Corporatism and Labor Quiescence."

148   "The members of the highly encompassing": Mancur Olson, *The Rise and Decline of Nations* (New Haven: Yale University Press, 1982), p. 48.

149   On Swedish industrial history: See Gösta Esping-Andersen, *Social Class, Social Democracy and State Policy* (Copenhagen: New Social Science Monographs, 1980).

151   Swedish labor market policy: Allan Larsson's interview with the author and the Swedish Labor-Market Board (AMS) Annual Report, 1983 (Stockholm).

152   Labor-market participation rates: "The Challenge of Unemployment," document (Paris: OECD, 1982).

153   "Solidarity wage policy": Willy Bergstrom, "Wage Policy, Economic Growth, and Structural Change" (paper delivered to the Meidner Symposium, Arbetslivscentrum, Stockholm, 1980), p. 9.

157   On Tax-based Incomes Policies (TIPs): See Sidney Weintraub, *Capitalism's Inflation and Unemployment Crisis* (Chicago: Addison Wesley Publishing Co., 1978).

159   Austrian economy: "Survey of the Austrian Economy, 1983" (Washington: Embassy of Austria, 1983).

160   Study of Austrian unionism: Robert J. Flanagan, David W. Soskice, Lloyd Ulman, *Unionism, Economic Stabilization, and Incomes Policies: European Experience* (Washington: The Brookings Institution, 1983), pp. 51–52.

161   Pay ratios: *OECD Observer,* March 1983, Appendix, "Take-home Pay" table.

162   German inflation: *OECD Economic Outlook,* July 1983.

164   Norwegian indexation: Flanagan et al., *Unionism,* p. 155.

166   Incomes policy in conditions of economic stagnation: Ted Hanisch, "Is There a Role for Incomes Policy?" (paper presented to the "Stagnation in the West" conference, Athens, June 2, 1983), p. 13. Comparison of economic performance in "labor corporatist" and laissez-faire nations:

Country	Average Annual Growth Rate		Average Annual Unemployment	
	1965–73	1973–80	1965–73	1973–80
Austria	5.5	3.0	2.0	1.7
West Germany	4.3	2.3	0.9	3.5
Norway	4.1	4.8	0.8	0.1
Sweden	3.4	1.8	2.0	1.9
United Kingdom	3.1	0.9	2.3	4.6
United States	3.8	2.4	4.4	6.7

Source: Jeffrey Sachs and Michael Bruno, "Labor Markets and Comparative Microeconomic Performance," from *A Study of Stagflation* (Cambridge: Harvard University Press, 1984).

170 Economic dualism: See the author's "The Declining Middle," *The Atlantic Monthly,* July 1983.

172 Bureau of Labor Statistics study: Peter Henle and Paul Ryscavge, "A Survey of Earnings Gaps," *Monthly Labor Review,* June 1980.

174 Electronics engineers' salaries: Martin Carnoy and Russell Rumberger, "Segmented Labor Markets: Some Empirical Forays," unpublished paper (Stanford University Center for Educational Studies), pp. 40–41.

175 Family income statistics: Bureau of the Census, *Current Population Reports,* Series P-60.
Bifurcation of jobs: Peter B. Doeringer and Michael J. Piore, *Internal Labor Markets and Manpower Analysis* (Lexington, Mass.: D. C. Heath, 1971).

177 Statistics on public employment service placements: See Robert Haveman, "European and American Labor Market Policies in the late 1970s" (Washington: National Commission on Employment Policy, 1982), p. 20.

178 Rising productivity and rising destitution: Wassily Leontief, "The Distribution of Work and Income," *Scientific American,* September 1982, pp. 188–205.

179 "Adam and Eve enjoyed": Leontief, Ibid., p. 198.

184 Partial pension programs: Allan Larsson, "Labor Market Reforms in Sweden" (Stockholm: Swedish Institute, 1980), p. 91.

5. TAXES

187 "It should be the policy of governments": David Ricardo, *On the Principles of Political Economy and Taxation* (New York: E. P. Dutton and Co., Everyman's Library, 1962), p. 96.
Data on comparative tax burdens: Public Expenditure Trends (Paris: OECD, 1978), especially chart at p. 16.

188 Germany: Bundesministerium der Finanzen, *Subventionsbericht* (Bonn, 1980).
United States: *Budget of the United States, FY 1983, Special Analysis G: Tax Expenditures* (Washington: Government Printing Office, 1982); *Setting National Priorities, the 1983 Budget,* Joseph Pechman, ed. (Washington: The Brookings Institution, 1982).

189 Change in tax burden on average family: Advisory Commission on Intergovernmental Relations, *Significant Features of Fiscal Feder-*

alism, 1980–81 edition (Washington: Government Printing Office, 1981), p. 49.

Increase in U.S. individual taxes: Robert McIntyre and Dean C. Tipps, *Inequity and Decline* (Washington: Center on Budget and Tax Priorities, 1983), p. 14.

190 British family: Joseph Pechman, "Taxation in the United Kingdom," in *Britain's Economic Performance*, Richard E. Caves and Lawrence B. Krause, eds. (Washington: The Brookings Institution, 1980).

Tax comparisons: OECD, *Public Expenditure Trends*, tables 12 and 18 (pp. 42 and 57).

Family allowances: *The Tax/Benefit Position of Selected Income Groups* (Paris: OECD, 1978), table 8, p. 98.

191 Taxes and redistribution: Joseph Pechman, *Federal Tax Policy*, fourth edition (Washington: The Brookings Institution, 1983), p. 6.

192 Incidence of capital-gains preference: *Tax Notes*, May 2, 1983, p. 464.

195 Effect of capital-gains cuts: "Comment" by Martin Feldstein, *Tax Notes*, May 2, 1983, p. 463, and "Reply to Feldstein" by Joseph Minarik and William Nordhaus, *Tax Notes*, May 9, 1983, p. 475.

197 Different approach of depreciation accounting: Alan J. Auerbach and Dale W. Jorgenson, "The First Year Capital Recovery System," *Tax Notes*, April 14, 1980, p. 515.

198 Effective tax rates on different industries: Robert S. McIntyre and Dean Tipps, *Inequity and Decline* (Washington: Center on Budget and Policy Priorities, 1983), p. 42. On such rates after enactment of ACRS, see *Tax Notes*, January 10, 1983, p. 173.

199 "While finding that the overall rate": "Tax Policy and Capital Formation," staff paper, Federal Reserve Board of Governors, Washington, D.C., 1981.

200 Loss to the Treasury: "General Explanation of the Tax Equity and Fiscal Responsibility Act (TEFRA) of 1982" (Washington: U.S. Congress Joint Taxation Committee, 1982).

201 Too much tax-shelter limited partnership money: "Public Limited Partnership Investment Up 50% in 1983," research report (Fair Haven, N.J.: Robert A. Stanger and Co., February 1984).

202 "Because deals are now layered": Real Estate Research Corporation report quoted in *Business Week*, October 24, 1983.

205 Estate taxation: George Cooper, *A Voluntary Tax?* (Washington: The Brookings Institution, 1978), p. 2.

206 Japanese taxation: Japanese Ministry of Finance, *An Outline of Japanese Taxes*, Tokyo, 1982.
Sir James Meade's view of the welfare state and the "trade union state": James Meade, *Efficiency, Equality and the Ownership of Property* (Cambridge: Harvard University Press, 1965), quote at p. 39.

208 Impact of Reagan cuts: "The Combined Effects of Major Changes in Federal Taxes and Spending Programs," staff memorandum (Washington: Congressional Budget Office April 1984).

209 British taxes: This section draws heavily on John Kay and Mervyn King, *The British Tax System*, second edition (Oxford: Oxford University Press, 1980).

210 British overseas industrial production: Stuart Holland's essay in *Deindustrialization*, Frank Blackaby, ed. (London: Heineman Education Books, 1978), p. 95.
Too much of British economy: Robert Bacon and Walter Eltis, *Britain's Economic Problem, Too Few Producers* (London: The Macmillan Company, 1976).

211 "There is justice": Kay and King, *British Tax System*, p. 62.

212 "Anyone who paid": Ibid., p. 43.

213 Shares of wealth: Report No. 4 of the Diamond Commission, Royal Commission on the Distribution of Income and Wealth (London: Her Majesty's Stationery Office, October 1976), p. 85.

214 Tax exhaustion: "Revamping Company Tax," *The Economist*, September 24, 1983, p. 41.

215 Tax rates on various investments vary widely: Ibid., pp. 41–46.

216 British statistics: Lord Kaldor, *The Economic Consequences of Mrs. Thatcher* (London: Duckworth, 1983), statistical appendix, p. 115.

217 The basic source for German data, except where otherwise noted, is *OECD Economic Outlook*, and OECD's periodic country reports. Unemployment data are from *The Challenge of Unemployment* (Paris: OECD, 1981).

219 West German depreciation deductions: George F. Kopits, "Tax Provisions to Boost Capital Formation," *Tax Notes*, November 17, 1980, p. 955; "Doing Business in Germany," a Price-Waterhouse pamphlet, 1980.

220 National Bureau of Economic Research study: Mervyn King and Don Fullerton, "The Taxation of Income from Capital: A Comparative Study of the U.S., U.K., Sweden, and West Germany," NBER Working Paper No. 1073, 1983.

Contrasting the gap: Ibid., p. 7.1.
"The results are surprising": Ibid., p. 7.6.

222   Japanese demographics: *The Economist,* May 15, 1983, p. 94.

223   Japanese revenue: Japanese Ministry of Finance, *An Outline of Japanese Taxes*; also Joseph Pechman and Keimei Kaizuka, "Taxation," in *Asia's New Giant,* Hugh Patrick and Henry Rosovsky, eds. (Washington: The Brookings Institution, 1976), p. 328; Jane Gravelle, "Comparative Corporate Tax Burdens in the United States and Japan and Implications for Relative Economic Growth" (Washington: Congressional Research Service, 1983).

224   Japanese depreciation formulas: *An Outline of Japanese Taxes* and Pechman and Kaizuka, "Taxation," p. 354.

226   "There is no evidence": Pechman and Kaizuka, "Taxation," p. 363

6. WELFARE

229   "The pursuit of equality is a mirage" (September 16, 1975): Quoted in David Keys, *Thatcher's Britain: A Guide to the Ruins* (London: Pluto Press, 1983), p. 2.

232   Social policy is the "charwoman" of the capitalist system: Rita Liljestrom, quoted in Alfred J. Kahn and Sheila B. Kamerman, *Family Policy: Government and Families in Fourteen Countries* (New York: Columbia University Press, 1978), p. 28.

234   Laborers "have nothing to stir them up": Bernard Mandeville, quoted in T. H. Marshall, *Class, Citizenship, and Social Development* (Garden City, N.Y.: Doubleday, 1964), p. 118.

235   "I wish to see the Poor House": Quoted in Norman Furniss and Timothy Tilton, *The Case for the Welfare State* (Bloomington: Indiana University Press, 1979), p. 98.
      Evolution of social insurance: See John Myles' fine *Old Age and the Welfare State* (Boston: Little, Brown and Company, 1984).

236   "It raised the floor-level": Marshall, *Class, Citizenship, and Social Development,* pp. 86–87.

237   "Benefit in return for contributions": William Beveridge, *Social Insurance and Allied Services,* American edition (New York: The Macmillan Company, 1942), p. 12.
      "The less social security": Martha Derthick, *Policymaking for Social Security* (Washington: The Brookings Institution, 1979), pp. 5, 416.

238   Beveridge on redistribution: Howard Glennerster, "A New Start for Labour," in *Socialism in a Cold Climate*, John Griffith, ed. (London: Unwin Paperbacks, 1983), pp. 8ff.
Child allowance statistics: David Piachaud, *The Distribution and Redistribution of Incomes* (London: Bedford Square Press, 1982), p. 54.

241   Cost of long-term benefits: *The Economist*, October 1, 1983, pp. 35–39.

242   OECD survey of pensions: "Public Expenditure on Income-Maintenance Programs" (Paris: OECD, 1976), p. 23.
Supplementary means-tested benefits: For Britain, see Piachaud, *Distribution and Redistribution;* for West Germany, see Stefan Liebfried, "Public Assistance in the United States and the Federal Republic of Germany: Does Social Democracy Make a Difference?" *Comparative Politics,* October 1978, p. 65.

243   Swedish pension statistics: "The Swedish National Budget 1983–84," Stockholm, 1983.
Universalism in Northern Europe and low proportion of means-tested aid: Gösta Esping-Andersen, "The State as a System of Stratification," unpublished paper, Harvard University, 1983, p. 27; forthcoming in Esping-Andersen and W. Korpi, *The Politics of Social Citizenship.*
Family allowances: "Social Security Programs Throughout the World, 1981," U.S. Department of Health and Human Services, Social Security Administration Research Report No. 58, 1982; also Alfred J. Kahn and Sheila B. Kamerman, *Not for the Poor Alone: European Social Services* (Philadelphia: Temple University Press, 1975).

244   History of French family policy: Nicole Questiaux in *Family Policy,* Kahn and Kamerman, eds.

245   On purchasing power of family allowances: Adrian Sinfield, "Poverty and Inequality in France," in *Poverty and Inequality in Common Market Countries,* Vic George and Roger Lawson, eds. (London: Routledge & Kegan Paul, 1980), p. 102.
Repeal of the income-disregard formula: Robert Kuttner and Phyllis Freeman, "Women to the Workhouse," *Working Papers,* September–October 1983.

246   Increase in French supplementary aid: Kahn and Kamerman, *Income Transfers for Families with Children* (Philadelphia: Temple University Press, 1983), p. 212.
Family allowance plus housing allowance as a percentage of the average production worker wage (single mother not in the labor force):

Country	Percentage
Sweden	93.8
France	78.6
West Germany	67.3
United Kingdom	51.7
United States	44.0
(The United States has no family allowance program. U.S. figure is based on food stamps plus AFDC, for a family in Pennsylvania.)	

Source: Kahn and Kamerman, ibid., p. 209.

247   Unemployment statistics: *The Challenge of Unemployment* (Paris: OECD, 1982).

248   Percentage of family income maintained in the first and second years of unemployment in selected countries (1982):

	Single Person		Married Couple with Two Children	
Country	Year 1	Year 2	Year 1	Year 2
Canada	51	0	56	0
France	67	67	69	69
West Germany	66	56	66	56
Sweden	63	28	69	37
United Kingdom	28	28	54	54

Source: Derived from *Employment Outlook*, 1983 (Paris: OECD), pp. 66, 60–61.

Unemployment compensation benefits as percentage of average production worker wage (one working parent, recently unemployed, with three dependents, 1979):

Country	Percentage
Sweden	91.6
West Germany	69.9
France	68.0
United Kingdom	49.5
United States (Pennsylvania)	42.4

Source: Kahn and Kamerman, *Income Transfers*, p. 222.

250   "In the NHS" (Klein quote): In *Challenge to Governance: Studies in Overload Politics*, Richard Rose, ed. (Beverly Hills: Sage Publications, 1980), p. 16.

251   Canadian versus American statistics: Paul Starr, *The Social Transformation of American Medicine* (New York: Basic Books, 1983), p. 412.

253   "What the Europeans apparently know": Kahn and Kamerman, *Not for the Poor Alone*, p. 172.

254   Danish home care: Author's interviews in Denmark; and Ernest Marcussen, *Social Welfare in Denmark* (Copenhagen: Det Danske Selskab, 1980), p. 90.
        Swedish home-care system: Kahn and Kamerman, *Not for the Poor Alone*, pp. 90–111. Statistical comparisons: Ibid., p. 105.

255   Swedish home-care outlays: Swedish 1983–84 State Budget, pp. 50 and 87.

256   "Workers on the front lines": Michael Lipsky, *Street Level Bureaucracy* (New York: Russell Sage Foundation, 1981), p. 38; see also Lipsky's "The Welfare State as Workplace," Working Papers, May–June 1980.

257   Warning in 1955 that welfare state was fragmenting: Richard Titmuss, "The Social Division of Welfare: Some Reflections on the Search for Equity," in *Essays on the Welfare State* (London: George Allen and Unwin, 1963), pp. 34ff.

260   U.S. wealth distribution statistics: Daphne Greenwood, "Age, Income, and Household Size: Their Relation to Wealth Distribution in the United States," paper delivered to C. V. Starr Center for Applied Economics Conference on International Comparisons of the Distribution of Household Wealth, New York University, November 11–12, 1983.
        Swedish distribution of wealth, 1920–1975:

	Wealth Held by Richest Households (as a Percentage of All Households)			
Year	Top 0.01	Top 0.1	Top 0.5	Top 1.0
1920	9	24	40	50
1935	6.5	18	33	42
1945	NA	15	29	38
1951	NA	12	25	33
1966	3.6	9	18	24
1975	2.2	6	12.5	17

Source: Derived from Roland Spant, "Wealth Distribution and Its Development in Sweden," monograph (Stockholm, 1980).

British wealth distribution: A. B. Atkinson and A. J. Harrison, *Distribution of Personal Wealth in Britain* (London: Cambridge University Press, 1978).

U.S. wealth distribution: James D. Smith, "Recent Trends in the Distribution of Wealth: Data, Research Problems, and Prospects," paper presented at the C. V. Starr Center Conference on International Comparisons of the Distribution of Household Wealth, New York University, November 11–12, 1983.

"Imagine a parade": Jan Pen, "A Parade of Dwarfs (and a Few Giants)," in *Wealth, Income, and Inequality*, A. B. Atkinson, ed. (Oxford: Oxford University Press, 1980), pp. 46–48.

262   "Transfers increase the total": Timothy Smeeding, "On the Distribution of Net Income: Comment," *Southern Economic Journal* 46, January 1979, pp. 932–44.

263   "Cash transfers reduced": Sheldon Danziger, Robert Haveman, and Robert Plotnik, "How Income Transfer Programs Work, Savings, and the Income Distribution: A Critical Review," *Journal of Economic Literature*, September 1981, p. 1008.

"Because of powerful demographic forces": Alan Blinder, "The Truce in the War on Poverty" (Washington: National Policy Exchange, May 1982), p. 12.

Urban Institute study: Frank Levy and Richard C. Michel, "The Way We'll Be in 1984: Recent Changes in the Level and Distribution of Disposable Income" (Washington: The Urban Institute, 1983), p. 3.

EPILOGUE: POLITICS

265   "As long as egalitarians assume": Christopher Jencks, *Inequality* (New York: Harper/Colophon Books, 1973), p. 265.

"The average American worker": Douglas Fraser in an interview with the author.

266   "The United States of America": Werner Sombart, *Why Is There No Socialism in the United States?* (White Plains, N.Y.: M. E. Sharpe, 1976 [first published in Germany in 1906]), pp. 1 and 109–10.

267   Interest groups and ideologies in America: See Walter Dean Burnham, *Critical Elections and the Mainsprings of American Politics* (New York: W. W. Norton, 1970); also "The Eclipse of the Democratic Party," *Democracy*, July 1982, p. 7. Also see Walter Korpi, *The Democratic Class Struggle* (London: Routledge and Kegan Paul, 1983).

268   Economy that remains fundamentally capitalist: Andrew Martin, "Is Democratic Control of Capitalist Economies Possible?" in *Stress and Contradiction in Modern Capitalism,* Leon Lindberg, ed. (Lexington, Mass.: D. C. Heath, 1975), pp. 45–46.

271   OECD study: OECD *Economic Outlook,* July 1983, pp. 44–49, especially table at p. 48.

ACKNOWLEDGMENTS

THIS BOOK grew out of a long article titled "Growth with Equity," which appeared in *Working Papers* magazine in 1981. *Working Papers,* published between 1973 and 1983, served as an eclectic forum of the practical democratic left. The theme of this book — democratic possibility in economic and social life — reflects that of *Working Papers,* which I was privileged to serve for three years. I learned much from the magazine's broad circle of contributors and friends, notably Paul Starr, Gösta Esping-Andersen, James Henry, John Myles, Ron Bloom, Sidney Blumenthal, Michael Lipsky, Paul Osterman, Richard Margolis, Bob Howard, and Kirk Scharfenberg. Without the opportunity afforded by *Working Papers* to discuss manuscripts, debate issues, make intellectual connections, and broaden horizons, this book could not have been written.

Many others in the greater Boston professoriat have taken time to acquaint me with a copious academic literature on equality and efficiency. These include Andrew Martin, Hugh Heclo, Douglas Hibbs, Martin Rein, James Medoff, Bob Reich, Lee Rainwater, and Deborah Stone. I was also very fortunate in receiving help from European scholars and trade unionists who are too numerous to list. Particular thanks to Peter Coldrick, Anna Hedborg, Roland Spant, Agit Singh, Nick Bosanquet, Adrian Sinfield, and Wolfgang Hager.

I had generous financial assistance from the Ford Foundation, which subsidized a year of research, and the German Marshall Fund, which underwrote three reporting trips. Special thanks to Robert Schrank, Gordon Berlin, Denie Weil; to my editors at Houghton Mifflin, Robie Macauley and Lois Randall; and to John Brockman.

Gratitude is also due the editors whose magazines have been hospitable to these somewhat heretical ideas, especially Hendrik Hertzberg of the *New Republic,* William Whitworth of the *Atlantic Monthly,* and Irving Howe of *Dissent.* Their exacting standards are exceeded only by their kindness. Some of the themes in this book have been previously treated in my *New Republic* and *Atlantic* articles.

Several colleagues and friends read and criticized portions of the manuscript: David Smith, Marc Landy, Samantha Sanchez, S. M. Miller, Barry Bluestone, and Bennett Harrison. As always, my most astute critic for consistency of ideas, plausibility of theme, and coherence of prose is Sharland Trotter Kuttner — living proof that the helping hand is not invisible and that equality is efficient.

INDEX